THE MADAM
AND THE SPYMASTER

Historian and journalist **Nigel Jones** is the author of eight historical books and biographies, including acclaimed lives of Rupert Brooke and Patrick Hamilton, *Peace and War: Britain in 1914* and *Tower: An Epic History of the Tower of London*. An authority on the poets of the Great War and the rise of Nazism and Fascism between the world wars, he has also guided historical tours of the Western Front, Germany and Italy for several years. A former deputy editor of *History Today* and a founding editor of BBC *History* magazine, he writes and reviews regularly for these and other national newspapers and magazines, and frequently appears in TV historical documentaries.

Urs Brunner studied History, Politics and Literature at the University of Zurich and the American University of Cairo, and worked as a freelance journalist. After moving to Thailand, he founded his own film content and finance company, which produced several feature films. He is presently involved in the development of an international TV series about the 'Salon Kitty'.

Julia Schrammel is an Austrian journalist who studied communication sciences at the University of Salzburg. She worked for radio and TV stations, in the state press office and now for various media companies as a freelance.

THE
MADAM
AND THE
SPYMASTER

The Secret History of the Most Famous
Brothel in Wartime Berlin

NIGEL JONES, URS BRUNNER, AND DR. JULIA SCHRAMMEL

PEGASUS BOOKS
NEW YORK LONDON

THE MADAM AND THE SPYMASTER

Pegasus Books, Ltd.
148 West 37th Street, 13th Floor
New York, NY 10018

Copyright © 2023 by Nigel Jones, Urs Brunner, and Dr. Julia Schrammel

First Pegasus Books cloth edition July 2023

ISBN: 978-1-63936-429-9

10 9 8 7 6 5 4 3 2 1

Printed in the United States of America
Distributed by Simon & Schuster
www.pegasusbooks.com

PUBLISHER'S NOTE

As is standard practice in English, this text uses double s to represent the German character *ß*, known as the *Eszett* or *scharfes S* ('sharp S'); for instance, Giesebrechtstrasse for Giesebrechtstraße.

CONTENTS

AUTHORS' FOREWORD

The legend of Salon Kitty is well known to historians, filmmakers, cinema goers, and indeed to anyone taking more than a passing interest in Nazi Germany. But until now, verifiable facts have been few, and myths, rumours and legends have accumulated. The bare bones of the story go something like this: Salon Kitty was a well-known and exclusive Berlin brothel catering to high-class VIP clients both under the Weimar Republic and after Hitler's rise to power. Shortly before the outbreak of the Second World War it was converted by the Nazi secret services into a sophisticated 'listening post' to spy on VIP visitors, both foreign and domestic, using a combination of sophisticated hidden microphone 'bugs', and specially trained 'amateurs': spy-prostitutes who would extract indiscreet information from their clients during pillow talk accompanying their erotic encounters.

Variously described by historian Hans-Peter Bleuel as 'the Third Reich's most prominent establishment of love for sale'; by the *Der Spiegel* journalist Fritz Rumler as 'a high-class brothel'; and by documentary film director Rosa von Praunheim simply as 'a place for spies to meet', the truth about the establishment's history and functions has proved tantalisingly elusive.

According to 'Peter Norden' (the pseudonym of journalist Joseph Fritz), author of the only previous book on the story, *Madam Kitty* (1973), which was the basis for the notorious Nazi sexploitation film *Salon Kitty* (1976), the brothel was utilised by the Nazi secret service under Reinhard Heydrich to spy on their friends and enemies after the brothel's owner and manager Kitty Schmidt was brutally coerced into co-operating with the project. The brothel was already up and running when the Nazis first took an interest in it, and its owner was no ordinary 'madam' but an intelligent and sophisticated socialite at the heart of inter-war Berlin society. If we are to believe Norden's account, Kitty was compelled into this clandestine collaboration after being brutalised in a cell at the notorious HQ of the Nazi secret police and security apparatus in Berlin's Prinz-Albrecht-Strasse, where she was threatened with being sent to a concentration camp if she did not co-operate.

The originator of the plan to convert the brothel into a listening post and surveillance centre was Reinhard Heydrich himself. The cruel, ruthless and utterly amoral Heydrich was creator and chief of the *Reichssicherheitshauptamt* (Reich Security Main Office) or RSHA, an umbrella organisation under which he was combining all the rival security and secret police arms of the Reich into one monstrous maw of repression and terror. Heydrich's plan for Salon Kitty was simple. His intention was to employ specially trained prostitutes to pull a Mata Hari-style stunt not only on important foreign diplomats and visitors, but also on the Nazi party's own top leaders and officials. The sex workers would extract information from their clients' conversations, which, unknown to them, would also be picked up on concealed state-of-the-art listening devices, recorded on wax discs or newly developed magnetic tapes, and constantly monitored by a team of SS technicians installed in the brothel's basement.

Urs Brunner first stumbled on this astonishing story in 2011/12 when his film production company, 'Angel & Bear Productions', was approached by the film producer Mark Boot, who was considering making a new film of the story. He was looking for a business partner to develop and produce the movie and his pitch was persuasive. Mark's portfolio included owning the licensing rights for the films of the Italian director Tinto Brass, including his 1976 movie *Salon Kitty*, dubbed by the *Frankfurter Allgemeine Zeitung* newspaper as 'the most sophisticated of all trash movies about the Nazis'.

We were encouraged to pursue the story because at the time film and television producers were showing renewed interest in Berlin during the inter-war years. Though perennially fascinating, the city of *Cabaret* and Weimar decadence on the cusp of Hitler's takeover was then presenting a more nuanced cinematic picture of the Nazis than had previously been the case. National Socialists were no longer just being paraded as the thuggish, one-dimensional bad guys in action flicks, or acting out their perversions in sexploitation films. Now they were the protagonists in serious films with Oscar ambitions such as *Downfall* (2005) and on German television. High-quality TV series about the Nazis and their incubation under Weimar such as *Unsere Mütter, unsere Väter* (2013) or *Babylon Berlin* (2017) were sold around the world. Likewise, Anglo-American productions such as *Valkyrie* (2008) starring Tom Cruise as Count Claus von Stauffenberg, Hitler's would-be assassin, and a distinguished British cast, or Quentin Tarantino's *Inglorious Basterds* (2009) were other successful examples of the genre.

The first and most urgent question facing us as we looked at the Salon Kitty story was to what extent there were historical documents in the public domain, and what was based on secondary sources or literature. As we started to search for the historically documented story, we made a startling and sobering discovery: there were practically no cast-iron sources for the events at Salon Kitty and the people who frequented the brothel at Berlin's Giesebrechtstrasse 11 in the western Charlottenburg quarter of the city. That at least was the result of our first round of – admittedly superficial – research. Instead of hard facts we came across a plethora of legends and wild rumours, spiced with lurid tales clearly designed for commercial exploitation. Initially, therefore, we were forced to agree with *Die Welt* newspaper, which, in 2004, concluded:

> There was indeed a brothel in Giesebrechtstrasse, and the women there may have given reports to the police. Anything else that's said about 'Salon Kitty' is probably invented, feeding on a combined smattering of historical knowledge, dirty imagination, and analogies with the methods of modern intelligence services.

Instead of just accepting this deflating conclusion, however, we were tempted to dig deeper. What led us on was Peter Norden's book *Madam Kitty* (1973). For all its invented scenes and imagined conversations, and the author's own admission that it was a 'documentary novel' somewhere between fact and fiction, it seemed to us to contain a core of truth that fitted the known facts. Norden also proudly labelled his book 'a true story'. With due respect for a writer's creativity and imagination it was hard to believe that he had merely invented all those 'facts'. In any case, it piqued our interest and curiosity, so we optioned the film rights for Norden's book and began our own serious investigation into Kitty Schmidt's murky past and the details of what went on at her establishment in the Giesebrechtstrasse.

We began by systematically scrutinising the available literature and archives, along with accounts by contemporaries, press articles, and film and photographic material. Our search took several years and proved to be exciting – if time consuming and demanding. In the end, as the material accumulated, we forgot our original intention to just make a film, and this book is the result.

The book traces the activities and biography of the owner of the eponymous salon – Kitty Schmidt herself – and through her tells the story of the brothel that she ran. We attempt to separate fact from fiction as precisely as possible, and based on the recollections of contemporaries as well as memoirs, photographs and numerous secondary sources we have shed light on a very murky story, and at last told the full story of the salon, its owner, her 'girls', and the 'guests' they entertained and spied upon.

The story of Salon Kitty cannot be adequately covered and completely comprehended without a fuller knowledge of the Third Reich, the society that produced it, and of the history and methods of its espionage, police and intelligence services. We have, therefore, explored this dimension and set the story firmly in the wider context of Weimar Berlin, its famously louche and decadent nightlife and prostitution scene, and the way that the Nazis used and misused sex and eroticism for their own dark ends.

We describe the role that sex and prostitution played in Germany as a whole in the 1920s and 1930s, looking behind the image of glamorous Weimar portrayed in films like *Cabaret* to the seedy reality beneath. We examine the astonishing range of clubs and sexual services available to those who paid in the economically depressed and politically desperate country. We show how the Nazis used and abused sex when they came to power in 1933, on the one hand repressing the more overt manifestations of eroticism, and on the other abusing it for their own perverse purposes – such as in the brothels of their concentration camps, and the *Lebensborn* (Fount of Life) programme derived from the Nazis' racist ideology, to breed a 'pure' Aryan race by encouraging women to produce children fathered by SS officers outside the 'bourgeois' confines of marriage.

We relate the story of the competing Nazi police and intelligence services – the Gestapo, the *Kripo* (Criminal Police), the Abwehr military intelligence agency, the SS and its own intelligence agency, the *Sicherheitsdienst* (Security Service or SD) created and run by

Heydrich. We tell of the dramatic rivalry and the strange love/hate relationship between Heydrich and his mentor, Admiral Wilhelm Canaris, head of the Abwehr. We show how the all-encroaching Nazi police state created a climate of fear and terror with its official encouragement of denunciations by ordinary citizens of those suspected of opposition or disloyalty. The Nazi state, as we clearly demonstrate, was by no means a smoothly running machine operating with ruthless efficiency. Rather it was a mishmash of fiercely jealous personalities and competing agencies which got in each other's way and bred mutual distrust and hatred.

Just as fierce were the personal feuds between the leading Nazi paladins themselves as they competed to win the ear and the favour of the Führer. The rivalry between Göring, Goebbels, Röhm, Ribbentrop, Bormann, Himmler and Heydrich was a constant battle, which materially contributed to the ultimate failure of the Third Reich. We look at the biographies of these brutal men to determine how their personalities and sexualities affected the disastrous course of German – and European – twentieth-century history.

The core of the book, however, remains the extraordinary story of Salon Kitty itself and the mysterious motivations of its owner. We investigate its origins under Weimar as Berlin's most exclusive 'house of pleasure' and how and why it morphed into a Nazi-run brothel where the regime spied on society at large. We trace the course of Kitty Schmidt's life, including the recollections of those who came into contact with her before, during and after her time as Germany's most notorious 'madam'. We question Kitty's motivations: was she a cynical opportunist; a willing stooge of the Nazis who infiltrated and controlled her establishment; or just a woman doing her best to survive amidst intolerable pressures and threats? And how did this Aryan woman, with many Jewish friends and customers, perceive the all-pervading anti-Semitism lying at the core of the Nazi regime?

Finally, we journey to Giesebrechtstrasse 11 itself to visit the building at the centre of our story as it is today. Though badly damaged by an Allied bomb in 1943, Salon Kitty survived the city's apocalyptic destruction in 1945, and resumed its chequered history. We enter the doors of the premises through which so many 'distinguished' (and undistinguished) feet trod before us; revisit the 'love rooms' where so many indiscreet secrets were spilled; and descend to the cellars where they were recorded by ever-listening ears. In uncovering the story of Salon Kitty we have told one of the very last untold stories of the Third Reich, its leaders and the Second World War.

NIGEL JONES, URS BRUNNER, JULIA SCHRAMMEL

CHAPTER ONE

'FUCKING FOR THE FÜHRER'

– The birth of Salon Kitty

SS-Gruppenführer Reinhard Heydrich had an idea. It was not an unusual event, for the feared head of Nazi Germany's *Reichssicherheitshauptamt* (Reich Security Main Office, the RSHA) – the umbrella organisation that would run the Hitler regime's chief organs of terror – was a constantly fertile source of schemes to better control, intimidate and persecute the country's cowed population. This plan, however, first formulated in Heydrich's mind shortly before the outbreak of the Second World War, was audacious and amoral even by the debased standards set by the man known as 'Hitler's hangman'.

It was, in the vulgar words of a modern German historian, to 'fuck for the Führer'. Heydrich intended to take over Berlin's most notorious and exclusive brothel, known as 'Salon Kitty'. Using a combination of hi-tech, state-of-the-art eavesdropping devices, and specially selected and trained women, distinguished both by their erotic charms and their devotion to the Nazi cause, the scheme would be to spy on the brothel's male clientele. Important foreign visitors to the Reich's capital would be cultivated by Heydrich's

1

agents and discreetly directed to sample the joys of the city's leading 'house of pleasure'.

With his cynical view of human nature and his knowledge of the moral frailties of his fellow Nazi leaders, Heydrich knew that visitors to the brothel would also include leading National Socialists – indeed, he himself made frequent use of such establishments. And he had no qualms about spying on his colleagues and rivals. The information thus gleaned would be added to the stock of damaging secrets gathered in the files that that were steadily accumulating in his office safe.

Heydrich envisaged that once through the doors of Giesebrecht-strasse 11 in Berlin's prosperous western Charlottenburg quarter, visitors would be warmly welcomed by none other than the establishment's famed owner and 'madam', Kitty Schmidt herself. After plying them with Champagne, fine wines or spirits in the relaxed high-bourgeois atmosphere of the salon's luxurious reception lounge – all plush velvet chairs and curtains, reproductions of Old Master paintings and ornate wall mirrors in the cosy Biedermeier style – Kitty would produce with the utmost discretion her special 'private' album.

This picture book would feature alluring photographs of the twenty girls who worked at the salon and – a fact unknown to the men eagerly turning the album's pages – who were also agents in the employ of Heydrich's SD (*Sicherheitsdienst*), the secret service of the SS. Rigorously chosen for their physical attractiveness, high sexual appetites and erotic skills – and with some originating from the upper reaches of the Reich's high society – these women were also selected for their intelligence, were fluent in at least one foreign language, and above all were blindly devoted and indoctrinated adherents of National Socialism. Specially selected for their roles, they would be initiated into the ranks of the SS and trained to combine professional 'business' with their more subtle secret work: extracting indiscreet information from their clients in post-coital pillow talk.

At the same time – and unknown to their unwitting clients – their conversations would be recorded on some fifty hidden microphones carefully placed in the salon's 'love rooms'. The sounds and words picked up by these bugs, then the very latest technology available in the armoury of the SD's surveillance weapons, would be fed down through hidden tubes to Salon Kitty's cellar. Here a staff of five SD technicians – sworn to secrecy on pain of death – would be on permanent round-the-clock duty, recording and monitoring the results on wax discs or more advanced magnetic tapes. This belt-and-braces approach to his project was typical of Heydrich's thorough perfectionism, making assurance doubly sure and doubly secure. All these plans were but gleams in Heydrich's narrow gimlet eyes on the day in 1939 when he summoned his subordinate Walter Schellenberg to his office to put the proposal to his most trusted and efficient lieutenant.

The meeting that was the genesis of Salon Kitty was held in Heydrich's office in the Prinz-Albrecht-Palais, a vast and sprawling eighteenth-century rococo palace that had once belonged to Germany's former ruling imperial family, the Hohenzollerns. After the Nazis came to power in 1933, the palace and surrounding buildings, including the former Prinz Albrecht Hotel and the neighbouring arts and crafts museum, had been taken over by the Nazi's mushrooming security services as the headquarters of their feared organs of terror. The Gestapo, the secret political police, had their HQ inside the complex, along with the SS – the Nazis' elite security force who staffed the regime's concentration camps and would provide the personnel to carry out its dirtiest future task, the Holocaust of Europe's Jews. Also located there were the SD, the SS's own intelligence and espionage division. The palace's cellars had been converted into narrow windowless cells in which the regime's open opponents – and those even suspected of being so – were imprisoned, abused, brutalised and sometimes executed. By the late 1930s the mere words 'Prinz-

Albrecht-Strasse' had become a feared euphemism known to every German as the location of terror, torture and disappearance into the *Nacht und Nebel* (night and fog) of the concentration camp system, and ultimately in many cases to their deaths.

The spider at the centre of this web of terror was Reinhard Heydrich himself. Fiercely bright, and just as fiercely brutal, cynical and ruthless, Heydrich was both a meticulous and permanently suspicious bureaucrat who imagined that everyone – loyal Nazis, obedient subordinates and open enemies alike – shared his own malign nature. He was therefore building a mountain of information about the character flaws and weaknesses of hundreds of officials who worked for him, ready to use it against them should the opportunity and necessity arise. The idea of converting an exclusive brothel into a spy centre suited such a purpose perfectly.

Answerable only to his own immediate boss, the SS overlord *Reichsführer* Heinrich Himmler, and to Hitler himself, in 1939 Heydrich was busy finalising his bureaucratic plans, which would be completed within the year, to centralise the organs of terror into a single umbrella organisation under his personal control: the Reich Security Main Office – or RSHA. As master of the Reich's machinery of terror, spying and repression, Heydrich, still only in his mid-thirties, thoroughly deserved Hitler's awed tribute to him as 'the man with the iron heart'. Feared and hated by even his closest colleagues – his intelligence service rival Admiral Wilhelm Canaris described him as the Reich's 'most intelligent monster' – the cruel and ice-cold Heydrich's formidable but twisted brain was forever devising devilish fresh schemes to spin his web of control over new areas; which is why he had called Schellenberg in to see him.

Walter Schellenberg was a man cast in Heydrich's own malign mould. Even younger than his boss, the thirty-year-old lawyer turned SD functionary came from a similar middle-class and musical milieu.

Where Heydrich's father Bruno had been a composer of unsuccessful Wagnerian operas and head of the musical conservatory in his native city of Halle, Schellenberg's father was a manufacturer of pianos in the western Saarland province. Both families had suffered the economic impoverishment caused by rampant inflation under the Weimar Republic in the 1920s. This had reduced many middle-class families like the Heydrichs and Schellenbergs to genteel penury, and had made them enemies of democracy and easy prey for the extremist message of the rising Nazi movement. The Schellenbergs had even been forced by economic need to leave Germany for neighbouring Luxembourg. Returning from there, Walter Schellenberg had been recruited by the SD as an informer while studying law at Bonn University. He joined the SS in 1933.

The young man's intelligence and his cynical willingness to put the demands of the party and his ambitions for his own career above formal legal restraints soon attracted Heydrich's admiring attention. After efficiently performing various espionage tasks in France and Italy by way of initiation into the secret intelligence world, Schellenberg joined Heydrich in preparing the ground for creating the RSHA as the central body of the Nazi terror state above and beyond the rule of law. It was Schellenberg who had suggested both the title and the structure of the RSHA, and it was during his work preparing this that Heydrich tasked him with the extra job of setting up Salon Kitty as a spy centre.

Heydrich and Schellenberg were hardly models of the official public line on sexual morality and marital fidelity preached but rarely practised by the Third Reich's leaders. Heydrich had been forced to resign from his first chosen career in the navy in 1931 by a court of honour for 'conduct unbecoming an officer'. He had broken his promise to wed the daughter of an influential friend of the head of the navy, Grand Admiral Erich Raeder. But that disgrace had led to the launch of his spectacularly stellar second career in Nazi intelligence when the woman he did marry that year, Lina von Osten, a keen Nazi, encouraged her unemployed husband to apply to Himmler for the job of creating an intelligence service for the SS. Though without any experience in the intelligence field – in the navy he had been a signals specialist – Heydrich, a keen consumer of spy pulp fiction, used that and his own innate intelligence to sketch out within half an hour the outline of what would swiftly become under his leadership the SD. Himmler was suitably impressed by the plan, and by the tall young man's blond and impeccably Aryan appearance, and gave him the job.

Though he remained married to Lina, and would father four children with her, Heydrich had a high sex drive and was a regular visitor to Berlin's brothels. It was almost certainly such visits that had planted the seed of his idea of using a bordello as a listening post. Schellenberg, though less of a sexual adventurer than his boss, was equally ruthless and amoral. He had recently ditched his first wife, a seamstress of humble origins who was eight years older than him, for being an unsuitable partner in his future career ambitions. The first Frau Schellenberg, Käthe Kortekamp, had generously paid his way through university. In dumping her, as a consolation prize for her loss, Schellenberg gave his jilted spouse a clothing company confiscated from its Jewish owners.

Schellenberg saw his second wife, Irene Grosse-Schönepauk, a tall and elegant middle-class woman whom he would wed in 1940 after divorcing Käthe, as a more suitable spouse for the future senior role he envisaged for himself. If he had any bourgeois misgivings about venturing into the underground world of commercial sex, Schellenberg was quite prepared to suppress them on Heydrich's orders in the higher interests of pleasing his boss and furthering his promising career.

According to Schellenberg's self-serving post-war account, Heydrich's first unexpected question at their meeting was to ask whether he was faithful to his wife. On Schellenberg answering in the affirmative – despite the fact that he was in the midst of exchanging his first wife for his next – Heydrich proceeded to unfold a sketch of his grand plan. He was finding it difficult, he told Schellenberg, to gather information via the usual methods and channels – reports from informers and paid agents. Wouldn't it be more effective and fruitful to overhear targets in an informal setting and atmosphere where tongues loosened by alcohol would be more likely to wag? What he had in mind, he added, was to post young and attractive women in a restaurant, or perhaps somewhere even more intimate, to listen to their drunken dates and pick up information that would be of value to the secret services.

According to Peter Norden, author of *Madam Kitty*, published in 1973, Schellenberg, after hearing these details, begged to be entrusted with the execution of the scheme. Heydrich was a busy man. He speedily ordered Schellenberg to produce his first preliminary report within a week and sent him on his way. There may have been another secret reason why Heydrich had selected Schellenberg for the task of setting up Salon Kitty, and one that would have appealed to the SD chief's devious and malicious nature: he suspected that his young protégé might have been enjoying a secret extra-marital affair with a young married woman. With delicious irony, the woman in question was none other than his own wife, Lina Heydrich.

There is no doubt that in the late 1930s the Heydrich marriage was in deep trouble. As he built his empire of terror, Heydrich spent less and less time with his wife and young children. Lina strongly suspected that her husband, with his strong sexual appetite, was taking time off to visit bars and brothels and indulge in casual erotic liaisons. Lina, for her part, was not a woman to accept her husband's infidelity without complaint and keep quiet as a good Aryan wife should. A forceful personality in her own right, Lina took her revenge by indulging in affairs herself. She is reported to have had relationships with the Nazi artist Wolfgang Willrich, who painted and drew portraits of her husband in 1935, and with an SS officer named Wilhelm Albert. Most significantly for the Salon Kitty story, however, was her 'friendship' with Schellenberg.

It is certain that Lina and Schellenberg had formed an intimate bond soon after they first met at an official function in 1935. After the war, Lina admitted that she had deliberately and publicly flirted with the handsome young functionary in order to arouse her husband's jealousy. But it is quite likely that the liaison went further than that. Certainly, Heydrich had good reason to think that it had. In his own post-war account, Schellenberg relates an extraordinary story. After enjoying a typical drunken evening letting off steam with his boss and another sinister police official, Heinrich Müller, Schellenberg claimed Heydrich told him that he had spiked his drink with a deadly poison and would only give him the antidote if he told the truth about his relationship with Lina. Schellenberg blurted out some sort of confession of intimacy, after which, he said, he decided that it would be best if he never saw Lina Heydrich again. If there is any truth in this story, it is highly likely that giving Schellenberg the Salon Kitty assignment was a twisted form of revenge that would have appealed to Heydrich's warped mind.

Juggling his secret schemes, and at the same time intriguing to advance his own inordinate and seemingly limitless ambitions to accrue more and more power to himself, was more than a full-time job for any man, and it naturally produced a state of extreme tension in Heydrich. Alongside his sedentary secret service office work, the young and manically active SS-Gruppenführer sought diversion and relaxation in his rare off-duty hours, at first in sport. He was an Olympic standard fencer and a keen swimmer and yachtsman. Naturally, though, it would be a bold, not to say foolhardy, opponent who would dare to best him with foil or sabre. Heydrich was also a skilled horseman, and like Hitler's deputies Hermann Göring and

Rudolf Hess, held a pilot's licence, which he used in an extraordinarily daring and reckless way for one of the Reich's top leaders.

When war came, the Gruppenführer flew combat missions on both the Western and Eastern Fronts. He flew as an air gunner in the Polish campaign in 1939, and was injured when he crashed soon after the launch of Hitler's attack on Western Europe in May 1940. Nothing daunted, Heydrich piloted one of the Reich's leading fighter aircraft, the Messerschmitt Bf 109 – decorated with the SS runes as his personal emblem – in combat over Russia after the launch of Operation Barbarossa, the invasion of the Soviet Union, in June 1941.

On 22 July, exactly a month after the launch of the invasion, his luck ran out again. Hit by ground fire, he managed to crash-land his plane. Heydrich was missing for two days in No Man's Land between the German and Russian lines, but finally made his way back to safety. When Hitler learned of the man with the iron heart's latest near fatal misadventure, he banned him from flying altogether, and the grounded Heydrich was once again forced to seek an outlet for his ever-tightening tensions back on earth.

Before the war, as he continued to extend his intelligence empire, Heydrich had enjoyed musical evenings and family meals with his rival Admiral Wilhelm Canaris who had known him during his naval days. The 'little admiral', head of Abwehr military intelligence, was a shrewd judge of character, and shared Heydrich's cunning – though, to his ultimate cost, not his amoral and brutal ruthlessness. Observing Heydrich at close quarters in his own home, Canaris sensed that his opposite number, under a superficially affable exterior, was quite literally a deadly enemy.

Such sedate soirees though, as he verbally crossed swords with the admiral, were not enough to satisfy Heydrich's unquenchable thirst for danger. Restrained by the Führer – along with Himmler, the only man in the Reich he dared not disobey – Heydrich fumed in frustration. He would round up small groups of colleagues and hit the streets and clubs of Berlin for drunken nights of dissipation. As often as not, such adventures would end in the small hours with the Gruppenführer in the arms of one or more whores. When the idea of utilising an establishment like Salon Kitty for espionage purposes occurred to him, Heydrich knew the milieu in which he was mixing. It was rumoured that after returning home from one such night on the tiles, catching sight of his reflection in a full-length mirror, and drunkenly mistaking himself for a hostile intruder, he pulled his pistol and shot out the glass. If true, for once Heydrich had got the right man.

In 1939, Heydrich was still in the midst of his meteoric career climb. One surviving eyewitness to the man and his methods was Eugen Dollmann, a diplomat and SS member who acted as Hitler's personal interpreter during the Führer's many meetings with his Fascist friend, puppet and partner in crime, Italy's dictator Benito Mussolini. As Dollmann recalled in an article in *Der Spiegel* magazine in 1967, he had met Heydrich in Rome and Naples in April 1938.

The Gruppenführer had been sent to check out the security arrangements for one such summit between the Führer and the Duce during a visit by Hitler to Italy. Struck by Heydrich's 'icy, blue-eyed coldness and the severity of the second highest police official in Germany', Dollmann was still unprepared for what happened next. One evening in Naples, Heydrich asked Dollmann to accompany him to a well-known Neapolitan brothel known as the 'House of the Provinces'. Dollmann claimed:

> He told me about his plans to become the patron of an undertaking in Berlin where influential friends, diplomats and other gentlemen of the Higher Society would enjoy nocturnal pleasures – all controlled by him, via in-built listening devices.

The discreet diplomat did not disclose whether he accepted Heydrich's invitation to visit the brothel.

If Dollmann is to be believed, the idea of using a brothel for his secret schemes had been brewing in Heydrich's brain for at least a year before he called in Schellenberg to put the plan into action. The diplomat's credibility is supported by the fact that the Naples brothel he mentions certainly existed, and was still in business in 1949. 'The House of the Provinces' was just one of 717 state-licensed brothels in Italy at the time, employing some 4,000 prostitutes. The system only came to an end in September 1958 when state-licensed brothels were closed.

Schellenberg was not the only henchman that Heydrich tasked with setting up the Salon Kitty operation. To set a spy to spy on a spy and act as the smooth lawyer's deputy, he appointed a much rougher and tougher character, one Alfred Naujocks, who would shortly rejoice in his unofficial sobriquet as 'the man who started the Second World War'. Originally a car mechanic from the north German port of Kiel, Naujocks had studied engineering at his home town's university. Handy with his fists, while still a student he became an amateur boxer and a Nazi and acquired a reputation as a street-fighting man in the murderous brawls between the Nazis and Communists that were tearing German cities apart in the early 1930s.

After the Nazis took power, Naujocks joined Heydrich's SD, originally as a lowly driver. In 1934, recognising the bruiser's propensity for violence and his readiness to carry out illegal and dangerous tasks, Heydrich gave Naujocks his first lethal assignment. Naujocks was ordered to travel to neighbouring Czechoslovakia – the country where Heydrich would eventually meet his doom – and there to eliminate a particularly troublesome and sharp thorn in the side of the new regime.

Nineteen thirty-four was the year when the festering conflict between Hitler and the *Sturmabteilung* (Storm department or SA) came to a violent head. The three-million strong SA militia were the brown-shirted paramilitary wing of the Nazis who had formed their thuggish muscle in the murderous street warfare between the party and their Communist and Social Democratic enemies during the *Kampfzeit* (time of struggle) that accompanied the party's rise to power. Led by the scar-faced ex-soldier Ernst Röhm, one of Hitler's oldest and closest cronies, the SA had always enjoyed a semi-detached autonomous relationship with the party, and after they had battered open the gates of power for the Führer with their fists, clubs and guns, they were eager to enjoy the fruits of their victory.

Hitler, however, had other ideas. Having not yet gained full control over the state, his first year in power was still a dangerous and delicate time for the new Chancellor. At any time the conservative partners in Hitler's ruling coalition, disgusted by the SA's brutish lawlessness, could ask their patron, President Hindenburg, to dismiss the man Hindenburg despised as a 'Bohemian corporal' and proclaim martial rule. Hitler was therefore coming under increasing pressure from the German army, the Wehrmacht, and more conservative Nazis like Göring, to curb or completely crush the anarchic, brawling Stormtroopers.

Röhm, blind to his increasing political peril, was anxious to absorb the army into the ranks of the SA and complete what he called a 'second revolution'. In his wilder moments, he even talked of getting rid of Hitler himself. Himmler and Heydrich saw their chance. Decapitating and emasculating the SA would offer them a golden opportunity to massively augment the power of their SS. An altogether more disciplined, elitist and ideologically driven force than the brutish Brownshirts, the largely middle-class black-clad SS despised their proletarian SA rivals.

Rudolf Formis, Naujocks' intended victim in Czechoslovakia, was an SA man from Stuttgart. A radio engineer by trade, he had fallen out with and been expelled by the Nazis when it was found that he had a Jewish grandmother. Thoroughly disillusioned, Formis retaliated by using his radio skills to sever a landline relaying one of Hitler's speeches, cutting the Führer off from much of his audience in mid-flow. Arrested by the Gestapo, Formis was severely beaten and sent to one of the new concentration camps, where the Nazis were imprisoning thousands of their enemies without trial and in brutally cruel conditions. Formis managed to escape and made his way to the Czech capital Prague.

Here he joined forces with Otto Strasser, another ex-Nazi renegade, who, like Röhm, was a former comrade of Hitler's who had fallen foul of the Führer. Röhm and Strasser took the socialist side of National Socialism seriously, and considered that Hitler had sold out to 'Reaction' – the name commonly given to the Nazis' conservative enemies – by consorting with the capitalists who had funded the party's rise. Expelled from the Nazi ranks, Otto Strasser had fled to Prague in 1933 and formed an exiled opposition movement called the Black Front.

In July 1934, Hitler had finally 'settled accounts' with both Röhm's SA and his conservative critics in a blood-drenched summer weekend known as 'The Night of the Long Knives'. One of the most prominent victims of the purge was Gregor Strasser, Otto's elder brother. Gregor Strasser had also been a courageous critic of Hitler's within the party. Like his younger brother Otto, he considered himself a socialist, and his organisational abilities had done much to build the party outside his native Bavaria. Hitler broke with him shortly before coming to power when Strasser was tempted to take his wing of the party into government without Hitler. Gregor Strasser retired from politics, but that did not save him from Hitler's vengeance. The instrument of that vengeance was Reinhard Heydrich.

Arrested in Berlin as the Long Knives purge got underway, Gregor Strasser was brought to the Prinz-Albrecht-Strasse and thrown into a cell. Heydrich ordered his immediate execution. However, the bullet merely severed Strasser's carotid artery, spraying his blood around the cell's walls. As Strasser lay weltering in his own gore, Heydrich looked in and jeered: 'Is he still alive? Let the swine bleed to death.' Strasser took an hour to die. His neighbour in the next cell heard him groaning in his death agony. When he finally expired, his body was bundled into a bag and, along with scores of other victims, he was anonymously cremated. As an extra sadistic refinement, Heydrich left the bloodstains on the cell walls as a warning to other inmates of what they could expect, and only had them washed off when his own staff complained.

Otto Strasser was incensed when he heard of his brother's gruesome end and redoubled his opposition activities. In December 1934 Rudolf Formis moved to the Czech town of Slapy, near the German frontier, where, with Otto's help, he set up a shortwave radio transmitter smuggled from Germany and began to broadcast on behalf of the Black Front. Tapping into the Nazi's own state broadcast wavelengths, Formis acted as a one-man technician, producer and broadcaster, and beamed a diet of anti-Nazi propaganda into the Reich.

Infuriated by the broadcasts, and after official protests to the Czech government had failed to stop Formis, in January 1935 Heydrich ordered Naujocks to silence him by any means – either by kidnapping or killing the renegade. Accompanied by a female agent in the guise of a couple on a skiing holiday, and tipped off by an SD informant inside the Black Front, Naujocks tracked Formis down to his studio. Then, assisted by a male accomplice, he broke into the studio to await his victim. Formis arrived, and, in the ensuing gun battle, was shot dead. Naujocks and his accomplice escaped back across the frontier to Germany, but the murder caused a diplomatic rumpus. Embarrassed by the botched abduction, Heydrich was reprimanded by Himmler, but Naujocks had got his man and proved his ruthlessness and his lethal skills.

The incident earned Naujocks the nickname 'Heydrich's errand boy' in the Prinz-Albrecht-Strasse, and he was promoted to become head of the SD's 'technical section' – a euphemism for dirty jobs, sometimes using the killer's engineering knowledge. That knowledge would be utilised in several future 'special operations' involving Naujocks. The most infamous such episode, the one that earned the thug the title of 'the man who started the Second World War', was an attack on another radio transmitter, this time on German soil, at Gleiwitz (today Glewice in Poland) in the south-eastern province of Silesia, on the Polish frontier.

After his successive occupations of the Rhineland, Austria, the Sudetenland and Czechoslovakia, achieved by his favoured methods of bullying, blackmail and intimidation, Hitler knew that he would have a harder task with his next victim, Poland. The country was well armed and determined to fight to maintain its independence, backed by guarantees from Britain and France that they would go to war if Poland was attacked.

After clearing the ground for his coming conquest with his cynical pact with Stalin's Russia, announced to a stunned world in August 1939, the Führer needed a *casus belli* to justify his attack on Poland. The excuse was provided courtesy of the SS in a series of 'false flag' operations along the Polish frontier, acting in co-operation with its fellow security and intelligence agencies, the Gestapo and the Abwehr. Of these, the most blatant was the incident at Gleiwitz, personally ordered and organised by Heydrich, using Naujocks – by now an *SS-Sturmbannführer*, or major – as his principal agent.

Gleiwitz was a local radio station with a tall transmission mast and substantial buildings. Heydrich's plan was to temporarily take over the station using an SS team, led by Naujocks, dressed in Polish military uniforms. The team would broadcast a provocative message in Polish and then depart. Goebbels' state-run National Radio would then claim that Polish 'provocateurs' had crossed the border and seized the station – thus providing Hitler with the perfect excuse for his war. The fiendish extra touch planned by Heydrich was to leave eight corpses, cynically codenamed 'Konserve' or 'canned goods', and also dressed in Polish uniforms, scattered around the station as 'proof' of the 'Polish' incursion, with their faces disfigured by acid to prevent identification.

The plan worked perfectly. As Naujocks testified to the Nuremberg tribunal trying the surviving Nazi leaders after the war, his men successfully seized the station on the night of 31 August. Using his radio knowledge, Naujocks hijacked the studio, a Polish speaker gabbled a short message over the airwaves and Naujocks fled into the night with his SS team. The uniformed dead bodies they left behind had been inmates of Dachau – one of the earliest Nazi concentration camps near Munich – who had been murdered with lethal injections administered by an SS doctor. Bullets were then fired into the lifeless bodies as evidence of Polish aggression. The Polish uniforms were provided by Admiral Canaris's Abwehr military intelligence agency, at that time still ready to co-operate with the SS and Gestapo.

The Gestapo's part in the plan had been to arrest and murder a local Silesian farmer, Franciszek Honiok, known as a Polish sympathiser, the night before the attack. Honiok was also dressed in a Polish uniform and murdered by lethal injection before his corpse too was riddled with gunshots. His body was then presented to both the local police and a gullible press corps as a single identifiable 'Polish' attacker. Hitler had his *casus belli*. The following day, German columns poured across the frontier and warplanes streaked across the Polish skies. The Second World War had begun.

There are several alternative versions of precisely how the Salon Kitty operation originated, but the essential elements are the same. Schellenberg and Naujocks, the two main actors in the Salon Kitty drama to survive the war, along with Kitty Schmidt herself, provided their own competing accounts of how the operation to bug the brothel began, while others originated in the unverifiable miasma of post-war rumour surrounding the story.

One version is that Naujocks and Heydrich arranged to meet Kitty Schmidt in the luxurious surroundings of the bar at the Hotel Adlon. The Adlon, opened in 1907 in the heart of Berlin in imitation of the Ritz hotels in London and Paris, was built on a prime site next to the Brandenburg Gate on the city's main tree-lined Unter den Linden avenue. Furnished with such touches as a palm court, barbers and cigar shops, and a music room, and designed in elegant French Second Empire style, the hotel had hosted such international VIPs as Albert Einstein, F. D. Roosevelt, Josephine Baker, Marlene Dietrich and Charlie Chaplin; it was the centre of Berlin's high society before and during the Nazi era.

According to this version, after an hour's polite chit-chat, Heydrich outlined his scheme to Kitty Schmidt, who wisely acceded to the proposal, replying: 'You call the shots, Reinhard. Your idea is fabulous.' Heydrich allegedly responded: 'We'll call the place Salon Kitty, after you.' Not hanging around, the very next day Heydrich purportedly ordered Naujocks to take over the brothel and install the listening equipment.

Naujocks' own story is slightly but significantly different. While confirming that he and Heydrich had met at the Adlon's bar to discuss the plan, he denied that Kitty had been present. According to him Heydrich, Schellenberg, four lesser members of the SD and Naujocks himself were there at an SD staff get-together. The drinks flowed, and an increasingly inebriated Heydrich accosted an attractive young blonde woman and slurringly asked her if she wanted to work for him. He explained to the others that this was exactly the type of woman – pretty and assured in high-society surroundings – he wanted to work in the luxury establishment he envisaged. Warming to his theme, it was time, he continued, to open a stylish brothel for diplomats, high-ranking officials, ministers and foreign visitors in order to elicit useful information from them.

Peter Norden, however, tells a different story again in *Madam Kitty*. Norden claims that in April 1939, Erich Kuhn, a detective superintendent from the Berlin vice squad – department M2 of the city's *Kriminalpolizei* (Criminal Police, or Kripo) – was tasked by his boss, Kripo chief Arthur Nebe, with approaching Kitty Schmidt with the idea of infiltrating her salon with undercover girls working for the police. Nebe's plan was similar to Heydrich's, but without the planted microphones to back up the reports of the girls. Norden alleges that Kitty politely stalled Kuhn, but, thoroughly alarmed, she accelerated her own plans to flee Germany for Britain.

Norden claims that Kitty had been mulling such plans ever since the Nazi takeover. In 1934, three of her regular customers, a trio of Jewish businessmen named Levy, Cohen and Herz, seeing that they had no future in Nazi-ruled Germany, had fled to London after Hitler had become Chancellor. Once established there, they invited Kitty to follow them to Britain, to set up a similar establishment to the brothel she ran in Berlin. Kitty took the plan seriously, not least because she already knew Britain well, having lived there during the First World War. During her visit to London, Kitty stayed at the expensive Dorchester Hotel on Park Lane, where she met her three friends to discuss their idea over dinner.

Still weighing her options, Kitty returned to Berlin, but gradually began to transfer sums of money in instalments to an account in Britain that her friends there had opened for her. In January 1937, the Nazi authorities became suspicious and began to query these regular cash transfers, so Kitty decided to adopt more clandestine methods of ensuring her own future and that of her daughter Kathleen. She arranged for young women who worked at her brothel to make regular trips to London with banknotes sewn into their underwear. Over the years, again according to Norden, these smuggled deposits, originating from the clients of the brothel, amounted to several million Reichsmarks.

As the international situation became more fraught with the run-up to war, Kitty again tried to use the legal route to move her money. This attracted the authorities' attention, and in July 1938 she was accused of currency smuggling. Kitty used her inside contacts with the Kripo to avoid being charged. The writing, however, was on the wall, and by March 1939, at the age of fifty-seven, Kitty had made up her mind to leave Germany for good. The final straw came when, on 4 April, she received the fateful visit from Superintendent Kuhn. She asked the vice squad detective, whom she knew well from his previous visits in the course of his duties, to give her a week to consider Nebe's proposal. In fact, she used the time to prepare her flight into exile.

As described by Norden, Kitty, helped by a wealthy client, Guido Brisalla, an Italian fruit importer, put her escape plan into action. Brisalla agreed to escort her daughter via Italy to London where one of her friends, Levy, who had anglicised his name to Samuel Lewis, would iron out any immigration problems and smooth the way for Kitty's arrival. Unfortunately, one of the coded telegrams that she sent to Levy in Britain was read by the authorities at the Post Office and found its way to Walter Schellenberg, who was in the early stages of carrying out Heydrich's order to find a suitable establishment for a listening post.

Schellenberg set a trap. He put an SD tail on the track of the maid who Kitty was using to send her telegrams. The man followed Kitty's maid back from the Lietzenburgerstrasse Post Office to the Giesebrechtstrasse. To continue monitoring Kitty, the SD agent chatted up and began an affair with the maid. Having established the link between Kitty and the mysterious messages to London, Schellenberg enlisted the aid of the Gestapo, who placed the brothel's madam under 24-hour surveillance. Meanwhile, Superintendent Kuhn returned to Giesebrechtstrasse to get a definite answer from

Kitty to Nebe's proposal. Backed into a corner, and knowing that she was about to flee, Kitty politely but firmly declined to co-operate.

Suspecting that she was being followed, but desperate, on the evening of 28 June Kitty packed a bag, concealed a stash of cash in her clothes, and Brisalla drove her to the railway station where she took a train to Hanover on the first stage of a journey that she hoped would lead her to a new life in freedom. Kitty was met in Hanover by a friend of Brisalla's, who drove her to Münster via Gütersloh, hoping to shake off her unseen watchers. At Oldenburg station she bought a ticket for Enschede, from where she intended to board a train to Amsterdam. As she awaited her connection in the station's waiting room, the polite young man who had helped carry her bag called Schellenberg to report on Kitty's progress.

The *SS-Obersturmführer* (lieutenant colonel) ordered that Kitty should be allowed to continue her journey as far as the Dutch border to provide the proof that she was trying to flee the Reich. At that point she was arrested and escorted back to Berlin. Once in her home city, she was taken to the Prinz-Albrecht-Strasse and unceremoniously locked into a windowless cell. It was a cheerless contrast to the comforts she had been used to in her heyday. The only furnishings were a cot with a thin straw mattress covered by a single stinking blanket. There was a latrine in one corner, and light was provided by a single dim bulb that burned all day between 6am and 6pm.

For the next fortnight, though she lost track of time, Kitty was subjected to an ordeal that she had only heard about as whispered rumours reported by fearful friends. Her confinement in the chilly cell was interrupted by repeated interrogations conducted in a bare office where harsh lights were shone in her face. She was questioned about her telegrams to Sam Lewis in London, and truthfully reported that he was a friend of some twenty years. The shouted questions were accompanied by slaps and blows when her answers failed to satisfy her interrogators. She was permitted to wash once daily, and the only other interruptions to the hellish routine were the arrival of scanty meals – watery soup and ersatz coffee with the occasional sparse *Eintopf* stew.

On 14 July, without warning, Kitty was taken in a prison van to an SD office at Meineckestrasse 11 and told to freshen up in a bathroom. Then, for the first time, she met Walter Schellenberg. The confrontation was a 'meeting without coffee'. Schellenberg was brisk, cold, impersonal and to the point. He made Kitty an offer that she felt unable to refuse. He assured her that he had more than enough evidence of her 'crimes': she had helped Jews escape the Reich and had illegally smuggled currency out of the country. The choice before her was a two-year stretch in a prison cell under conditions similar to those that she had just endured, or, even worse, immediate dispatch to the feared terrors of a concentration camp – to disappear into the *Nacht und Nebel* from where few returned. Or, Schellenberg continued, she could save herself from this fate by co-operating with the plan he had in mind.

Schellenberg proceeded to outline the scheme that he and Heydrich had devised. If she agreed to collaborate with the SD in allowing the installation of sophisticated listening equipment to spy on some of her 'guests' of interest to the authorities; and if, furthermore, she raised no objection to the addition of a score of extra employees to her usual cast of girls, her past crimes would be forgiven if not forgotten. Moreover, she would be assisting the Reich, and there could, of course, be no question of her emigrating to England. According to Peter Norden, Kitty felt that she had no alternative but to comply. Weakened by her incarceration and frightened by the deep interrogations that she had suffered, she buckled. 'I'll do everything you ask me to,' she allegedly told Schellenberg.

There is one more unverified story that further muddies the already murky waters surrounding the birth of the Salon Kitty spy centre.

According to an unsigned article that appeared in *Der Spiegel* news magazine on 15 December 1949, there was a second 'Kitty': a woman who managed a similar brothel in Landhausgasse in the Austrian capital Vienna. This woman, named Kitty Schröder, was allegedly an acquaintance of the police chief and *SS-Sturmbannführer* Arthur Nebe when he was posted in Vienna before the war. Kitty Schröder had allegedly moved to Berlin where Nebe supposedly gave her a task 'of high importance to the Reich': to open another brothel on the city's Bayerischer Platz under the guise of a high-class pension, or boarding house.

Nebe, alleged the article, had a special interest in such establishments as overall head of Berlin's vice squad. And, like many Nazi leaders, he had questionable sexual morals himself. (After opportunistically taking part in the July 1944 bomb plot on Hitler's life, Nebe would go into hiding on an island on Berlin's Wannsee lake, only to be betrayed to his death by a discarded mistress.) It is likely that Nebe's police deliberately used spies at other brothels besides Salon Kitty to collect and pass on information. The uniqueness of Kitty Schmidt's establishment was that it was 'wired for sound' by the SD using the most sophisticated listening equipment then available, and that it was staffed by specially trained SD spy professionals.

In our research we have failed to find any trace of 'Kitty Schröder' or her brothels in Berlin or Vienna. Our belief is that the anonymous author of the *Spiegel* article was deliberately camouflaging the real Kitty Schmidt – possibly at her request – by inventing a fictional persona and history. Given that in 1949, when the article appeared, Salon Kitty was back in business in the Giesebrechtstrasse, and again being run by its original owner, there was every reason for the real Kitty Schmidt to draw a veil over the dark past.

So what were the reasons that caused Heydrich and Schellenberg to hit on Kitty's salon as the locale for their spying operation? Firstly, the house at 11 Giesebrechtstrasse was in a very good location: just off the main Kurfürstendamm avenue, yet in a quiet and discreet street where any observers on the 'Ku'damm' could not see those entering or leaving the premises. Secondly, after the official Nazi crackdown on the teeming clubs and bordellos that had flourished under Weimar, there were very few similar establishments left in business by 1939. Thirdly, it can be assumed that Kitty Schmidt herself had good relations with leading Nazis in the regime, given that some of them were already her regular customers. Fourthly, and finally, if Norden's account has any credibility, Kitty Schmidt had laid herself open to blackmail and coercion by Heydrich and Schellenberg because of her 'crimes'. We will examine Kitty's motivations more closely in a later chapter.

In his post-war memoirs, written under the shadow of his imminent death from cancer, Walter Schellenberg owned up to the part he had played:

So I went about renting a suitable house via an intermediary . . . Double walls, modern listening devices and automatic transmissions ensured that every word spoken in this 'salon' was recorded and transmitted to operational headquarters. The technical maintenance was done by officials from the SD, under oath (i.e., sworn to secrecy), and all personnel, from the maids to the waiter, were secret service agents.

However, Schellenberg considered the task of actually finding the 'beautiful women' who would staff the spy brothel somewhat beneath him. By his own account, as we shall see, he tasked Naujocks and vice squad boss Arthur Nebe with the distasteful job.

There is another piece in the confusing jigsaw of conflicting evidence to consider. Felix Kersten, the personal physician and masseur to Heydrich's boss, Reichsführer Heinrich Himmler, recounts in his post-war memoirs a meeting he had with Heydrich on 24 February 1941. During their conversation, the masseur claimed, the SD chief invited Kersten to 'inspect' what he called the 'elegant house in the Giesebrechtstrasse':

> If you are interested – from a strictly medical point of view of course – to have a look at the house in the Giesebrechtstrasse, it is always at your disposal. Just give me a call. I may even show you around myself. You can come wearing a white coat; that always looks good. I will also put one on and assist you.

According to Kersten, Heydrich added the titbit that Salon Kitty had been created with the co-operation of the Reich's Foreign Minister Joachim von Ribbentrop:

> . . . in particular so as to have something to offer to the foreigners in Berlin, who frequented it in high numbers. For the time being it still required support, but he was hoping that soon it would finance itself.

Moreover, wrote Kersten, Heydrich mused that he was considering establishing a similar venue specifically catering to homosexuals.

Heydrich's widow, Lina von Osten, who had first pointed him in the direction of his career as a spymaster, also mentions Salon Kitty and its finances in her 1976 memoirs *Leben mit einem Kriegsverbrecher* (*Life with a War Criminal*), claiming that the bugged brothel was not necessarily her husband's idea:

> I presume it was Walter Schellenberg. They set up an establishment at the highest level for diplomats and employed the elite of Berlin's ladies of pleasure. Occasionally, if there was no money to be had, the state paid their fee. An intelligence

operation was established that could never have been set up with regular official means. Here, too, they installed state-of-the-art technology – in the walls and in the furniture.

Amidst all these varying accounts, one thing is clear. All the accumulated evidence from a variety of sources makes certain that there was much more to Salon Kitty than a mere 'legend' concocted from a mishmash of scurrilous rumour. The truth of the matter as far as it can now be established, and the context in which the salon operated, we can now reveal.

CHAPTER TWO

LOVE FOR SALE

– Sex and prostitution in the
Weimar Republic

Not for nothing was the German capital on the eve of the Nazi take-over known as 'Berlin Babylon'. Few cities – not even Paris in the Belle Epoque of the late nineteenth century – have established such a well-deserved reputation as a centre of sexual indulgence. Prostitution, wild perversion and a network of brothels, bars and clubs tailored to cater for every erotic taste flourished in an atmosphere of free licence shading into decadent dissolution. The revolutionary upheavals that accompanied the collapse of Imperial Germany at the end of the First World War, followed by the inflation, mass unemployment and economic misery of the 1920s and early 1930s had led to social dislocation, widespread impoverishment and bewildering political instability. Berlin was a city of extremes.

The image of the city as a centre of crime, depravity and dissolution was first portrayed in the stark pictures of artists like George Grosz, Otto Dix and Max Beckmann, who together with others formed the *Neue Sachlichkeit* (New Objectivity) movement. Their portraits of a society on the edge are peopled by ugly, raddled whores and the fat, complacent bourgeois and military men who used them and exploited their services. An atmosphere of cruelty, violence, despair and decay saturates these images of a city which, according to these painters, was populated by impoverished war cripples, gangsters, sex killers, racketeers and the scar-faced capitalists and monocled officers feeding off the decadence like carrion crows.

George Grosz, the artist who satirised the Berlin of the 1920s most savagely, also portrayed the putrid atmosphere of the city in words, recalling in his autobiography *A Small Yes and A Big No* (1955):

> The times were certainly out of joint. All moral restraints seemed to have melted away. A flood of vice, pornography and prostitution swept the entire country . . . The city was dark, cold and full of rumours. The streets were wild ravines haunted by murderers and cocaine peddlers, their emblem a metal bar or a murderous broken-off chair leg.

This portrayal of Berlin, half wickedly glamorous and half dangerously perverse, was first popularised in the film *The Blue Angel* (1930), one of the first 'talkies' shot at Berlin's Babelsberg studios. Directed by the brilliant Austrian filmmaker Josef von Sternberg, and loosely based on a novel by Heinrich Mann, it starred Emil Jannings as a respectable schoolteacher brought down to degradation and eventual death by his infatuation for Lola, a sultry nightclub singer. Lola's role was played by an unknown actress, Marlene Dietrich, whose seductive pose, lolling back in black stockings and top hat as she performed her signature song 'Falling in Love Again', seemed to sum up the camp and sensual erotic charms of the city – and launched her stellar international career.

The club in the film was based on a real Berlin cabaret club, The Stork's Nest, whose customers could pay extra for a seat on the stage to ogle the singers at close quarters. The club was one of scores of similar venues offering erotic entertainment, ranging from sophisticated nightclubs to sleazy strip joints, and spanning a wide gamut of sexual tastes, including gay, lesbian, cross-dressing and S&M specialities. The clubs, bars and cafés had names like Heaven and Hell, Cosy Corner, and Dorian Gray. The portrayal of a Berlin teetering on the edge of the abyss and striving to forget its troubles in erotic obsession were most famously set in stone and propagated by the Berlin stories of the expatriate British writer Christopher Isherwood, later successfully glamorised and sanitised in another musical made into a movie – *Cabaret*.

The elegant atmosphere of the nightclub portrayed in the film – made from the stories that 'Herr Issyvoo' observed with an ironic and half-amused camera-like eye – were some way from the sordid reality of sex for sale in the city. Berlin was a teeming metropolis where even previously respectable middle-class women and young girls were forced to sell their bodies after the economic ruination they had suffered in the year of rampant inflation in 1923. This was the terrifying time when a hundred paper mills across Germany worked round the clock to print banknotes that became worthless before the ink on them was dry; when workers collected their wages in wheelbarrows; and the price of a cup of coffee in a café tripled while it was being drunk. The inflation had wiped out the life savings of the German middle class, and with it the moral values of the stable pre-First World War society.

In an essay titled 'Berlin is Becoming a Whore', the writer Thomas Wehrling captured the desperation of a period that had debauched the morals of the previously prosperous middle classes along with their savings.

A University Professor earns less than a streetcar conductor, but the scholar's daughter was used to wearing silk stockings. It is no accident that the nude dancer Celly de Rheidt is the wife of a former Prussian officer. Thousands of bourgeois families are now being forced, if they want to live respectably on their budgets, to leave their six-room apartments and adopt a vegetarian diet. This impoverishment of the bourgeoisie is necessarily bound up with women accustomed to luxury becoming whores . . . The impoverished noblewoman becomes a barmaid; the discharged naval officer makes films; the daughter of the provincial judge cannot expect her father to make her a present of her winter clothes.

In the phrase 'the discharged naval officer makes films', Wehrling was being more prophetic than he knew. One such naval officer, Reinhard Heydrich, dishonourably discharged from the navy at the height of the Great Depression, may not have made films, but took up a new career as intelligence chief of Himmler's SS, a role in which he would not only go on to initiate the Holocaust, but forge a straitjacket of terror, repression and surveillance across Germany and most of conquered Europe.

That earlier 1923 inflation – fuelled by the huge reparations that Germany had been forced to pay by the deeply resented Treaty of Versailles as compensation for the ravage its aggression had wrought during the war – also attracted a host of foreigners, like Isherwood, keen to sample the dubious delights of the city on the River Spree. These visitors found that their money in hard foreign currency went much further than in their home countries. Some were shocked by the scale of the open prostitution on the capital's streets, with underage girls competing for custom with their senior sisters. Arriving in Berlin to direct *The Blue Angel*, Josef von Sternberg, saw schoolgirls '. . . flaunting pigtails and schoolbooks, paraded to appeal to those who hurried to meet them with clenched jaws and set fists'. The American film writer Anita Loos, author of *Gentlemen Prefer Blondes*, was struck by the ambiguous atmosphere of cross-dressing and gender fluidity she found during a visit to Berlin from Hollywood: '. . . any Berlin lady of the evening might turn out to be a man; the prettiest girl on the street was Conrad Veidt, who later became an international film star'.

Conrad Veidt is a figure who exemplifies the step change in German culture between the repressive Wilhelmine Empire and the liberal Weimar Republic. The star of the quintessential Weimar expressionist film *The Cabinet of Dr Caligari* (1920), the pansexual Veidt, who married three times despite his cross-dressing tendencies, was, like Marlene Dietrich and the writers Heinrich and Thomas Mann, one of the hundreds of German artists forced to go into exile when the Nazis took power. One of his earliest film roles was a collaboration with Dr Magnus Hirschfeld, a pioneer of the sexual liberation that Weimar represented, in a movie now regarded as the first plea for tolerance of homosexuality shown on the silver screen. In the 1919 film *Anders als die Andern* (*Different from the Others*), Weidt played a suicidal gay patient of Hirschfeld who funded and co-wrote the film's script and played himself in the part of a sympathetic psychiatrist.

Hirschfeld was a courageous campaigner for worldwide sexual liberation who had been agitating for reform of Germany's repressive laws on sexuality since the nineteenth century – a stance which saw him twice almost beaten to death by anti-Semitic thugs. Hirschfeld had managed to win the support of the powerful Social Democratic Party (SPD) for removing the notorious Paragraph 175 forbidding male homosexuality from the German Penal Code, although the attempt was defeated on the floor of the Reichstag parliament.

After the First World War, and the collapse of the monarchy, in 1919 Hirschfeld established his *Institut für Sexualwissenschaft* (Institute for Sexual Science), the world's first such sexology centre, in a large building complex with some sixty-five rooms overlooking the Tiergarten park in central Berlin. The institute combined physical and psychiatric treatment of patients suffering sexual problems with research into the subject. It had a large library – including Europe's biggest collection of pornographic and erotic literature – along with more scientific works on sexology and a museum of sexuality. During the decade that the institute remained open, it was visited by 20,000 people a year, ranging from curious celebrities to the sexually troubled and the simply desperate. Visitors could also rent rooms to stay. One who did so during one of his earliest trips to Berlin in 1929 was Christopher Isherwood.

At that time, Isherwood was still repressed about his own homosexuality and regarded the earnestness with which Hirschfeld and his colleagues treated the subject with embarrassed English humour. Hirschfeld's lover Karl Giese and the friend who had introduced him to the Institute showed Isherwood round his new home, as the latter recalled in his autobiography *Christopher and His Kind* (1977):

> Christopher giggled nervously when Karl Giese and Francis took him through the institute's museum. Here were whips and chains and torture instruments for the practitioners of pain-pleasure; high-heeled, intricately decorated boots for the fetishists; lacey female undies which had been worn by ferociously masculine Prussian officers.
>
> Here were the lower halves of trouser-legs with elastic bands to hold them in position between knee and ankle. In these and nothing else but an overcoat and a pair of shoes, you could walk the streets and seem fully clothed, giving a camera-quick exposure whenever a suitable viewer appeared . . . Here were fantasy pictures, drawn and painted by Hirschfeld's patients. Scenes from the court of a priapic king who sprawled on a throne with his own phallus for a sceptre and watched the grotesque mating of his courtiers. Strange sad bedroom scenes in which the faces of the copulators expressed only dismay and agony.

Another visitor to the city, the Austrian writer Stefan Zweig, linked the trashing of previous strict moral codes forbidding premarital sex and frowning on homosexuality to the mass outbreak of commercialised sex.

> All values were changed, and . . . Berlin was transformed into the Babylon of the world. Bars, amusement parks, honky-tonks sprang up like mushrooms. Along the entire Kurfürstendamm [Berlin's main western throughfare] powdered and rouged young men sauntered, and they were not all professionals; every high-school boy wanted to earn some money and in the dimly lit bars one might see government officials and men of the world tenderly courting drunken sailor[s] without any shame. Even the Rome of Suetonius had never known such orgies as the pervert balls of Berlin, where hundreds of men costumed as women and hundreds of women as men danced under the benevolent eyes of the police. In the collapse of all values a kind of madness took hold, particularly in the bourgeois circles which until then had been unshakeable in their probity.
>
> But the most revolting thing about this pathetic eroticism was its spuriousness. At bottom the orgiastic period which broke out in Germany simultaneously with the inflation was nothing more than a feverish imitation . . . The whole nation, tired of war, actually longed only for order.

The nation was to get its unconscious wish for 'order' soon enough.

It is impossible to put a precise figure on the numbers of people engaged in prostitution in Berlin in the years between the downfall of the Kaiser in November 1918 and Adolf Hitler's appointment as Chancellor in January 1933. The usual guesstimate is that some 120,000 girls and women and around 35,000 boys and men sold their bodies professionally in a city with a population of just over four million. Given the blurred lines between 'amateurs' willing to 'moonlight' and full-time sex workers, the actual numbers so engaged were almost certainly much higher.

The laws governing prostitution in the Weimar Republic had been introduced under Kaiser Wilhelm II in an effort to regulate the sex trade and confine it to certain clearly defined areas. Known as *Kasernierung* (barracking), the idea was to separate whores from the 'respectable' run of the general population and lock them away in barrack-like brothels, mainly in the impoverished industrial eastern side of the city. The police dedicated specific streets for such brothels, and the areas where prostitutes and their clients could meet and mingle freely had been originally designated since medieval times by physical lines – known as *Striche* – painted on the ground. This gave rise to the popular slang term for sex workers: *Strichmädchen* or *Strichjunge* (the latter term technically referring to male prostitutes). To take up prostitution was popularly termed '*auf den Strich gehen*' – literally 'to walk the line'.

In 1914, when the First World War broke out, only 4,000 prostitutes were officially registered with the Berlin Police. These professionals were subject to monthly health checks by the eight doctors in the city tapped for the task. After the war prostitutes were still strictly forbidden to verbally solicit potential customers and were obliged to signal their specialised services by other means such as the colour coding of clothes, shoes and boots. Customers seeking flagellation, or other varieties of S&M, for example, knew by looking at the footwear of *Stiefelhuren* ('booted whores') that if green boots were worn, they could look forward to a session of slavery and humiliation with a scatological happy ending. If the boots were red or maroon, they signalled an evening of discipline administered with whips or canes.

A favoured spot for 'dominas' to pick up clients was the area west of Wittenbergplatz in south-western Berlin. Here, eight years apart, the writers Klaus Mann – son of the novelist Thomas Mann

– and Curt Moreck (a pseudonym of the writer and Berliner Konrad Haemmerling) encountered two examples of the species at the same spot. In 1924, at the height of Weimar's hyperinflation, Mann met

> . . . fierce Amazons, strutting in high boots made of green, glossy leather. One of them brandished a supple cane and leered at me as I passed by. 'Good evening, madam,' I said. So she whispered into my ear: 'Want to be my slave? Costs only six billion and a cigarette. A bargain. Come along, honey!'

In 1932, Moreck, author of guidebooks to Berlin's sexual underworld, had a similar experience, encountering a troop of strapping six-foot 'boot girls' resplendent in scarlet and black clothes like nineteenth-century horsewomen. Cracking a horsewhip, the tallest of them bellowed threateningly: 'Who will be my slave tonight?' Brothels and prostitutes specialising in sadomasochism were not confined to Berlin. In 1927 the Anglo–American high-society diarist and Tory MP Henry 'Chips' Channon was visiting Cologne and counted twenty-four brothels in a single street. At one of these Channon sampled a beating himself, administered by a muscular blonde woman wielding a birch.

Under Weimar, prostitution influenced women's fashions: the garish colours worn by prostitutes were widely adopted by women wishing to be modish. The popular short 'bobs', or *Bubikopfs* ('boyheads'), for example, which were the hallmark of many streetwalkers, became the mainstream hairstyle of the 'flappers' – fashionable young women in the early 1920s.

The Weimar Republic, in a conscious effort to shed the restrictive culture of Wilhelmine Germany, made an effort to liberalise the laws governing prostitution. In March 1924, the Reichstag parliament in Berlin called on the Reich government to close all state-licensed brothels throughout Germany and abolish the *Kasernierung* regulations. Prostitutes should no longer be confined to barracks under the watchful eyes of landlords, but be allowed to live and work among the general population. One effect of this liberalisation was that sex workers who did not already have their own accommodation – and were reluctant to try their luck with clients on the streets – had to find their own, usually overpriced, flat or room as private tenants.

In Berlin there was a general distinction between more affluent call girls who worked 'inside' from their own property, and less prosperous 'outside' street girls – nicknamed *Bordsteinschwalben* ('kerbstone swallows'). Beyond these broad differences there were many sub-categories, which reflected a city catering to every conceivable variety of vice. *Grashüpferinnen* ('grasshoppers') were women who serviced clients in grassy nooks of the Berlin Tiergarten, the city's huge central park, or in shady corners on Bulow Platz, a large public square. *Halbseidenen* (those wearing 'half-silk' fabrics) were unregistered amateurs, reputedly moonlighting from their day jobs such as secretaries or salesgirls, who wanted to earn extra money on the side in their free time. Halbseidenen are estimated to have numbered between 40,000 and 55,000 – making them the biggest sub-group among Berlin's sex workers.

By 1930, numbers of the 4,000 pre-war state registered *Kontrollmädchen* ('control girls') had more than doubled to 8,750. Like their pre-war sisters, they had to report regularly to the vice department of the Berlin Criminal Police, the Kripo, to be checked for sexually transmitted diseases by public health officials. A dozen areas of the city were especially noted for prostitution, of which the most open and notorious was the 'Alex' – the area around the Alexanderplatz, a large square on the city's proletarian eastern side, where the headquarters of Germany's Communist Party, the KPD, was located, along with Berlin's central police station. The Alex district housed an astonishing 320 brothels, ranging from a dozen sophisticated establishments of the Salon Kitty type to scores of cheap 'knocking shops' where sordid rooms could be rented by the hour by women who had picked up their clients in the street.

Pregnant sex workers and girls who thronged under the lanterns of Münzstrasse to await their suitors were nicknamed *Münzis*, while the crop-headed boyish teenagers engaged in the same profession were called *Nutten*. Deformed, disabled or unattractive women, perhaps hunchbacked or missing a limb, were known as *Steinhuren* ('stone whores') or *Murmeltiere* ('marmots'). Mistresses specialising in domination, and typically clad in fur coats and knee-high patent leather boots, officially numbered 850 in 1930. So-called *Tauentzien-girls* were named after another well-known Berlin street: the Tauentzienstrasse, and often operated in mother-daughter teams.

Moving up the social sexual scale from the street girls to the 'insider' women who worked in brothels or private apartments, *Chontes* was a disparaging term derived from Yiddish for Polish–Jewish women working from home. *Demi-castors* or *mannequins* were terms used for *Belle de Jour*-style women from wealthy families fallen on hard times who wanted to earn extra pocket money by prostitution. The Russian journalist Ilya Ehrenburg, passing through an impoverished Berlin soon after the First World War, described his encounter with one such family:

> We travelled by underground . . . and finally found ourselves in a respectable flat. On the walls hung portraits of members of the family in officers' uniform and a painting of a sunset. We were given 'champagne' – lemonade laced with spirits. Then the host's two daughters appeared – naked – and began to dance. One of them talked of Dostoyevsky's novels. The mother hopefully eyed the foreign guests: perhaps they would be tempted by her daughters and would pay: in dollars of course . . .

Fohsen were sex workers who kept off the streets and advertised their services as 'masseuses' in local newspapers and magazines. *Fremdspracheninstitute* were S&M brothels masquerading as foreign language institutes whose staff, dubbed 'racehorses', were willing to be whipped and beaten by clients. Another variety of sex workers catering to their clients' sadistic tastes were called 'minettes' – young women prepared to indulge in bondage games or satisfy their clients' cross-dressing fantasies.

There were no limits to the depravity of the sex trade in inter-war Berlin. One of its most disturbing aspects was the abuse of underage children as prostitutes. Adolescents, some as young as twelve, worked as 'telephone girls' under the names of famous film stars such as Marlene Dietrich who could be ordered over the phone by depraved customers and delivered to their destinations by taxi. Likewise, the coded sub-category known as 'medicine' was another form of child prostitution. Pimps acting as 'pharmacists' noted the sick desires of their 'patients'. When ordering, the 'patients' listed the number of 'sick days' that corresponded with the age of the girls they wanted to abuse, and the colour of the 'pill' required referred to the desired hair colour of the girls.

The *Tischfrauen* ('table ladies') were sophisticated courtesans who frequented the exclusive western nightclubs around the Kurfürstendamm. This sub-category offered 'looks' specific to certain countries. Usually stunningly beautiful, multilingual and well-educated, they would dress as Spanish ladies, elegant Nordic blondes or exotic Russians according to their clients' choice. Prospective clients would pay an exorbitant table fee for the pleasure of the company of such ladies, and would be served expensive Champagne before adjourning for a more intimate encounter in separate booths.

In 1930, the author Willy Pröger, conducting a survey of Berlin's lower depths, spoke of the 'gruesome conditions' that he found in the sleazy dosshouses where prostitutes and their clients rented rooms by the hour. He conducted his readers on a tour ranging from the miserable dives around the Schlesischer Bahnhof train station and the Alexanderplatz, to the more luxurious venues near the Friedrichstrasse and on the Kurfürstendamm boulevard. His report included an urgent appeal to the authorities to increase health education and raise awareness of the dire situation in the cheap bordellos that were 'predestined to spread sexually transmitted diseases'.

Pröger underlined the clear distinction between the two groups of prostitutes. A 'lady of class', he wrote, could afford to service just two clients a day in a transient hotel and lead a tolerable life. But a 'cheap slut' had to satisfy at least six men a day in order to maintain a bare level of subsistence. A prostitute existing at such a marginal level earned two to three Reichsmarks per customer (roughly ten euros in today's value). In such transient hotels, and even in private apartments, Pröger found sheets and towels were rarely changed after use, which meant that STD contagion and diseases like syphilis, gonorrhoea and tuberculosis were widespread. Although such sex hotels were officially illegal, the police and health authorities had no power to close them down, and the tax authorities treated them as if they were legal. *Kriminalrat* Kunze, a senior official working at the headquarters of the Berlin Police in Alexanderplatz, told Pröger in an interview: 'If we close down one of these coupling houses three new ones open up elsewhere.'

CHAPTER THREE

LOVE SUPPRESSED

– The Nazi crackdown on Eros

Adolf Hitler's appointment as Reich Chancellor on 30 January 1933 signalled not only the seizure of political power by his Nazi Party, but an abrupt end for the free-ranging sex and prostitution characterising Berlin. The erotic underworld of the old Weimar Berlin had already received an advance warning of the coming crackdown in the spring and summer of 1932 when pornographic publications and some of the city's more extreme drag clubs and clip joints were shut down by the authorities. Hitler himself had already made his attitude to prostitution quite clear in his autobiography/manifesto *Mein Kampf*, where he branded them 'a disgrace to humanity'.

The official Nazi Party line was that prostitutes were the very opposite of their ideal of the true role of women as monogamous, faithful wives, whose sole purpose was to keep well-run homes and breed and raise children. According to the Nazis, the moral depravity of whores revealed the inferior genetic make-up of these 'asocial beings' who were 'aliens in our communities', and often 'morally feeble-minded'.

In several large German cities, such as Essen, Lübeck and Karlsruhe, the concept of *Kasernierung* – physically separating prostitutes from the general community, expressly abolished under Weimar – was reintroduced. In other cities – Munich, Hamburg and Stuttgart, for example – police handed out warning leaflets to prostitutes to inform them of the *Strichverbot*: a ban on walking the line. Those who ignored the ban and continued to publicly ply their trade risked being taken into *Schutzhaft* – protective custody – the sinister term for unlimited detention without trial, which frequently meant consignment to one of the new concentration camps being set up across Germany by the Nazi regime.

The Nazis wasted no time in enforcing their crackdown on vice. On 26 May 1933, four months after Hitler's appointment as Chancellor, they introduced a 'Law Amending Provisions of Criminal Law', stipulating that it was no longer necessary to explicitly prove a 'violation of decency and morals' to forbid prostitution. On the contrary: street prostitution was to be actively suppressed in police raids. The new law stipulated: 'Anyone who solicits fornication, or offers to engage in the same, in public and in a conspicuous manner likely to cause annoyance to individuals or the general public' was to be punished by six weeks in jail and subsequent confinement in a workhouse.

In Hamburg, which as a busy port city had long been notorious for prostitution, 1,500 women were temporarily taken into 'protective custody' between March and December 1933. The rules of the Hamburg Police were clear: the first time that a woman engaged in prostitution was picked up, she received a warning. The second time that this happened, she had to spend eight days in jail. And a third offence committed within a year resulted in three months' detention. In Berlin, too, the open sex trade disappeared almost entirely in the summer months of 1933 as the Nazis consolidated their rule.

Prostitution was branded as something disgusting and dangerous, and brothels were seen as synonymous with a source of infections and a breeding ground of chronic venereal diseases like syphilis and gonorrhoea. Purportedly, in 1934, someone in Germany was infected with a STD every two minutes, of which gonorrhoea was the most widespread, with 175,000 new cases reported each year, and the real figures much higher still.

After the elimination of public prostitution, the authorities turned their attention to clamping down on private brothels. The Reich Minister of the Interior, Wilhelm Frick, issued a decree on 12 July 1934 that explicitly made the reopening of brothels illegal. Even before the decree was issued, by the spring of 1934 there were only around twenty brothels remaining in Berlin – a city that had only recently hosted hundreds of such establishments. The few surviving bordellos had to comply with a long list of stringent regulations.

Stairwells had to be brightly lit by day and night; prostitutes could no longer show themselves in the entrances, in corridors or windows, or on the street outside wearing 'objectionable clothing'. The brothel landlords had to put up a table displaying their full name by the entrance door, and it was forbidden to establish a welcoming 'salon' lounge. The rooms had to have consecutive numbers and landlords had to provide clean sheets and towels and regularly change them. If there was no central heating in the building, every room had to be equipped with a stove. If a brothel was on the ground floor it had to have heavy curtains shielding the lewd goings-on inside from the view of passers-by. Drinks and any other beverages could only be served by prostitutes in the privacy of their own rooms. All told, these regulations were designed to make brothels as unattractive as possible to their customers, workers and owners alike.

Along with its campaign against prostitution, the new Nazi state waged war against moral laxity more generally. Health authorities and the police worked hand in hand to combat 'commercial fornication'. In addition to women who followed prostitution as their profession, the health authorities across Germany were officially observing approximately 20,000 so-called 'h.w.G' women (h.w.G standing for *häufig wechselnder Geschlechtsverkehr*: 'frequently changing sexual partners'). The state snooping often led to diagnosis, by means of tests, of those classed as 'morally feebly minded'. Such women were subjected to legal constraints that could include detention, sterilisation and even murder by euthanasia.

Once a woman was officially classed as a prostitute, she became an 'asocial', a category branded *arbeitsscheu* ('workshy'), which included habitual criminals, alcoholics, the long-term unemployed and conscientious objectors to military service. After the setting up of concentration camps, this category was in danger of being sent to the camps alongside Jews, Communists, homosexuals, Roma and Sinti, Jehovah's Witnesses and other victims of the Nazis. In the camps asocials had to wear black triangles sewn on their striped blue and white pyjama uniforms to distinguish them from racial, religious, homosexual and political prisoners. Of the 110,000 non-Jewish Germans sent to concentration camps between 1937 and 1943, 70,000 were registered as asocials and 40,000 as political prisoners.

Any woman who did not follow a respectable bourgeois lifestyle, had previously suffered from a sexually transmitted disease, frequently changed their lovers or simply refused to conform to narrow or Nazi moral ideology was in danger of being confined under *Schutzhaft*. Such women were seen as 'unable to live in society', and inherently genetically diseased and inferior. Actually proving that such women had an STD became of minor importance.

Once a woman was declared 'legally incapable' under the German Civil Code they effectively became an unperson at the mercy of an all-powerful state. A municipal official was appointed as her legal guardian and could decide the fate of their 'ward'. 'Legally incapable' was defined as a 'person being legally incapacitated due to feeble-mindedness no longer capable of taking care of his or her affairs'. 'Feeble-minded', in turn, were those 'whose intellectual capacities are severely restricted'. A typical example of such a case of 'incapacitation' can be read in a judgement handed down by a Hamburg district court:

> The plaintiff has repeatedly failed in her emotional life and in exercising her will. Her moral values and her ability to lead a life determined by a sense of ethical responsibility are withered to a degree that clearly points to feeble-mindedness . . . She has given in to constitutionally degenerate appetites, without fail and without consideration for possible consequences, indiscriminately and displaying a below average intelligence.

This mainly affected women who 'as a consequence of their moral guilt, become an increasing burden on public welfare, stubbornly refuse to work, and engage in fornication'. The vague term 'public welfare' was used as a catchall pretext to persecute such women. Even an unpaid hospital bill could be enough to lock up a young woman in a so-called workhouse. Some twenty-six such workhouses had existed across Germany under Weimar but had stood half-empty.

When the Nazis took over in 1933, workhouses rapidly filled up as internment facilities for 'asocial elements'. A 'Law Against Dangerous Habitual Criminals and on Measures to Secure Them and Improve Their Character', passed in 1934, permitted the detention of beggars, vagrants, prostitutes and pimps for an indefinite period of not less than two years. In detention, so that they would not be even more of a burden on the state, the women were compelled to work in nursing or old people's homes, or on menial tasks such as cleaning, laundry, sewing, darning or gardening. After a series of so-called 'beggar raids' by the police, 1,800 such people were interned in workhouses in 1934. Once concentration camps came on stream, these 'asocials' were increasingly sent to them.

The fate of Else Krug, a Düsseldorf prostitute specialising in sadomasochism, who had plied her trade for ten years without undue official interference, was typical of many. A police raid launched at 2am on 30 July 1938 on the brothel in Corneliusstrasse in the city's Bahndamm red-light quarter where Else lived and worked, ignored the clients, who fled half-dressed into the night, but Else and twenty-three of her fellow sex workers were detained and officially classed as asocials. The raid was part of an unreported nationwide round-up of prostitutes named *Aktion Arbeitsscheu Reich* ('Reich Workshy Action') under which some 20,000 'asocials' – beggars, vagrants, petty and habitual criminals, along with prostitutes and their pimps – were arrested and consigned to concentration camps. Else ended up in Ravensbrück, the camp primarily for women prisoners near Berlin that opened in 1939.

In Hamburg, the city with the largest number of sex workers after Berlin, the welfare authority in charge of prostitutes encouraged the 'welfare guardians' of such women to sterilise one of them each week. Between 1936 and the end of the war in 1945, Käthe Peterson, head of the Hamburg Welfare Authority, assumed the legal guardianship over a total of 1,450 women who had been legally incapacitated due to their 'feeble-mindedness' and were deemed to be 'estranged from society and at risk'. In the first months of her duties alone, by July 1936, 80 per cent of the 230 women under Peterson's charge were sent into institutional 'care'. Peterson described her charges as 'weak-willed and dull, making it impossible for them to get used to an orderly lifestyle'.

In addition to their 'moral degradation' denounced by the regime, prostitutes under the Third Reich were increasingly regarded as workshy degenerates. Another draconian law, the 'Fundamental Decree for the Prevention of Crime', passed on 14 December 1937, proscribed preventive detention of all those 'who, short of being a professional or habitual criminal, put the community at risk by means of their asocial behaviour'. By April 1938 the concept of 'asocial' included prostitutes and anyone suffering from an STD who 'evade measures by the public health authorities'. By the war's end, those detained in concentration camps under this measure numbered tens of thousands.

Despite their increasingly repressive campaign against vice and prostitution, the National Socialists were well aware that the phenomenon could never disappear entirely. Indeed, in some special circumstances they encouraged it to continue. In order to lure as many foreign visitors to Berlin as possible for the 1936 Summer Olympics, for example, commercial prostitution was actually promoted by the regime. For the duration of the Games, the Nazis issued special permits to some 7,000 prostitutes licensing them to ply their trade in the city. In another temporary fake 'liberalisation' at this time, the women of Berlin were permitted to raise the seams of their skirts by a modest five centimetres!

In the following year, the head of the SS, Reichsführer Heinrich Himmler, in a private speech addressed to SS group leaders in February 1937, declared: 'In this area [i.e., prostitution], we will be very generous, because we cannot on the one hand try to prevent our youth drifting into homosexuality, and on the other hand bar every way out of this. That would be insane.'

In a typical example of double standards, it was only the prostitutes' clients who benefitted from the Nazi government's 'generosity' rather than the women themselves. When the Second World War began, the persecution of surviving prostitutes was stepped up, and their living and working conditions deteriorated drastically. Many were permanently interned in the surviving brothels themselves, while others were forcibly conscripted to serve in brothels established in concentration camps or in military brothels set up for the benefit of Wehrmacht soldiers. They were subjected to the strictest regulations, registered with the police, and stringently monitored by the health authorities.

After the Wehrmacht's conquest of much of Europe early in the war, some 500 military brothels were set up to serve German soldiers and sailors in the conquered countries – 100 of them in France alone. Most of the military brothels were located in large buildings such as former hotels, but in at least one case, in the port of Brest in Brittany, a brothel was established in a former synagogue. In Western Europe, the brothels were staffed by professional prostitutes, but in occupied Poland and the Soviet Union, young women and teenage girls were snatched off the streets in mass kidnaps, abused, raped, brutalised and forced to serve in the military brothels.

Inside Germany, the police employed brutal methods to control prostitution completely and comprehensively. Open soliciting on the streets and squares was forbidden entirely under a circular issued on 16 March 1940, shortly before Hitler's Blitzkrieg on Western Europe began. The circular extended the existing ban on open prostitution in the Reich to all areas occupied by the Wehrmacht with the exception of the Czech lands in the Protectorate of Bohemia and Moravia.

With the imposition of this measure prostitution could only be practised in dedicated brothels. If such houses were not already available, the police had to provide them, following the 'general racial principles'. This meant in practice that 'prostitutes of non-German blood' were allowed to work in brothels – except for Jewish women who were banned entirely from such work to prevent them from 'polluting' the Aryan race.

One week after the war began, on 9 September 1939, the Reich Ministry of the Interior decreed that all remaining prostitutes and their landlords had to be registered with the police. A confidential circular to police accompanying the decree stipulated that in future streetwalkers would only be allowed to solicit custom in dedicated rooms; that at night they would be confined to their accommodation;

and during the day they were not allowed to frequent certain public locations: all prostitutes had effectively become prisoners of the state.

The long arm of the Nazi state extended into the private practices of the world of prostitution. Whores were forbidden from contacting their pimps, and any use of sado-masochistic instruments was banned. Any change of address had to be reported to the authorities and regular visits to a doctor for check-ups were made compulsory. Moreover, the prostitutes had to employ contraceptive protection during intercourse – even though these had been officially banned since long before the war, supposedly to ensure the continued procreation of the German race.

This ban, introduced in May 1933 soon after the Nazi takeover, forbade the import, advertising and sale of contraceptives, along with abortions. However, the law was widely and openly flouted. Contraceptives continued to be readily available from dispensers in locations such as subways and railway stations, public toilets and pharmacies. Statistics show that in 1938, 38 million condoms were used. A Nazi doctor, Ferdinand Hoffmann, blamed this figure for a decline in the birth rate. Consequently, the enforcement of the contraceptive ban was tightened up and any form of sex education in schools was 'forbidden to Aryans'.

Allowing contraceptives in brothels was not only intended to maintain sexual hygiene, but also to ensure that those 'asocial persons' staffing the brothels did not themselves procreate and contaminate the pure Aryan genes with their 'impure' blood. Himmler, who outdid even Hitler and all the other chief Nazi paladins in his crazed racial manias and theories, was anxious to have the male sperm collected in the condoms subjected to scientific research. To this end, for example, prostitutes in Stuttgart's Klosterstrasse were ordered to keep their semen-filled contraceptives stored in special containers after sex, waiting to be picked up and studied in SS laboratories.

On 18 September 1939, new measures were announced to step

up the fight against sexually transmitted diseases. But despite all the precautions, in 1942 Propaganda Minister Joseph Goebbels deplored the fact that 15 per cent of all women picked up during raids in that year carried STDs – including syphilis. Clandestine, uncontrolled prostitution was seen as the biggest threat to sexual and racial purity. So-called *Fürsorgestreifen* (joint 'welfare patrols' of police and health officials) were ordered to be on the lookout for the 'h.w.G persons' with frequently changing sexual partners.

On 5 May 1941, Reinhard Heydrich, now head of the security police, and the SS's own security service, the SD, sent a circular to all branches of the Kripo. Heydrich demanded a list of all existing brothels, including information on whether the bordellos conformed to Nazi racial policy. He also required the names and nationalities of the prostitutes they employed. Those who evaded registration or were arrested walking the streets were threatened with preventive detention in a concentration camp for 'asocial behaviour'. In setting up Salon Kitty, the 'man with the iron heart' knew all there was to know about such establishments.

Prostitution was not the only target of the Nazis' crackdown on sexuality. Male homosexuality was officially despised by the regime because such behaviour was thought to be effeminate, weak, and encouraged intimate relationships and male bonding that could endanger the hierarchical structure of National Socialist society. Above all, for an ideology that proclaimed the heterosexual nuclear family as the ideal, homosexuality was seen as running counter to the aim of breeding children to serve the Fatherland.

Paradoxically, however, the misogynistic masculine ethos of Nazism, which celebrated the beauty of male bodies in its official art, and encouraged male comradeship in the party organisations, could be seen as homoerotic. Hitler himself had tolerated the open homosexuality of his closest and oldest comrade, the SA leader Ernst Röhm, during the party's rise to power. After the Night of the Long

Knives purge of the SA in the summer of 1934, however, with the execution of Röhm and other gay SA leaders, the Führer's attitude changed. The 'decadent and debauched' sexuality of the SA was proffered as one of the main excuses for the purge by Hitler and Goebbels, and tolerance changed to condemnation.

Heinrich Himmler, whose SS had been the prime killers in the Röhm purge, enthusiastically carrying out the executions of their rivals, was even more rabidly homophobic than the Führer. In a speech to party leaders at Bad Tölz in 1937, Himmler declared: 'For homosexuals, love of the erotic replaces emphasis on individuality and accomplishment.' In the same speech, Himmler bemoaned the fact that the medieval German practice of drowning homosexuals in swamps had died out. This was a deficiency that he would soon rectify.

Himmler's fear that young men might be drawn towards homosexuality for the lack of heterosexual outlets was one reason why brothels were not banned outright by the National Socialist regime. Homosexuality itself was rigorously punished in the Third Reich, and between 5,000 and 15,000 homosexuals found themselves sent to concentration camps to wear pink triangles as their distinctive brand alongside Jews, asocials, political prisoners and other nonconformists. Within the camps, they were isolated and, along with prostitutes, subjected to particularly vicious treatment, and given harder tasks than other inmates. As a result, homosexuals were two-thirds more likely to die in the camps than other categories – with the exception of Jews sent to the death camps of Poland.

Within the SS, and the police, homosexual relationships were strictly forbidden and even made punishable by death from November 1941 on Hitler's personal orders. Himmler's decree on the 'Purification of SS and Police', issued on 15 November 1941, stipulated that:

. . . in order to cleanse SS and police from weaklings with homosexual inclinations, the Führer has decreed that any member of the SS or police who commits sodomy with another man or who permits another man to commit sodomy with him will be punished by death, irrespective of his age. In case of mitigating circumstances, he may be sentenced to jail for not less than six years.

CHAPTER FOUR

THE END OF LOVE

– Sex in concentration camps, military brothels
and the Lebensborn project

The brothels set up in concentration camps and the military bordellos established for the use of the Wehrmacht could not have been further removed from, on the one hand, the often primitive *Nuttenbetriebe* ('slut dens') for the asocials and lower-ranking soldiers, and the luxurious plush salons – such as Salon Kitty – reserved for the high and mighty on the other. Despite, or perhaps because of, this contrast, these special utilitarian brothels offer interesting insights into the contradictory and sometimes clearly sadomasochistic attitudes of the top Nazi paladins like Himmler and their henchmen regarding male sexual drives which – official ideology notwithstanding – could often only be satisfied by those working in the sex trade. And, as so often in Hitler's state, economic considerations over how to improve performance, productivity and profit – how to maximise human resources in a 'rational' albeit inhumane manner – played a central role.

In the concentration camps run by his SS, Heinrich Himmler saw the prospect of a trip to the brothel as an incentive for prisoners to better their work performance. During an inspection tour of

Mauthausen concentration camp in Austria in June 1941, Himmler gave the order for a brothel to be set up for inmates. Within a year, the camp brothel was up and running. 'I do consider it necessary that those prisoners showing diligence in their work have access to women in brothels, in as liberal a form as possible,' Himmler wrote to Oswald Pohl, head of the Central Administrative Economic Office for the camps in a letter of 23 March 1942.

Himmler intended to motivate camp inmates to put in extra efforts not only by pitifully small rewards of money and goods, but also by providing 'incentives of a natural kind': his euphemism for sex. This was to be achieved by means of a three-tier prize system, to be rolled out in all concentration camps by 1 May 1943 at the latest. In another letter to Pohl on 5 March 1943, Himmler wrote: 'If I have this natural incentive at my disposal, I think we are obliged to make use of it.' According to this scheme, the first tier provided incentives such as cigarettes or other small perks for inmates. Those in the second tier would receive tiny daily financial payments of ten to twenty Reichspfennige – worth less than one euro today. Finally, the third tier of 'prizes' meant, added Himmler, that '. . . in every camp, it should be possible for the men to visit the camp brothel once or twice a week.'

In obedience to Himmler's command, on 15 May 1943, Pohl authorised the 'Service Regulations Regarding Privileges for Inmates'. According to these regulations, increased work performance could only be achieved by 'guiding and educating the inmates'. 'In future,' Pohl's directive continued, 'inmates who stand out due to their diligence, prudence, good behaviour and exceptional work performance shall receive privileges. These consist of 1) An easing of the conditions of imprisonment.' (This meant, for example, that a prisoner could receive more mail or decide how he wanted his hair cut.) '2) Increased food rations.' (In reality this might mean an extra helping of the unappetising 'Buna soup' made from potato peelings and swedes.) '3) A financial bonus.' (Monetary rewards in the camps were often distributed arbitrarily and, in reality, had nothing to do with a prisoner's 'diligence'.) '4) Tobacco products.' (Cigarettes were the currency in the camps used to obtain food and other extra perks.) '5) A visit to the brothel.'

Pohl's directive specified that visits to the brothel should be granted only to 'top workers' and could be applied for to the camp commandant once a week. The fee for such a visit was two Reichsmarks – worth around seven euros today – and was paid for in the form of a *Prämienschein*, or coupon. In comparison, the going price for twenty cigarettes sold in the camp canteens was three Reichsmark. In practice, visits to camp brothels were usually granted mostly to kapos or block elders – inmates, often criminals, who were granted a privileged position to supervise, bully and control their fellow prisoners.

Implementing Pohl's regulations saw camp brothels rolled out and opened in 1943 at Auschwitz, Buchenwald and Sachsenhausen camps. The brothels were mainly staffed by women who were already prisoners in camps. In July 1943, for example, eleven women from the Ravensbrück female camp near Berlin, were selected as suitable for prostitution and taken to the Buchenwald camp brothel. Other batches soon followed: twelve to Mauthausen and Flossenbürg, four to Dachau and so on.

At first, most of the women sent to staff the brothels at the camps came from Ravensbrück, which had a high proportion of 'asocial' inmates, amounting to two-thirds of the estimated 132,000 women who passed through the camp between 1939 and 1945. In 1944, further brothels were established at Neuengamme and Mittelbau-Dora camps. For the SS running the camps, the tier prize system had the positive effect of dividing the prisoners into brothel visitors and those denied the privilege, thus increasing obedience and compliance with the rules, and lessening solidarity among the inmates.

If access to camp brothels was considered a privilege for the minority of male prisoners who 'enjoyed' it, for the women concerned it was unmitigated hell. Consequently, recruiting 'volunteers' posed an increasing problem for the SS, and persuading women prisoners from Ravensbrück to staff the brothels was something of a final resort. The SS claimed that they had first attempted to recruit 'ordinary' prostitutes on a voluntary basis to go to the camps. When this failed, they turned to the 'asocial' women already detained. However, these women were not given any information about their future work, only a vague – and later broken – promise of early release if they co-operated.

After the war, in 1947, a Buchenwald doctor, Gerhard Oskar Schiedlausky, who had also worked at Ravensbrück, stated under oath: 'The first women who came to Mauthausen had purportedly been given the promise of being released after working as prostitutes for six months.' Schiedlausky, who would be hanged for his crimes, testified at his post-war trial that 'The women had to be pretty, with good teeth, and with no venereal infections or skin disease.' The women selected for the camp brothels were allowed to choose their own clothes from the camp stores 'in order to look their best'.

By the summer of 1944, the supply of suitable recruits from Ravensbrück for the brothels in other camps was drying up. The remaining women in the camp were deemed too ill, starved or worn out to do the job. Foreign women, Poles, Ukrainians, Frenchwomen and Russians, were increasingly reluctant to leave Ravensbrück for an uncertain future in other camps. Rumours of the hellish life suffered by the women in the brothels had reached Ravensbrück, and the lies and blandishments of the Nazis about an early release were no longer believed.

In some desperation, the SS lined up the women from the Polish block and asked for volunteers. They were greeted by a 'thunderous silence'. When, eventually, one stepped forward, she was booed and hissed by her comrades. Later, ten women cut off the hair of the volunteer and beat her up. Four of the women responsible were punished with twenty-five lashes on the flogging *bock*. A delegation of Poles lodged an official protest with the camp commander, Fritz Suhren, who 'gaped . . . and didn't know what to do'. Finally, the Polish women were deprived of food parcels as a collective punishment for their defiance.

One woman did return to Ravensbrück after six weeks in a camp brothel used by the SS. She described her experience as 'a horror of rape and abuse'.

> Every morning the prostitutes had to get up and let themselves be cleaned by the female guards. After the coffee the SS would come and start to rape and abuse the women. It would go on for sixteen hours a day, and only two and a half hours off for lunch and dinner.

Friederike Jandl, an Austrian woman prisoner, had a friend from Vienna who believed that she would be freed after a short time in the brothel and made the mistake of volunteering. 'I tried to stop her,' Jandl recounted, 'but she told me "I have nothing to lose".' Six months later, instead of freedom, she was returned to Ravensbrück. 'She was finished. Totally used up. Destroyed. She said she wished she'd listened to me.'

A group of French prostitutes, including the entire staff of a brothel in Rouen, newly arrived at Ravensbrück, had not learned the truth about the conditions that awaited them in camp brothels and several duly volunteered for such service. They were dissuaded from doing so by more sophisticated and knowledgeable political inmates. Jacqueline d'Alincourt, a nineteen-year-old veteran of the French Resistance, described the arrival of her fellow countrywomen in her Ravensbrück block:

At first they didn't understand, these women. They were uneducated. They had nothing to hold on to – no religion, no values. I remember one of these poor creatures lying on her mattress saying, 'Why am I here? Why am I here?' We in the resistance, we knew why we were there. We had a superiority of spirit . . . We had the desire not to die in Germany and to see France again. But these creatures had no idea why they were there. It was a question of spirit. So we political women got together and decided to make a list of everyone who had volunteered to go. And we told them not to take this work. We said 'No! There's no question of that!' We were very severe. And we watched carefully what they did.

Detailed information on the 'asocial' women imprisoned as prostitutes is more difficult to come by in comparison to other categories of concentration camp victims such as Jews and political prisoners for fairly obvious reasons. In general, such women were less articulate than their fellow inmates. Moreover, many of those that survived were reluctant to go public about their suffering because of the nature of their former profession, and their shame at the degradation they had endured in the camps. Ironically, such information as we do have often comes from the meticulous bureaucratic record-keeping of the Nazi authorities themselves.

One such typical case is that of Anna Sölzer, a twenty-year-old part-time prostitute from Cologne. Surviving official records tell Anna's sad story in briefly bleak bureaucratese. They show that she was arrested in her single room in 1941 after being bombed out of her previous home by a British air raid. Her police file states that she was alone when the police called, but they found evidence that men had visited her there.

Anna had not had much luck in her short life. She had never known her father, and her mother had died when she was six. At the age of eight she had been sent from an orphanage to work as a domestic servant in a private house. The pay was so poor that she started work in a factory and supplemented her meagre wages of twenty Marks a week with prostitution.

Five months pregnant when she was detained, Anna was placed under a curfew until her baby was born. Her police report branded her as coming from a 'genetically worthless family' and showed 'wilful, cheeky behaviour' – such as refusing to get out of bed when the police came calling. She had appealed for help to her unborn baby's father, but as he was a married man, he had refused. Defiantly refusing to give up working as a prostitute, she told police that she had to support her child. She was not given that opportunity. Instead, after her son Bodo was born, she was sent to Ravensbrück. Records show that Anna died in the camp in 1944 – officially from tuberculosis, which was often a euphemism for murder.

Moving to work in brothels in male camps must have seemed a desperate last hope of improving their dire situation for women such as Anna. Interned under atrocious conditions, the bargain of agreeing to offer up their bodies in return for their eventual freedom appeared to be the only possibility of survival. But when such promises and inducements failed to provide enough volunteers, the SS resorted to brute force and compulsion. They made women go to the brothels who, according to their twisted ideology, had already become 'unpersons' excluded from the Nazi *Volksgemeinschaft* ('People's community') because of their immoral way of life.

Not all 'asocial' women sent to the camps were prostitutes, though they were often treated worse in Ravensbrück than other asocials. One rare example of a survivor who spoke out about her experiences was a woman named Käthe Datz, who told a researcher in the 1990s that she had been branded as workshy for taking a day off work in a factory without permission to visit her sick mother.

They said I was a traitor and had committed a crime. Then I was put on a mass transport [to Ravensbrück], so I cried. Amongst our group were many working girls – prostitutes. I remember them walking in their high heels across the cobbled streets . . . on the way to the camp. I can tell you how they went for those women. 'You swine. We will teach you a lesson' – and then came the kicking and the beating.

Himmler underlined the point that only the lowest of the low were fit for such a role as camp prostitutes, telling Pohl that only such 'harlots' could be chosen:

. . . for whom, given their previous life and behaviour, all hope is lost that they might return to an orderly life so that, if we submit our choices to a strict scrutiny, we will never have to reproach ourselves of having ruined a human being who could possibly have been saved for the benefit of the German people.

According to reports by prisoners who survived the camps, most of the women working in the brothels were Germans, with Poles making up the second largest national group, followed by Frenchwomen. Many such women had been previously detained for persistent prostitution, but they also included non-prostitutes. Such non-professionals included those detained for a lifestyle of frequently changing their sexual partners, or merely refusing to comply with the prevailing Nazi ideas of sexual or social conventions. Some of the interned women had indeed volunteered for brothel duties, while others had been forced to do so against their will.

Some prostitutes interned in Ravensbrück were promoted to become kapos, exchanging their black 'asocial' tags for green ones as mere criminals to denote their new status. Else Krug, for example – the experienced S&M dominatrix from Cologne, who had taken younger working girls under her wing during her ten years in that city – reprised her caring role when she became a kapo. Else, arrested in 1938, had been among the first arrivals when Ravensbrück opened its gates in May 1939. She soon found her feet amidst the savage Darwinian struggle for survival in the camp, and was assigned a job supervising a work gang of fellow asocials in the kitchens – which gave her easy access to the extra rations necessary for bare existence.

Else's powerful personality not only enabled her to control and dominate her kitchen work gang, but she also succeeded in seeing off an attempt to infiltrate and take over the much sought-after kitchen duties by Communist fellow inmates. One of the most insidious intentions of the Nazi division of their concentration camp captives into categories was to encourage hostility between the various groups. The Communists, with their experience of tight party discipline and secret underground work against the Nazis, were particularly skilled at these internal battles among the inmates, and it is a tribute to Else's strong character and personal skills that she successfully resisted them.

The secret of Else's popularity with her work gang was the fairness with which she divided up the perks of their job. Work gang members had ample opportunity to help themselves to illicit extra portions of the vegetables that they had to peel and prepare, such as carrots, cabbages, potatoes, swedes and turnips, that made up the basic camp diet. Else would arrange the smuggling out of delicacies such as canned food and jam to their starving friends outside their block. She saw to it that these extras were shared out justly. After the outbreak of war, camp rations were reduced to one ladle of soup a day, and Else's smuggling became essential for some to survive for another day.

Else befriended Grete Buber-Neumann, a political prisoner doubly damned by the Nazis as being both Jewish and a former Communist. Grete had suffered the unenviable unique distinction of being imprisoned in the concentration camp systems of the twin totalitarian tyrannies of Stalin's Russia and Hitler's Germany.

A dedicated Communist, she had fled Germany for France after the Nazi takeover. In France, she had worked for the international Stalinist Communist organisation, the Comintern. Summoned to Moscow, she had witnessed the disappearance of her husband Heinz Neumann in Stalin's Great Terror, before being arrested herself and sent to a labour camp. Thoroughly disillusioned with Communism, she had survived three gruelling years in the Gulag, only to be sent back to Germany by Stalin along with other dissident German Communists during the brief alliance between Nazi Germany and the Soviet Union in February 1940.

Immediately consigned to Ravensbrück, Grete was rescued from a threatening mob of fellow inmates in the camp kitchens by Else Krug, as Grete recalled in her memoir *Under Two Dictators*:

> A powerful woman with lively brown eyes, a determined chin and a voice like a Sergeant Major . . . suddenly jumped up on a stool and bellowed: 'If you don't line up properly and stop mobbing the new Blockova the pots will go back to the kitchen and no-one will get anything.' It worked like a charm.

The unlikely friendship between prostitute and political activist blossomed, as Else fondly recalled to her shocked puritanical friend the lurid details of her S&M activities in Cologne:

> Up to then I had considered myself a fairly enlightened person and I'd read a certain amount of scientific literature on the subject, but Else's stories of the requests she met with in the course of her profession and how she complied with them made my hair stand on end. She told her stories in a dry, matter-of-fact way, and there was a certain professional pride in her attitude. She knew what she was, and she insisted that she was good at what she did.

Proud of her career as a prostitute, Else, observed Grete, never 'whined' about her fate nor made false promises to reform her behaviour in order to be released from Ravensbrück.

Such an independent and courageous spirit as Else was bound to clash with the pitiless officials who ran the camp, and her downfall and death, as witnessed by Grete Buber-Neumann, was precipitated by her brave refusal to take part in the most brutal divisive tactic of all those used by the Nazis: punishments inflicted on offenders not by the SS, but by their fellow inmates. The prisoners licensed to inflict merciless thrashings were those already in the *Strafblock* (punishment block). They were promised release from the Strafblock if they agreed to beat their fellow sufferers.

A group of Jehovah's Witnesses – persecuted by the Nazis and sent to the camps for their steadfast refusal to take part in any form of military activity – discovered in Ravensbrück that Angora wool they were sent to collect was to be used to line soldiers' coats. They therefore refused the work. Scores of the women were sentenced to a flogging. Such beatings in camps were unspeakably cruel and could often result in the deaths of victims – doctors would examine potential victims before the beatings to make sure that they could survive them. Typically, the condemned were strapped over the 'bock' flogging bench and received twenty-five strokes, delivered by a variety of instruments ranging from thick sticks to thin whips.

The Ravensbrück camp commander, Max Koegel, ordered Else Krug to take part in the punishment of the Jehovah's Witnesses in return for being freed from the Strafblock where she was undergoing a sentence on starvation rations. 'No, Herr Camp Commander,' Else stoutly replied. 'I never beat a fellow prisoner.'

'What!' screamed Koegel in a rage. 'You dirty whore! You think you can pick and choose? That's refusal to obey an order!' Else shrugged but maintained her resistance in stony silence. 'Take the whore away,' snarled Koegel. 'You'll have cause to remember me, I promise you.'

Koegel kept his word. Soon afterwards, Else Krug was removed from the camp. She never returned. After the war it was found that she had been gassed at Bernburg, a facility near Berlin where exterminations under the Nazis' T4 euthanasia programme were carried out.

A French prostitute known only as 'Simone', who arrived at Ravensbrück in 1944, demonstrated similar courage and generosity towards her fellow inmates as Else Krug. Simone had been working in a brothel in Le Havre where downed American airmen were being hidden from the Germans – who were using the brothel's usual services in an adjoining room. Simone fell in love with one of the pilots who promised her that if they both survived the war he would return, find her and marry her. Remarkably, he kept his word. In 1946, after her return from Ravensbrück, the US flier came back to Le Havre, married the woman who had saved his life and they started a new life together in America. During her time in Ravensbrück, Simone had been put to work at Zwodau, a sub-station of the main camp, where she toiled in the laundry. She was able to use her job to smuggle out warm clothing to her fellow inmates to help keep them alive.

By no means all prostitute prisoners had the nobility of character shown by Else Krug and Simone – rather the reverse. Philomena Müssgueller, a 41-year-old brothel madam from Munich, for example, and Elfriede Schmidt, a Cologne prostitute who had been netted in the same round-up as Else, became much feared and hated kapos. They surrounded themselves with a gang of green-tagged criminals and delighted in lording it over fellow prisoners, especially the 'red-triangled' Communists.

Müssgueller and Schmidt enthusiastically took part in punishments of other prisoners, and their gang of asocials acted as spies for the SS, reporting one inmate for the 'crime' of stealing half a carrot. Such was their moral degradation that these two were among the Ravensbrück inmates sent by Himmler as kapo guards to Auschwitz when the women's section of the Polish camp was opened. Here, the gang disgraced themselves by having affairs with male kapos who decorated them with jewellery stolen from Jews arriving at the camp to be exterminated.

At Buchenwald camp, near the city of Weimar, work in the brothel was organised on military lines almost like a factory assembly line. Before visiting the brothel, privileged male prisoners had to hand in their application to their supervising kapo or block elder. The request was passed up the chain of camp command to the *Schreibstube* (camp orderly office), and the applicant would be medically examined in the camp hospital barracks. During the evening *Appell* (roll call), the SS would read out the numbers of the prisoners whose brothel application had been approved. These men were then marched to the brothel barrack, where they received an injection from the duty doctor and had salve applied to their penises. They were then assigned a room and had to wait in line outside the door.

Once admitted, the prisoner had to remove their wooden clog shoes and trousers before commencing copulation. The time allotted for satisfying their sexual desires was strictly limited to fifteen minutes. Sex was only allowed in the missionary position, and SS guards watched through peepholes in the door to ensure compliance with the rules. Once the time was up, the guards would call out and physically pull and beat the prisoner from the room. After intercourse, the doctor gave the prisoner another injection. The woman had to douche herself after every visit and then immediately receive the next prisoner.

To guarantee that the women working in the brothels remained 'attractive', they were given bigger and better food rations than their fellow inmates. They carried out their sex work in day and night shifts, lived isolated from other inmates, and were not allowed to move freely around the camp. They were forced to work a seven-day week, and were not permitted to have Sundays off, as was the case for other inmates. If a brothel woman became pregnant, she was forced to have an abortion – although terminations were illegal for all other women in the Reich. According to an interview in 1990 with 'Ms W', a surviving witness at Buchenwald, contraceptives were not provided for the working women:

Our clothing consisted of a white pleated skirt, flimsy knickers and a brassiere. Every evening we had to let eight men mount us in the course of two hours. That meant they came in, went to the doctor's office, got an injection, got their number – for us female prisoners – did their thing; they went inside, up, down, out, went back outside, got another injection, and left.

Ms W was one of sixteen women working at the Buchenwald brothel. She had been arrested by the Gestapo in November 1939 because she had been having an affair with a half-Jewish man, a criminal offence under the notorious Nuremberg Laws of 1935 that had forbidden sexual relations between Aryans and Jews. Sent to Ravensbrück in 1943, she was selected for work in a camp brothel by the SS and taken to Buchenwald. Here she endured two years of violence, sexual assault and physical and psychological abuse and humiliation before being liberated at the war's end.

Describing her pitiful existence in the camp, Ms W said:

Your senses become dull. Life simply doesn't matter anymore, because they have destroyed everything that counted for you as a human being. You become indifferent to everything, what can I say . . . nothing moves you any more. Limitless apathy; they could have done whatever they wanted; we knew we were entirely at their mercy.

Driven beyond the limits of despair, Ms W attempted suicide. Her attempt failed.

Those privileged prisoners permitted visits to the brothels were in better physical shape than their starved fellow inmates, enjoying higher food rations and performing easier labour. Usually, they worked as hairdressers, in the camp kitchens, in the hospital barracks or the butchers – where such prisoners had opportunities to engage in illicit bartering. Only very few inmates reached this highest level of privilege. For the vast majority of other inmates, the top priority was to save their energy in order to simply survive. Only between 100 and 200 prisoners out of the overall 30,000 prisoners in the main camp at Auschwitz, for example, were allowed to visit brothels.

The ultimate objective of the Nazi drive to force sex underground and persecute those who would not or could not conform to their ideological mindset was to mould the minds and behaviour of the younger generation of Germans. Controlling and steering the sex lives of the mostly young soldiers of the conscripted Wehrmacht was also a consequence of the negative experience in the First World War. In the four years of that conflict, no fewer than two million soldiers had contracted a sexually transmitted disease.

The Nazi authorities were worried about the dangers of what they termed 'clandestine prostitution', which led to much increased risks of infection, but they were also concerned about 'the manifold ways in which military secrets are carelessly revealed'. Though sexual fraternisation between soldiers and civilians in countries occupied by the Wehrmacht was forbidden, human nature being what it is, it naturally took place on a large scale. In occupied France, for example, German soldiers are estimated to have fathered some 60,000 children with Frenchwomen who engaged in 'horizontal collaboration' between 1940 and 1944. A group of French prostitutes were sent to Ravensbrück as a punishment after they were found to have infected Gestapo officials with VD.

In order to guard against both rampant sexual disease and also to protect the Wehrmacht's secrets from careless talk, it was deemed necessary to 'set up appropriate houses . . . for the exclusive use of German soldiers' in towns and cities wherever the army was billeted. Despite the precaution of limiting soldiers to strictly controlled military brothels, it is estimated that one in ten German soldiers during the Second World War contracted syphilis. It is ironic that the Nazis who were so worried about secrets being shared in unlicensed brothels would later appropriate Salon Kitty for precisely the purpose of listening in to such post-coital pillow talk.

Such was the demand on the 500 official military brothels set up in Poland, France, Norway, the Netherlands, Belgium, Greece, Croatia, Rumania, Russia and the Ukraine that in some cases, the military authorities were forced to use unlicensed bordellos too. In occupied Paris, for example, there were twenty 'official' Wehrmacht military brothels, but a further ten civilian brothels in the French capital were utilised by the occupiers. Responsibility for running all these establishments was vested in German military officers who could decide unilaterally when and whether to open or close them.

The military brothels were controlled at least as strictly as those left open in the Reich. Every brothel had house rules that forbade loud noise and violence, regulated the sale of alcohol, determined opening hours and set the fees – usually between two and five Reichsmarks, or eight to twenty euros in today's money. Half the fee went to the proprietress of the brothel, and half to the working girls. Sex was permitted only with contraceptives, which the proprietress had to provide for free. Trade in the most frequently used brothels in larger cities was brisk. Prostitutes who serviced up to fifty men a day could earn as much as 200 Reichsmark (or 800 euros) a day.

Brothel madams also had to keep a logbook or album with photos, ages and personal and medical records of all the women working for them. Before and after visiting a brothel, soldiers had to report to a medical office for a check and have their names recorded along with the name of the woman he had seen. Local civilians in the vicinity of the bordellos were forbidden to use the Wehrmacht brothels, and German soldiers were strictly banned from using unlicensed local prostitutes or casual streetwalkers – though obviously this rule was frequently breached.

When the tide of war turned ever more decisively against Germany, necessity compelled the Nazis to relax and even reverse some of their ideological fanaticism. With millions of men fighting on far-flung frontiers, the shortage of labour in the Reich was remedied by employing women in factories and offices – removing them from the child-bearing and -raising role that was the Nazi ideal. The labour shortage was also met by armies of slave labourers working in horrendous conditions in concentration camps, and on such projects as the manufacture of the V1 and V2 weapons in underground facilities and the construction of the Atlantic Wall defences in France. 'Volunteer' workers were also recruited in France and Italy to work in the Reich, and even Himmler recognised that biological reality dictated that their natural needs had to be met. He therefore decreed that they be allowed access to brothels in the Reich.

Adolf Hitler was not the most fanatical Nazi leader when it came to manipulating the lives and loves of the Reich's citizens – that dubious honour belonged to Heinrich Himmler. Though the bespectacled, chinless failed chicken farmer was hardly the model of an Aryan superman himself, the master bureaucrat who built the SS from Hitler's personal Praetorian Guard into the all-powerful secret state at the heart of Nazi Germany was dedicated to the goal of purifying the German race. To achieve this aim, he was prepared to overturn all limits of law and morality in manipulating the physical, racial and personal characteristics of those under his rule. At first, this only applied to those selected to join the SS's ranks, but when the Nazis took power, he extended his crackpot theories to the party's racial and political enemies who were herded into the concentration camps.

When the Second World War began, Himmler's murderous obsessions were further extended to most of the continent of Europe that fell under Nazi conquest, ending in the attempted extermination of the continent's entire Jewish population in the Holocaust. In the Reich itself, anyone not deemed to meet the correct standards of bodily and mental health – primarily the physically and mentally handicapped, but also including the blind and deaf – were in severe danger of being eliminated by deliberate forced euthanasia.

The other side of Himmler's mania, the drive that went in parallel with the mass murder of the racially and physically 'unworthy', was the procreation of those considered fit enough to meet the Reichsführer's exacting standards. In the words of historian Catrine Clay:

> There were two parallel routes to the supreme goal: the racially impure had to be exterminated while the racially pure were encouraged to multiply. The Final Solution would be achieved only when both the negative and positive objectives had been fulfilled.

The idea that a purer and healthier race could be achieved by manipulation of human breeding had been around for centuries, and Himmler's notions were an extreme and twisted perversion of the late nineteenth-century evolutionary theories of Charles Darwin – advocated as the pseudoscience of eugenics by Darwin's cousin Francis Galton. Eugenics had been enthusiastically taken up by doctors, scientists and progressive thinkers dedicated to 'improving' humanity in the early twentieth century. As a result, criminals and the incurably insane were sterilised in several Western countries, notably the United States and Scandinavia. Never before the advent of Hitler and Himmler, however, had a state deliberately and ruthlessly pursued a policy of extermination of the 'unfit' allied to mass breeding of the 'fit'.

The Social Darwinists such as Galton advocated that healthy young people should be encouraged to marry each other and have large families. They were worried that modern medical advances were saving large numbers of the less fit and unhealthy, and that they would reproduce their 'unworthy' genes in great numbers, thus diluting and contaminating the 'superior' human stock. Such theories were given an explicitly racial twist by the Nazis, who identified the Jews as inferior stock who had infiltrated and undermined Nordic states. And the man who gave such theories their lethal form in the real world of the Third Reich was Heinrich Himmler.

Once he had established himself as master of the Reich's police and security services, Himmler wasted no time in putting his racial theories into murderous action. Not content with setting up the concentration camp system to corral and finally eliminate the perceived political and racial enemies of the Nazis, the Reichsführer put the 'positive' side of his programme into effect with the foundation of the *Lebensborn* ('Fount of Life') Society in December 1935.

Lebensborn's official aims at first were to care for unmarried mothers 'of good blood' made pregnant by SS members. The offspring of these unions were either adopted by childless SS families, or the fathers were induced to marry the women they had impregnated. The first Lebensborn maternity home was opened at Steinhöring, near Munich, in 1936, and others soon followed across the Reich.

Very soon, the original stated purpose of Lebensborn was widened, and the Lebensborn homes became human stud farms where SS members stayed for R&R holidays with extra benefits: sex with suitable Aryan women of child-bearing age. One witness and participant on such occasions was the war criminal SS-Gruppenführer Jürgen Stroop, the man who commanded the suppression of the Warsaw Ghetto uprising in 1943 during which more than 50,000 Jews were massacred. In conversations with his Polish cellmate Kazimierz Moczarski after the war while awaiting his trial and execution in Warsaw, Stroop fondly recalled his times at a Lebensborn home. They had all the thrill, said Stroop, of a snatched dirty weekend with a secretary or mistress. He added that he kept knowledge of such stays secret from his wife.

Himmler, who though married himself, made his secretary Hedwig Potthast his mistress and fathered two children by her, thoroughly approved and encouraged the extra-marital liaisons in the Lebensborn homes. He had no time for 'bourgeois' concepts of marital fidelity, or the teachings of the Christian churches on sexual morality. The only thing that mattered to him was producing pure Aryan children to guarantee the future of the race. Himmler even threatened an unmarried senior SS colleague, 44-year-old *Hauptsturmführer* Franz Schwarz, with dismissal if he had not married by the war's end.

Before being allowed to copulate, the women who volunteered to be Lebensborn mothers were thoroughly investigated to ensure that their physical and mental health was sound, and their racial ancestry was purely Aryan, and free from any taint of Jewish blood or hereditary defects. The would-be fathers had already been subjected to such tests and inquiries before joining the SS.

Himmler took an obsessively deep personal interest in every detail of life in his pet project – even down to ordering the diet of the pregnant women and deciding on the decoration of the maternity wards. One of his more bizarre commands was that the Lebensborn mothers should have porridge every day for breakfast since he believed that the daughters of the English aristocracy maintained their trim figures by such means. Later in the war, as privations bit into the Reich's economy, he reluctantly ordered that the porridge oats should no longer be made with full or skimmed milk but could be mixed with water.

In October 1939 Himmler publicly issued a general order to the SS which gave a broad hint as to what was already taking place in the strictly secluded Lebensborn homes:

> . . . beyond the boundaries of otherwise perhaps necessary bourgeois laws and customs, even outside marriage, it can be a lofty task for German women and girls of good blood, not lightly, but in deepest moral seriousness, to become mothers of children of soldiers called to war, of whom fate alone knows whether they will return home or fall for Germany. Also, the men and women who serve the state in the homeland have at this precise time the sacred obligation to become again mothers and fathers of children.

Perceptive members of the public, reading between the lines of this ambiguous order, took it to mean a licence for women and girls to desert the marriage bed and surrender their virginity to willing SS warriors, and to men in safe cushy jobs at home to cuckold absent soldiers away fighting for the Fatherland at the front. Small wonder, then, that publication of the order caused many to wonder what the future held for them and their errant wives and daughters.

One reason for the order probably lay in the Reichsführer's realisation, after unexpectedly high losses in the Blitzkrieg conquest of Poland, that the war would make substantial inroads into Germany's sacred breeding stock, which would have to be replenished. Another reason, in the words of Himmler's biographer Peter Padfield,

> . . . that it was yet another manifestation of the desire for blood and death which lay at the root of this war. Perhaps it was also an expression of the thwarted sexuality that surely drove him,

probably Hitler, and perhaps the entire male collective of the Nazi Party, even all strata of this masculine warrior state.

The conquest of Poland, rapidly followed by the occupation of Denmark, Norway, Belgium, Luxembourg, the Netherlands and France, and in June 1941 by the invasion of the Soviet Union, led to a much more severe haemorrhage of precious German blood, and hence to a massive expansion of the Lebensborn concept. Himmler called his new project *Eindeutschung* ('Germanisation'). Simply put, this was to be a programme of mass abduction of children from the conquered countries who fitted Himmler's standards of being Aryan – primarily having blonde hair and blue eyes.

The programme, as with many of the Nazis' most fiendish policies, was to be rolled out in strictest secrecy. Under the guise of health checks, children were to be examined by SS doctors to determine their suitability for Germanisation. Those selected were then divided into age categories. Children aged from two to six were taken to Lebensborn homes in Germany from where they would be farmed out to be raised by childless SS couples. Children aged from six to twelve would be sent to state-run boarding schools to be thoroughly indoctrinated with Nazi ideology. Poland, the first country conquered during the war, was where the scheme was first introduced, as many Polish children presented as Aryan in appearance, though once in Germany they were vaguely described as 'children orphaned in the east'.

By these means thousands of children were kidnapped and taken to the Reich. Some were genuine orphans, while others were simply stolen from their parents and shipped to Germany. There was no shortage of Nazi families willing to adopt children they were told were war orphans, and the demand outstripped the available supply.

Poland was not the only country to supply children to Lebensborn. Suitably Nordic women who were impregnated by German soldiers stationed in countries such as Norway – and who were ostracised by their own people as a result – were also sent to Germany to have their babies in the Lebensborn homes. Anni-Frid Lyngstad, a member of the Swedish pop band Abba, who was born in November 1945, was the offspring of a relationship between her Norwegian mother and a German Wehrmacht sergeant stationed in Norway at the end of the war.

After the assassination of Himmler's deputy Reinhard Heydrich in occupied Prague in 1942, the Czech village of Lidice was razed in reprisal. All 199 men in the village over the age of sixteen were murdered, and all the women sent to concentration camps. Thirteen of the village children who were deemed racially valuable were adopted by Lebensborn. Those children assessed as non-valuable were shuttled from camp to camp and almost all died of starvation, neglect or exposure.

CHAPTER FIVE

THE HYPOCRITES

– Sex and the secret lives of
the Nazi elite

Once Hitler had seized power, the liberal and sexually relaxed lifestyles of the Weimar Republic were largely stifled and suppressed. National Socialist ideology vehemently condemned the culture of sexual freedom, which they characterised as 'Bolshevist infestation of our sexual morals'. Rather than the free choice of individuals, now it was up to the state to determine who had intimate relations with whom, and in particular how sexual relationships should be conducted. Nazi ideologues emphasised that sexuality had only one purpose: namely that 'of family, of matrimony, to produce healthy children for the German people and to raise them to become healthy, respectable German women and men'.

There were a few token exceptions to the rules and pressures restricting women and confining them to the homebody limits of 'Kinder, Küche, Kirche' ('children, kitchen and church'). Notably, the film director Leni Riefenstahl was given special privileges, and granted every help – including lavish funding – to make her pioneering propaganda masterpieces *Triumph des Willens* (*Triumph of the Will*) and *Olympia*, her films of the 1934 Nazi Party Nuremberg rally and the 1936 Berlin Olympic Games respectively.

Hitler, dazzled by Riefenstahl's exceptional directing skills demonstrated in her earliest film *Das blaue Licht* (*The Blue Light*), personally selected her to direct a film of the 1933 Nuremberg rally, *Der Sieg des Glaubens* (*The Victory of Faith*), and ordered Propaganda Minister Joseph Goebbels – who had reputedly made an unsuccessful pass at her – to put all the resources of his propaganda empire at her disposal. But because that film prominently featured Ernst Röhm, the SA Brownshirt leader, at Hitler's side, copies were pulped after Röhm was murdered in the Night of the Long Knives in the summer of 1934, and he was airbrushed from Nazi history.

Riefenstahl was given the same job for the 1934 rally, and the result was a propaganda triumph. Her innovative technical filmmaking won international plaudits and prizes, but also glamorised the Nazis, and Hitler personally, as the star of the show. Though never a Nazi, Party member, Riefenstahl returned Hitler's adoration, and continued to publicly praise him even after she had personally witnessed a massacre of Jews during the 1939 invasion of Poland. After the war, she unconvincingly denied her Nazi sympathies but failed to relaunch her career as a director. She died in 2003 at the age of 101, having cemented her reputation as the most influential female filmmaker of the twentieth century despite her films having served an evil cause.

One woman who never denied her Nazi affiliations, and who remained an unrepentant National Socialist until her dying day, was Gertrud Scholtz-Klink, the leader of the official Nazi women's organisation, the *NS-Frauenschaft*. Having fulfilled her maternal role by producing six children with her first husband, Scholtz-Klink was appointed head of the Nazi Women's League, and in her many speeches made it clear where the duty of women lay: 'The mission of women is to minister in the home and in her profession to the needs of life from the first to the last moments of Man's existence.' Though used by the Nazis as a public figurehead for their policy towards women, her real influence was negligible, and she never attended the key all-male meetings of the party elite.

During the war, having buried her first husband and divorced her second, Scholtz-Klink married an SS-Obergruppenführer, August Heissmeyer, and visited concentration camps to address female inmates in an attempt to persuade them of the wickedness of their ways. At the war's end she and her husband attempted to disguise their identities, but they were arrested, and she served seven years in jail. She retired into obscurity, but in 1978 published a book on women in the Third Reich in which she upheld and attempted to justify her Nazi views. She died in 1999 at the age of 97.

Two more women who, because their special skills were useful to the Nazi regime, achieved prominence denied to other members of their sex were the aviators Melitta von Stauffenberg and Hanna Reitsch. Melitta was racially Jewish on her father's side, but despite this 'handicap' she became a skilled test pilot in the Third Reich, flying dive-bombers and experimental aircraft. She married the historian Count Alexander von Stauffenberg, elder brother of the man who attempted to assassinate Hitler on 20 July1944. Her husband and the rest of the Stauffenberg clan were arrested after the plot's failure. Melitta's skills, however, were too valuable to waste, and she was permitted to continue flying, although she fully shared the family's anti-Nazi views. In the last days of the war, attempting to trace her husband, she was shot down by an American aircraft and died of her injuries.

In stark contrast to her fellow flyer, Hanna Reitsch was a convinced Nazi and an avid admirer of Hitler, who decorated her with the Iron Cross, 1st and 2nd class. A petite blonde and blue-eyed woman, Reitsch was much feted in the Nazi press as an example of the Aryan ideal. Her affair with Wernher von Braun, the scientist behind the V1 and V2 rocket programmes, was covered up even after she secretly bore him a daughter, Alicia. Reitsch was a daring aviator who test-flew most of the Reich's fighter aircraft before they came on stream, and she survived several crashes. Politically naïve, during the war she asked Göring and Himmler whether the rumours were true that the Nazis were killing Jews. She swallowed their denials without question. She convinced Hitler to form a Kamikaze-style 'suicide squadron' but the factory making the aircraft involved was bombed before it came into operation.

At the end of the war, accompanied by her possible lover, the air ace Ritter von Greim, Reitsch flew into embattled Berlin. Greim was wounded by Russian anti-aircraft fire, but Reitsch took over the controls and landed on an improvised airstrip in the Tiergarten park – part of the dwindling enclave in the city centre still held by Nazi forces battling the invading Red Army. The pair made their way to the Führerbunker where von Greim's wound was dressed and he was promoted to head the Luftwaffe in place of Hermann Göring – dismissed, disgraced and arrested for attempting to usurp the trapped Hitler's place as Führer.

Having failed to persuade Hitler to escape the bunker and flee with them, Reitsch and von Greim flew out again. Before bidding them farewell, Hitler had issued the couple with capsules of cyanide poison to take their own lives if necessary. Von Greim swallowed his capsule after he was captured by the Americans and told he would be handed over to the Russians. Surviving the Reich's collapse, after a brief spell in Allied captivity, Reitsch became something of an international celebrity despite refusing to renounce her hero-worship of Hitler. She travelled to India and the US, and ran a gliding school in Ghana. Her stay in Africa may have caused her to rethink her racist ideas. Leni Riefenstahl had a similar experience late in life when she stayed with and photographed the Nuba people of Sudan. In 1979, aged sixty-seven, Reitsch died suddenly. It is believed that she may finally have used the cyanide phial given her by her idol, Hitler.

Despite these rare exceptions, the overwhelming majority of

women in the Reich were systematically pushed out of certain professions, as Nazi morality saw the ideal, faithful and conformist German wife as running a beautiful clean home and being responsible for the upbringing of her Aryan progeny. In order to boost this policy, as early as August 1933 every married German woman who gave up her job could claim support from the state in the form of the so-called *Ehestandsdarlehen* (marriage loan), and every time she bore a child, 25 per cent of the loan repayment was waived. Later on, women who had more than four children were decorated with the *Ehrenkreuz der Deutschen Mutter* (Cross of Honour of the German Mother) medal.

Men were under no less pressure to father as many children as possible: civil servants without children were considered to be saboteurs or suspected of being homosexual, and an apprenticeship was frequently only possible if the young man in question promised that he would get married at the end of his indentured training period. Values like love and spiritual communion between spouses were subordinated to the biological primary purpose of procreation and securing progeny to serve the new Nazi state. In 1936, the Family Law Committee of the Academy of German Law defined the term 'marriage' as:

> . . . a permanent union of two racially identical, genetically healthy persons of different genders, recognised by the national community and based on mutual loyalty, love and respect, for the purpose of safeguarding and promoting the common good through mutual co-operation and for the purpose of producing racially identical, genetically healthy children and raising them to become diligent community members.

Increasing birth rates on the one hand, and prohibition of certain births on the other were two sides of the same coin, since support for procreation could only apply to the Aryan population, as Hitler put it quite clearly in *Mein Kampf*: '. . . as if it was up to every individual how they treat their body! There is no such thing as the freedom to sin at the expense of future generations and thus of race.' Mixing and intercourse with non-Aryans, 'asocials' or 'degenerates' would only bring forth 'inferior' progeny and was strictly forbidden. Not only was sex with Jews outlawed under the notorious 1935 Nuremberg Laws, but during the war sexual relations with the thousands of foreign workers brought to Germany along with prisoners of war was also totally banned and severely punished.

There was an inherent contradiction between Hitler's published views on the importance of 'purity' in sexual relations for the future of the Aryan race, and his private tolerance of the louche behaviour of his senior Nazis. Although normally known as being rather uptight and repressed – for example refusing to let even his valet and doctor see him naked – Hitler repeatedly insisted that he didn't expect party members like the thugs of the SA to behave like young ladies at a finishing school. Indeed, according to one of his early intimates, Hermann Rauschning, he went further and was far from a 'spoilsport' about the 'frolicking' of his fellow Nazis:

> I loathe this prudishness and moral sleuthing . . . I will not spoil my men's fun. If I demand them to do the utmost for me, then I also have to give them their freedom to let off steam the way they want to, not in the manner deemed proper by some churchy types. My men are no angels, God knows, and they don't have to be. They are ruffians and that's how it should stay. I have no use for sneaks and moral do-gooders. I don't care about their private lives, just like I will not tolerate any meddling in my private life.

Hermann Rauschning was a conservative Nazi leader in the Free State of Danzig, a German enclave within Poland created after the

First World War. He became disillusioned with the Nazis after they came to power, whereupon he fled into exile. He published a series of books, one of which, *Hitler Speaks*, became an influential bestseller and purported to offer the Führer's real views expressed in private conversation. After Rauschning's death, Holocaust deniers smeared him and claimed his conversations with Hitler never took place. However, the views he reports accord entirely with what we know were Hitler's true opinions.

In principle, Hitler did not care about the morals – or lack of them – of his most important paladins, so long as they did not interfere with his plans. However, nobody really knew where the limits of Hitler's tolerance lay, and so the Nazi elite had a sword of Damocles hanging over their heads: only the Führer himself determined who had violated his unwritten moral laws and who should be punished accordingly.

Hitler's own puritanical view of sexual morals was not always uncritically accepted – even among his own closest acolytes. Some top Nazis saw the institution of marriage as a necessary condition for the much-desired increase of the Aryan race, while others – notably Himmler – saw Holy Matrimony as 'the satanical work of the Catholic Church' (to which both he and Hitler had been born into). Marriage, in the eyes of Himmler and his followers, could be an obstacle to the primary objective of sexual procreation. There was no clearly defined code for sexual behaviour for the Aryan citizen beyond the bans on sex with Jews, homosexuality, or sex with those condemned as asocial degenerates. Mores and morals were often quoted but never defined.

Amidst this confusion, with the unlimited power now in their hands after 1933, many of the leading National Socialists took their own steps to satisfy their erotic tastes and needs, which often contradicted the official party line. Hardly any members of the Nazi elite complied in private with the moral cliches that they preached to the people, such as the injunction to be 'modest, honest and faithful, you approach the loom to weave the tapestry of the new Germany'. On the contrary: behind the scenes, party fat cats lived the high life of luxury in a 'Nazi den of sins with double, even triple moral standards'.

One of the most notorious offenders, saying one thing in public while doing precisely the opposite in private, was Propaganda Minister Joseph Goebbels. Despite this, his voracious sexual appetite was widely known, earning him derisive nicknames such as 'tadpole' (all head and dick – a play on the German word *Schwanz,* which means both a tail and is slang for a penis). Goebbels was also dubbed the 'Noble Buck of Babelsberg' – a reference to him giving aspiring film actresses the casting couch treatment at Babelsberg, the suburb west of Berlin where Germany's major film studios were located. Another nickname was 'the cock of Schwanenwerder' – a reference to the wealthy area on west Berlin's Wannsee lake where, in 1936, Goebbels acquired a substantial villa and secluded estate where he entertained his conquests. Ironically, as Gauleiter (a political official in charge of a Nazi *Gau* or district)' of Berlin before coming to power, Goebbels had inveighed against the many Jews who owned properties in the area, which he called 'Schweinenwerder' ('Isle of Pigs').

Goebbels was born into a poor Catholic family in the Rhineland in 1897. Precociously intelligent, he was puny and suffered from a congenital club foot, walking with a limp, which excluded him from military service in the First World War. Small and dark, like most of the Nazi leaders, he was physically very far from the tall blond Aryan ideal. A gifted student of literature with an unsuccessful novel and a doctorate in philosophy to his name, Goebbels grew up in the economic shadows of Weimar, and failed to find a secure place in life until he joined the Nazi Party in 1922. His bitingly vituperative articles in the Nazi press and his talents as a rabble-rousing orator were second only to those of Hitler.

At first, Goebbels took seriously the 'socialist' aspects of the National Socialist programme and became a follower of Hitler's leftist

Nazi rival Gregor Strasser – even calling for the 'petit bourgeois Adolf Hitler' to be expelled from the party. When he met Hitler in person, however, he was dazzled and completely won over, and became one of the leader's most passionate and besotted followers. Hitler recognised Goebbels' organisational and oratorical talents and made him district party leader – or Gauleiter – in Berlin in 1926, tasked with the mission of changing the city's traditional left-wing orientation and winning the capital for the Nazis.

Goebbels set about his work with a will. A rabid anti-Semite, he denounced the decadence of the Weimar Republic's capital, and his Berlin newspaper *Der Angriff* ('The Attack') linked the Jewish population with corruption and vice in the city. Goebbels' rabble-rousing oratory as the Great Depression set in won recruits in the city's working-class areas. During his years as Nazi boss in the capital, Goebbels demonstrated his genius for propaganda, turning Nazi militants such as the Stormtrooper Horst Wessel, murdered by Communists, into martyrs of the movement. A few lines of doggerel written by Wessel became the ubiquitous anthem of the Nazis, the 'Horst-Wessel-Lied', and Goebbels staged spectacular funerals for him and other Nazis killed in clashes with the Communists.

Goebbels was put in charge of Nazi election campaigns as the economic crisis worsened and the party scored spectacular victories with the voters. Using such unprecedented publicity stunts as flying Hitler between political meetings in a plane, staging theatrical giant torchlit rallies, and using the new tool of radio to relay Hitler's speeches, Goebbels was the major architect of the party's rise to power. When Hitler was appointed Chancellor in 1933, Goebbels reaped his reward and was appointed as Minister for Propaganda and Public Enlightenment.

In the newly created post, Goebbels had complete control of the press, broadcasting and publishing, along with the theatre and cinema. As the Nazis tightened their grip on the Reich, propaganda played a major part in setting the tone of the new state, and Goebbels literally became the voice of the Nazi regime. Newspaper editors took their line from daily briefings at the Propaganda Ministry in the heart of Berlin. Opposition newspapers were simply suppressed. People were provided with cheap radio sets – the *Volksempfänger* ('people's receiver') – which could not pick up foreign stations.

Writers such as Thomas and Heinrich Mann and Bertolt Brecht; and performers, artists and actors including Marlene Dietrich, Fritz Lang, George Grosz, Max Beckmann and Otto Dix were forced into exile or banned from exhibiting. Their works were held up to mockery and ridicule in special shows of *Entartete Kunst* ('Degenerate art'). Goebbels was the new cultural dictator of the Reich, and within a short space of time he extirpated the free and easy atmosphere of Weimar and put Germany into a cultural straitjacket in which any deviations from the official line in print, in broadcasting, on stage and in film were suppressed. The economic deprivations of Goebbels' early life, coupled with his physical disability, had bred a profoundly cynical mindset in the young man, together with an inferiority complex. When he became Germany's cultural overlord with all the power that came with it, he gave his strong erotic desires full rein.

Even in his early youth Goebbels had demonstrated a keen sexual appetite. From his teens he had a series of passionate infatuations with a constantly changing cast of girlfriends – one of whom he dropped on discovering that she was Jewish. He breathlessly recorded his sexual successes and failures in the diaries he compulsively kept from his youth until his suicide in the ruins of Berlin in 1945. In 1926, the year he took up his Gauleiter's job in Berlin aged just twenty-eight, Goebbels confessed in his diary: 'Every woman tempts me to my very core. I storm about like a hungry wolf. Even though I am as shy as a child! Sometimes I hardly understand myself. I should marry and become bourgeois! And hang myself after eight days. Good night!'

Six years later Goebbels took his own cynical advice and did become 'bourgeois' by marrying. His bride, Magda Quandt, was a wealthy divorcee with a son from her previous marriage. Despite her fanatical devotion to the Nazi cause, and to Adolf Hitler in particular, Magda's complicated family background epitomises the absurdities and contradictions of Nazi family and racial policy. Her parents, Oskar Ritschel and Auguste Behrend, were unmarried when she was born in 1901, and though they married after her birth, they very quickly divorced. Magda's mother then married a wealthy Jew, Richard Friedländer – who may actually have been her biological father. Brought up by her mother and stepfather (who was to perish at Buchenwald in the Holocaust), in 1920 Magda married Günther Quandt, a wealthy member of the immensely rich family that still owns stakes in the BMW and Daimler-Benz car companies. Magda gave birth to a son, Harald Quandt, but the marriage foundered after Quandt discovered that his bored and neglected wife was having an affair.

In 1930, living in Berlin, Magda attended a Nazi Party meeting and was swept away by the oratory of both Hitler and the city's Gauleiter, Joseph Goebbels. Despite her Jewish background, she joined the Nazi Party and began an affair with Goebbels. The relationship was fraught from the outset, punctuated by fierce quarrels and passionate reconciliations. There was also a mutual attraction between Magda and Hitler, and it is possible that Hitler encouraged his propaganda chief to marry Magda so that he could be close to her without marrying her himself. Goebbels wed her in 1931 on the Quandt family estate with Hitler acting as best man.

Goebbels had made it perfectly clear to Magda that he had no intention of being a faithful husband, and Magda, too, indulged in extra-marital affairs. Despite this, she publicly played the role of the ideal Nazi wife and mother, and gave birth to six children by Goebbels in rapid succession – five girls and one boy – whose forenames all began with the letter 'H' in blatant homage to Hitler. When the Nazis took power, Hitler would regularly relax in the bosom of the Goebbels family, doting on both the children and their mother who acted as the 'First Lady' of the Reich.

Goebbels was far from an ideal husband. He spent little time in the family home, showed scant interest in his wife and children, and used his position as boss of the Reich's cultural realm to have constant affairs with attractive film and theatre actresses. The most serious such relationship – and the one that came close to derailing Goebbels' entire career – was his liaison with the Czech film star Lída Baarová.

Baarová had come to Berlin from her native Prague in 1935 and landed a role in a musical movie *Barcarole* opposite Gustav Fröhlich, one of Germany's leading stars since his part in the Weimar expressionist film *Metropolis* directed by Fritz Lang. At the premiere of *Barcarole* the eighteen-year-old Baarová met Hitler, who stared at her without speaking, but soon invited her to a tête-a-tête meeting at which he told her that she reminded him of his niece, Geli Raubal whose mysterious suicide in 1931 had blighted Hitler's rise to power and raised disturbing questions about his own sexuality and their relationship. Hitler – despite his disdain for the Czechs – invited Baarová to stay in Germany and take up German citizenship.

The young actress had begun an affair with her co-star Fröhlich and moved in with the actor. The following year, 1936, aged just nineteen, she met Goebbels who was instantly attracted to her. At first in the company of Fröhlich, she was invited to the 1936 Nuremberg rally and to sailing weekends at either of the two select properties that the propaganda minister had acquired on the lakes in the leafy suburbs west of Berlin. Flattered that the man who could make or break her career had fallen for her, Baarová succumbed to his open infatuation. When Fröhlich discovered the couple in a compromising position in the minister's car a blazing row ensued, during which the actor is reported to have slapped the minister's face.

Despite his cynicism and heartless philandering, Goebbels had genuinely fallen in love with his young mistress. When Magda Goebbels discovered what was going on, she started to collect information against her husband. She was helped by Goebbels' right-hand man Karl Hanke, undersecretary of state in the Propaganda Ministry. Hanke compiled a list of thirty-six occasions when Goebbels had committed adultery with actresses and various high-society ladies. Armed with this evidence, Magda went to see Hitler and demanded his permission to divorce Goebbels.

Hitler's reaction was predictable. He held Magda in great esteem, and he valued Goebbels' services far too highly to let him be disgraced in a public scandal. The Führer summoned Goebbels and pointed out that as Propaganda Minister he had to set an example of morality and probity to all Germans. Moreover, he added, Baarová was a Czech, and at that point, 1938, his campaign of intimidation against the Czechs – that would end with the Munich agreement and the eventual dismembering of the country – was reaching its climax.

At first, and for perhaps the first time in his slavish relationship with Hitler, Goebbels stuck to his guns. He accepted, he said, that he would have to quit as Propaganda Minister, but he still wanted to divorce Magda and marry Baarová. He even suggested that he should go to Japan with her to take up the vacant post of ambassador in Tokyo.

Hitler would have none of it. At the end of a stormy two-hour confrontation, Hitler issued a 'Führer directive' – an official order – to Goebbels that he would not see Baarová for a year. If, at the end of that period, he and Magda were still set on divorcing, then he would reluctantly agree. Eventually, just as reluctantly, Goebbels buckled and complied. To ensure that Goebbels obeyed the edict, Hitler had Himmler keep the promiscuous propaganda chief under police surveillance. In the meantime, to complicate matters still further, Magda herself had fallen in love with Hanke and even wanted to marry him. Stung to the quick, Goebbels hypocritically demanded a reconciliation. Hitler commented: 'When it comes to women, Goebbels is a cynic.'

Meanwhile, a not-so covert campaign was launched to end Baarová's career. The premiere of her next film was infiltrated by SS men in mufti who, on Himmler's orders, hissed and yelled 'Goebbels' Whore!' whenever Baarová appeared on screen. Contracts for her future films were abruptly cancelled, and a director who proposed to show her past movies was beaten up. Running out of money, and realising that her relationship with Goebbels was doomed, Baarová returned to Prague.

In the autumn of 1938 Goebbels and Magda were called to Hitler's Bavarian mountain retreat at Berchtesgaden to publicly demonstrate that their marriage was back on track. The photos of the far from happy couple, wanly grinning, with Hitler between them as boss cupid, were prominently displayed in the press. But this reconciliation was purely for public consumption. Both Goebbels and Magda resumed their secret lives of constant covert affairs, and behind the scenes lived largely separate lives until their gruesome ends in Hitler's bunker in 1945.

As we have seen, Heinrich Himmler's personality was very different from the libidinous womaniser at the Propaganda Ministry. Sexually repressed, puritanical and moralistic by his own standards, Himmler probably had little or no previous sexual experience when he proposed to his wife Margarete in 1927. His bride was a divorcee and nurse who shared her husband's beliefs in herbal medicine and racial purity. Margarete was eight years older than Himmler, and the future Reichsführer largely left his wife alone to run their home after the birth of their only child, Gudrun, while he concentrated on building his successful career in the party.

Though lacking Goebbels' hungry sexual appetites, Himmler was by no means wedded to conventional marital morality, and was happy to junk such Christian values in favour of the primary goal of breeding Aryan children to serve the Reich. He enjoyed at least one extra-marital affair with a Munich singer, Karoline Diehl, before making his long-time secretary Hedwig Potthast, whom he called 'Häschen' ('little bunny'), his mistress around the time that the Second World War broke out.

Himmler was notably hypocritical about his own double life and domestic arrangements. His chief of staff, Karl Wolff, repeatedly sought his boss's permission to divorce his wife and marry his mistress – and was just as repeatedly refused. Finally, in March 1943, Wolff went over Himmler's head and sought Hitler's permission to make the move – which the Führer granted. As a result, a furious Himmler sacked him.

Himmler set his mistress up in a house on the Obersalzberg mountain – close to Hitler's own Bavarian mountain retreat. She gave birth to a son, Helge, in February 1941; and to a daughter, Nanette-Dorothea, on 20 July 1944. Himmler missed the birth of his last child, as on the same day he was called to Berlin to deal with the aftermath of Count von Stauffenberg's unsuccessful attempt to assassinate Hitler with a bomb. Himmler was often absent from both his marital and his mistress's homes, preoccupied as he was with his major mission: building the SS into the network of terror that carried out the enormities of the Holocaust, and fashioning his malign vision of a racially purified Reich.

If Goebbels, with his six impeccably Aryan blonde children, lived up to Himmler's ideal of breeding the Aryan race more fruitfully than Himmler himself, he was outdone by Martin Bormann, the Nazi Party *Reichsleiter* (organisation leader) and Hitler's secretary. Bormann's wife Gerda produced no fewer than ten children. Bormann was a master of intrigue and empire building to put even Himmler to shame. By dint of staying literally by Hitler's side at all times he became his master's gatekeeper, controlling all access to the Führer. He ran Hitler's household and property portfolio on the Obsersalzberg, compulsorily buying up nearby land, expelling residents, and creating a veritable mountain fortress that became the 'second capital of the Reich'. He and other Nazi grandees such as Hermann Göring and Albert Speer built their houses close by. Along with Goebbels, Bormann was with his master in the Berlin bunker until the very end. Intriguing to the last, he persuaded Hitler to dismiss Göring and Himmler from the party at the war's end when they showed signs of wanting to negotiate a peace with the western Allies.

A brutal and violent thug, who had taken part in the murder of a political opponent in his youth, Bormann was also a man of unbridled sexual desires. His major mistress was the actress Manja Behrens, who, unusually, had spurned Goebbels' own advances before succumbing to Bormann. (She said that she would rather sweep the streets than sleep with the propaganda minister.) When Gerda Bormann learned of the affair, she actually encouraged her husband's liaison. Bormann was suitably grateful, writing to Gerda: 'Oh my sweet, you cannot imagine how happy I am with you both . . . all the happiness that you gave me, and all our children, and now I also have M.'

Gratifyingly for Bormann, Gerda responded: 'It is such a pity that gorgeous girls like her should not have any children. In this case you have the power to change that, but you should see to it that one year M bears a child and the next year I do, so that there is always one woman available for you.' Despite this helpful encouragement, Manja Behrens proved less fecund that Gerda Bormann and failed to bear her lover any offspring.

Another top Nazi with a penchant for the acting profession was Robert Ley. The boss of the unified Nazi workers' organisation, the *Deutsche Arbeitsfront* (German Labour Front), which had replaced the outlawed trade unions, Ley was a notorious alcoholic who was rarely seen sober in public. He went by the nickname *Reichstrunkenbold* ('chief Reich drunkard'). In 1937 Ley acted as host when the Nazi-sympathising Duke and Duchess of Windsor, the former British King, Edward VIII, and his bride Wallis Simpson, visited Germany and met Hitler at Berchtesgaden. During the tour, an inebriated Ley managed to crash the duke and duchess's car.

Ley indulged in unrestrained affairs, usually with very young girls, which soon provided ample material for public gossip. For three years the womanising Ley enjoyed an affair with actress and soprano singer Inga Spilker, the tall, blonde and beautiful daughter of opera singer Max Spilker. In 1938, when his lover got pregnant, Ley demanded a divorce from his sick wife Elisabeth, who was hospitalised with a heart condition. The same year he married Inga, who was twenty-six years his junior. Hitler – who overlooked Ley's drunkenness because he valued his total loyalty – was guest of honour at the wedding.

Marriage didn't stop Ley from continuing to indulge his sexual cravings. He was constantly unfaithful to his bride who sunk into drink and depression as a result. He was brutally violent too. Himmler's masseur, Felix Kersten, was present in Ley's home when the drunken oaf tore off his wife's clothes to show his guests 'the wonders of German female beauty'. In tears, Inga called her husband a wild animal. 'He treats me without shame. He will kill me, one day.'

A year later, on 29 December 1942, Inga Ley killed herself. By that time a morphine addict – like Hermann Göring – soon after the birth of her daughter Lore, Inga watched through a window while her husband took a flirtatious farewell of a female guest in a car. She placed her baby on her bed and took out the pistol that her husband had given her as protection against a possible attack from one of the armies of foreign labourers that Ley had imported into the Reich. She then shot herself in the head.

At the funeral, Ley, who had suffered a stammer since sustaining a head injury in the First World War, stuttered, 'M-m-my Führer, n-n-now you have all of me again.' Hitler had ignored Ley's infidelity and marital strife, just as he ignored his public drunkenness, even though it had ended in Inga's suicide. In his formal letter of condolence, he claimed that years of illness had broken the young woman's will to live.

Ley did not mourn for long. The grieving widower soon found solace in the arms of an underage Estonian, Madeleine Wanderer. According to official Nazi laws and principles this liaison, too, was a crime, but Hitler and the judiciary turned a blind, benevolent eye. Hitler was apparently even amused by Ley's antics. In one incident, Ley turned up at the offices of the town planning administration – a department where he had no authority. Drunk as usual, and dressed in an elegant tailored suit and Panama hat, the minister ordered the architects working there to build brothels. 'I will have this entire block built,' he slurred, 'and we need whores too! Lots of them, a whole house, modern furnishings. We will use what it takes, a few hundred million [marks] to build this, it doesn't matter.' Despite such outrageous behaviour Ley remained in office until the end of the war. Indicted at the Nuremberg tribunal for his use of slave labour, it was Ley's turn to take his life. He strangled himself in his cell with strips torn from his towel.

Joachim von Ribbentrop, a latecomer to the Nazis and a client at Salon Kitty, was a social-climbing snob who used his marriage to a wealthy German wine heiress, Anna Henkell, to advance his career and was deeply unpopular with his fellow senior Nazis. Ribbentrop earned Hitler's gratitude by brokering the key meeting at his house with leading conservatives that led to his master's appointment as Chancellor. Hitler mistakenly believed in Ribbentrop's expertise in foreign affairs, acquired as a travelling Champagne salesman, and made him successively Ambassador to Britain and then Foreign Minister. Equally unpopular in London, where he was derisively known as 'Herr Brickendrop' for his social gaffes, Ribbentrop was reputedly one of Mrs Wallis Simpson's lovers before her liaison with King Edward VIII, and reportedly sent her a bouquet of seventeen carnations to represent the number of times they had made love.

If rumours of her promiscuous early life are to be believed, Wallis Simpson had the unique distinction of being the lover of two of Salon Kitty's later clients – Ribbentrop and his Italian counterpart Count Gian Galeazzo Ciano, son-in-law of Benito Mussolini and Italy's Foreign Minister. As a young diplomat in the 1920s, Ciano was stationed in China and met Wallis, at the time unhappily married to the first of her three husbands, Earl Winfield Spencer, a drunken and abusive US naval officer. Ciano was a libidinous lifelong philanderer, and the couple are said to have had an affair which resulted in Wallis falling pregnant and a botched abortion that left her unable to have children.

The snubs he had endured in London made Ribbentrop an embittered enemy of Britain, and he encouraged Hitler to pursue the pact with Stalin that precipitated Germany's invasion of Poland and the Second World War. After the western Allies declared war, he steadily lost influence with Hitler, who distrusted the Foreign Office. Ribbentrop went into hiding with a woman in Hamburg at the war's end but was discovered and tried at Nuremberg with the other surviving Nazi leaders. He was condemned to death and hanged in October 1946.

Almost uniquely among the Nazi leaders, Herrmann Göring was a faithful husband. A high- scoring air ace in the First World War, he was a valued early recruit to the party because of his war record and high-society contacts. Wounded in the Beer Hall Putsch, he went into exile where he became addicted to morphine and met his first wife, a Swedish aristocrat named Carin von Kantzow. Returning to Germany, as the Nazis gained electoral popularity, he became in succession

President of the Reichstag and Prime Minister of Prussia. After the Nazi takeover he became economics overlord and chief of the rapidly expanding Luftwaffe. Combining brutal violence with jovial charm, he played a leading role in setting up the Gestapo and destroying the SA in the Night of the Long Knives. After Carin's death he built an extravagant mausoleum and country house, Carinhall, where he indulged his love of hunting, and was named *Reichsmarschall* in recognition of his position as Hitler's leading lieutenant.

In 1935, the widower Göring married the actress Emmy Sonnemann – who would vie with Magda Goebbels for the unofficial position of First Lady of the Reich. By no means as fertile as her rival, Emmy gave birth to Göring's only child, Edda – named after Mussolini's eldest daughter, Edda Ciano. After Göring's Luftwaffe failed to win the Battle of Britain in 1940, the fire seemed to go out of the Reichsmarschall. Increasingly obese, he gave himself up to his passion for looting art from across conquered Europe. Stripped of his party positions by Hitler at the end of the war after he attempted to usurp power from the Führer, he surrendered to the US Army and became the leading defendant at the Nuremberg trials. Sentenced to death, he cheated the hangman on the eve of his execution by swallowing a concealed cyanide capsule.

The sexuality and love life of Adolf Hitler himself remains a mystery. Despite a plethora of psychiatric reports, books, films, allegations by his political opponents and uncorroborated rumour, even the basic facts are still uncertain. Depending on which source is referred to, Hitler was either an asexual puritanical neuter who found all forms of sexual contact repellent; a coprophile pervert; a sadomasochist; an effeminate homosexual; or a sentimental romantic who enjoyed a 'normal' erotic life with his long-term mistress and finally wife Eva Braun. All that can be done is to set out what facts can be ascertained.

Hitler's family originated in the Waldviertel district of Austria, in the nineteenth century a poor and remote area inhabited by a mainly peasant population where illegitimacy and incest were rife. At the time of his birth 40 per cent of all babies here were born outside wedlock. His family inheritance reflected this background, with physical deformity, infant mortality and mental handicaps being common. One of his aunts was a hunchback, another was schizophrenic, and his sole surviving full sibling Paula was believed to have learning disabilities. Of the six children born to Hitler's parents – who were themselves distantly related – no fewer than four died in infancy or childhood.

Hitler was ashamed of his family background and, as Führer, did what he could to cover it up. He was especially troubled by the possibility that his tangled ancestry included Jewish antecedents, and he commissioned a secret study of Austria's ancestral records to establish whether this was true. In 2018 a scientific study of the DNA of Hitler family members in the United States and Austria concluded that the family did indeed possess Jewish and even Moorish African genes.

Hitler, like his fellow dictator Josef Stalin, had an abusive childhood in which he was frequently beaten by his drunken father, Alois. He sought comfort and reassurance from his mother Klara, often sharing her bed. Mother and son formed a close and cloying bond, and when Klara died of breast cancer, Hitler's grief – according to Eduard Bloch, the Jewish family doctor who treated her in her final illness – was overwhelming.

In his youth Hitler had few close friends, apart from a relationship with a young man called August Kubizek, with whom he shared rooms in Linz and Vienna and an intense devotion to the music of Richard Wagner. Kubizek's account of their youthful friendship – *Young Hitler* (1953) – includes an episode when at Hitler's suggestion he and Hitler visited the Spittelberggasse, Vienna's red-light district, but only to look rather than to participate – the impoverished youths could not have afforded to be patrons. As they paraded past the illuminated windows where the women displayed their charms, according to Kubizek, Hitler shuddered in revulsion, and once back in their lodgings delivered an impassioned homily against the world's oldest profession.

This incident may be related to Hitler's lifelong fear of venereal disease. His enemies spread rumours that he had contracted syphilis from an encounter with a Viennese – possibly Jewish – prostitute, and though such rumours were never substantiated, as Führer he chose as his personal physician a Dr Theodor Morell, whose speciality was VD and skin disease.

Another of Hitler's lifelong neuroses related to his genitalia. Again, ribald rumours propagated by his political opponents spread the story that he was deficient in the genital department. Specifically, rumour had it that he suffered from monorchism (a missing testicle) and/or that his penis was abnormally small – there was even an absurd story that a goat had nipped off the tip of his penis as a child.

The missing testicle rumour was so widespread that it became a song sung by British soldiers in the war: 'Hitler has only got one ball . . .' Once again, there may well be an element of truth in the rumours: the five Russian doctors who carried out an autopsy on Hitler's half-incinerated corpse in Berlin at the end of the war could find no trace of his left testicle; and photos of the Führer in his pomp frequently show his hands defensively clasped in front of his genitalia in a psychologically protective default gesture. Against this, we have the testimony of Dr Morell, who, on the rare occasions when he was permitted to examine Hitler naked, said he found no abnormality of his genitals, and his valet Heinz Linge, who testified that the Führer's penis was of normal dimensions when he glimpsed the organ as they were urinating together against a tree.

Psychologically, circumstantial evidence strongly indicates that Hitler was both a sadomasochist and suffered from real or imagined impotence. Instances of his cruelty are numerous, from his delight in shooting rats with an airgun as a child, to his insistence on filming the slow strangulation and humiliation of the plotters who had planned his assassination on 20 July 1944. He was proud of his ability to keep his arm stiffly extended in the Nazi salute at parades for lengthy periods, which it has been suggested was a substitute for real erections. In 1943 his mistress Eva Braun allegedly asked whether he could be given aphrodisiacs to boost his potency. Around the same time, he suggested to her that she should take another lover as he was no longer able to satisfy her sexually. By the war's end, he was a physical wreck, prematurely aged, with trembling limbs and possibly suffering from Parkinson's disease. He took no exercise, and was stuffed full of a cocktail of damaging drugs prescribed by the quack Dr Morell, and it is difficult to believe that he was capable of having any sort of sex.

During his vagrant years in Vienna before the First World War, Hitler lived in men-only hostels and mingled exclusively with other men. This male-only world continued during his war service on the Western Front, when he reportedly indignantly refused his comrades' invitations to join them on visits to brothels, and afterwards in barracks when he remained in the army acting as an informer on political groups in Munich. The German historian Lothar Machtan, in his book *The Hidden Hitler* (2001), has concentrated on these years, suggesting that Hitler had homosexual relationships in the army, and among his early political associates, but there is no solid evidence for these claims.

According to August Kubizek, in his teens Hitler had a romantic crush in the Austrian city of Linz on a girl named Stefanie Isak, who was of Jewish descent. He followed her and constructed a detailed fantasy life around her, wrote love poems to her, and even sent an anonymous love letter, but was too shy to actually approach her. They never met, and Stefanie apparently remained blissfully unaware of her tongue-tied and timid suitor's devotion.

During the Nazi Party's early years in Munich in the 1920s, Hitler was 'adopted' by a number of married wealthy high-society hostesses, including Helene Bechstein of the famous piano manufacturing family; Elsa Bruckmann, wife of the publisher Hugo Bruckmann; and Winifred Wagner, the British-born wife of Siegfried Wagner, only son of Hitler's musical idol, who regularly invited Hitler to the Bayreuth Festival of her father-in-law's works. These women made Hitler *salonfähig* – teaching him the mores and manners of polite society. They also smartened his eccentric dress style, showered him with gifts and money and promoted the young Nazi Party. Hitler treated his patronesses with the same old-world courtesy he would always show in public when meeting women, but there is no evidence of any romantic links between them. Interestingly, in view of the allegations of Hitler's S&M proclivities, Bechstein and Bruckmann both presented Hitler with whips, which he regularly carried around and was frequently photographed brandishing.

In Munich, Hitler was also befriended by a wealthy German–American married couple, the music publisher Ernst 'Putzi' Hanfstaengl and his wife Helene. Hitler valued the Hanfstaengls for their international contacts and promoted Ernst to be his foreign press manager because of his US links. (Hanfstaengl had been educated at Ivy League US universities and had spent much of his life as his family firm's representative in America.) In an early foretaste of his later relationships with Joseph and Magda Goebbels, and his cultured architect and armaments minister Albert Speer, Hitler also privately valued 'Putzi' for his piano playing, which soothed the future Führer's jangled nerves while he paid romantic but platonic court to Frau Hanfstaengl and petted their young son Egon. On one occasion he grovelled on his knees before Helene and begged to be her slave, although she put this behaviour down to his nerves. After the failure of the Beer Hall Putsch in 1923, Hitler sought refuge at the Hanfstaengls' house. Here, Helene reportedly saved a despairing Hitler from committing suicide by snatching his pistol and hiding it in a flour bin.

It was during the formative Munich years in the 1920s that we have the only documented account of a love affair involving Hitler from a surviving partner: a woman named Maria 'Mimi' Reiter. Ironically the daughter of an official of the left-wing Social Democratic Party, Mimi met Hitler in 1925 in Berchtesgaden, the Bavarian mountain resort where he took his holidays and which he was later to make the site of his rural retreat, the Berghof. Mimi was just sixteen and working as a shopgirl in her family's clothes store opposite the hotel where Hitler was staying. Hitler was thirty-seven when he shyly asked her elder sister to introduce him. At their first meeting he was carrying his ubiquitous whip and walking Prinz, the first of the German Shepherd dogs that would be his favoured pets to the end of his life. Their initial conversation – like Hitler's table talk at the last meal he ate with his staff in the embattled Führerbunker at the end of his life – concerned the correct breeding and training of dogs.

At the time he started to court Mimi, Hitler was rebuilding the Nazi Party after the hiatus following the 1923 Beer Hall Putsch when it was banned, and he was imprisoned. He invited Mimi to attend a party meeting at which he was speaking and seated her next to him at the dinner that followed. According to Mimi's later account, Hitler combined Viennese charm – feeding her cakes like a child – with a crude sexual advance, playing footsie under the table. The date ended awkwardly – Hitler savagely beat his dog, and then clumsily attempted to kiss the teenage girl who was upset by his brutal violence to the animal. When she refused, he stormed off with a curt 'Heil!'

The courtship continued, initially conducted by Nazi intermediaries sent to see Mimi on Hitler's behalf, who told her that their boss was 'on fire' for her. Despite her doubts, Mimi was persuaded to go on another date, and Hitler took her on an excursion to the picturesque Starnberger See lake in a car driven by his chauffeur, Emil Maurice – the man who would later fall out with the Führer over Maurice's romance with Hitler's niece Geli Raubal. En route, on the back seat of the car, the couple schmoozed, with Mimi experiencing her first kiss with her middle-aged suitor.

The third date was bizarre – Hitler, once again wielding his whip, took Mimi to visit Leonding, where his beloved mother was buried. Mimi – who had lost her own mother at a young age – was reduced to tears by Hitler's obvious emotion as he stood at the graveside. Their next date was a more conventional lovers' rendezvous – he took her for a walk in the woods. It was on this occasion that Hitler asked Mimi to call him 'Herr Wolf' – his usual alias when he sought anonymity. For his part, he called her 'Mimilein' – an affectionate Austrian diminutive. His behaviour, too, was that of a passionate lover. He posed her against a tree and called her his *Waldfee* (wood fairy), covered her with kisses, and protested his undying devotion – but told her that they could only marry and have 'blonde children' when he had fulfilled what he called his 'mission'.

Then, abruptly, there was silence. For some two years, Mimi heard nothing from Hitler. By then she was thoroughly infatuated with her increasingly famous lover, and was ready to wait for him as he had asked her. But as the weeks turned into months, and then years, she was driven to such despair that she made an attempt to commit suicide. She attached a clothesline to a door handle, wrapped it around her neck and sank into unconsciousness. At the last moment, when semi-comatose, she was found and saved by her brother-in-law. Coincidentally or not, Mimi thus became the first of several women whose associations with Hitler led to attempted or successful suicides.

Envoys from the party in Munich explained to Mimi that Hitler's silence was caused by poison pen letters and rumours spread by his political opponents alleging that he was conducting an improper relationship with an underage girl. Finally, in 1928, Mimi's patience ran out. She married a hotelier and moved to Innsbruck. But her marriage soon failed and her fascination with the rapidly rising politician continued.

In 1931, after a visit from one of Hitler's closest acolytes, Rudolf Hess, who assured her of Hitler's continuing interest in her, Mimi went to Munich with the intention of asking her absent admirer for a job. She called Hitler's adjutant, Julius Schaub. Hitler told Schaub to bring Mimi over to the luxury nine-room apartment that his admirers had acquired for him in the city's wealthy Prinzregentenplatz. It was here, at last, according to Mimi, that the relationship was finally physically consummated.

In her account of these events in 1959, in an interview given to Günter Peis, a journalist for *Stern* magazine, Mimi rhapsodised about her seduction by Hitler in gushingly romantic, schoolgirlish terms:

He pulled me towards him and kissed me. It was well after midnight. He leaned back on the sofa, further and further. He held me more and more firmly. I let everything happen. I had never been as happy as I was that night . . . around 2 a.m. he got up. After a while he said, 'Mimilein, I am rich now. I can offer you everything. I can remove any obstacles for you. Stay with me. My beautiful darling, dear Mimi. You must stay with me.'

Mimi claimed that she refused to become Hitler's live-in mistress and held out for marriage. He then had one of his sudden mood swings, and began to shout at her, angrily declaring that for political reasons he could not marry a divorcee. Despite his temper tantrum, Hitler did follow through on his promise to help her, sending his personal lawyer, Hans Frank, to Austria to handle her divorce from her husband.

After this sofa seduction, two more silent years passed, during which, as we shall see, Hitler became involved with two other young women: Geli Raubal and Eva Braun. By the time that Mimi met Hitler again in 1934, momentous changes had taken place in his fortunes and he had become Germany's Führer. Mimi went to Berlin and met her distant but now all-powerful lover. Once more, Hitler sang his familiar song: he still loved her and wanted her to become his mistress, but he could not marry her until he had fulfilled his 'mission'.

Once again, Mimi's patience ran out. In 1936 she married an SS officer, Hauptsturmführer Georg Kubisch. Hitler raised no objections to the match, and even publicly congratulated Kubisch at an SS parade in Munich. Two more years went by before Hitler and Mimi met again, in 1938, for the final time. At this meeting, according to Mimi, Hitler again assured her of his lasting love and expressed dissatisfaction with his mistress Eva Braun. When her husband was killed in 1940 during the Nazi conquest of France, Hitler sent Mimi a bouquet of a hundred red roses. It was the end of the affair.

Mimi Reiter's account of the affair, which remained completely unknown until her interview with Günter Peis, gained credibility as it was confirmed by none other than her friend Paula Hitler – the Führer's younger sister. Paula, a simple woman who lived a quiet life throughout the Third Reich and took no part in her infamous brother's rise to power, told Peis about Mimi and introduced them. Paula expressed the opinion that Mimi was Hitler's only true love, and that if the relationship had prospered, she might even have restrained him from the regime's excesses. However, it was not to be. Mimi Reiter became an alcoholic and died in 1992, aged eighty.

If the on-off affair with Mimi was privately conducted in the shadows, and remained a secret until long after his death, Hitler's simultaneous relationship with his niece Geli Raubal was a public scandal that nearly derailed his rise to supreme power and raised disturbing questions about his sexuality that have divided historians ever since.

Hitler had taken little interest in his family after leaving Austria for Munich in 1913. But in 1927, with his political star on the rise, he felt that he needed a housekeeper to manage Haus Wachenfeld, the country house he had rented on the Obersalzberg, overlooking Berchtesgaden, that he later enlarged to become his official rural residence, the Berghof. He turned to his widowed half-sister Angela Raubal, his elder sibling by his father's second marriage. Angela arrived and was soon joined by her two daughters: 'Geli', a lively nineteen-year-old just out of school, and her quieter younger sister Elfriede.

Though not conventionally pretty, the chubby-faced Geli, with brown hair and sparkling eyes, was chatty, cheeky, charming and laughingly vivacious. She quickly won over the moody man she called 'Uncle Alf' and lifted him from his frequent bouts of despondency. She took familiarities with him permitted to no other members of his inner circle, such as throwing her arms around his neck and demanding to be taken on picnics. At first, while they were living in the country, the relationship between uncle and niece seemed innocent enough, but gradually his escalating enchantment with his niece turned to an unhealthy and possibly sinister obsession. When he moved to his new Munich apartment in the Prinzregentenplatz, Angela and Elfriede were left behind on the Obersalzberg, but he brought Geli to Munich with him, with the excuse that she needed to be in the city to take music lessons. At first Geli was allowed her own room, but quite quickly, in 1929, she moved into Hitler's flat.

Geli was a high-spirited girl, and as she matured into a woman, she naturally embarked on relationships with a series of young suitors. Claiming to be *in loco parentis* in Angela's absence, Hitler kept a strict watch on such relationships, insisting that Geli was too naïve and inexperienced to be given a free rein. There was little doubt, however, that his ostensible regard for Geli's moral welfare masked his own growing erotic interest in her. He showered her with gifts of jewellery, and aides noticed that he behaved like a love-struck adolescent in her company, even patiently trailing after her on shopping expeditions, waiting while she tried on endless successions of hats and dresses.

Hitler also took his niece with him to social and Nazi Party occasions, such as the 1929 Nuremberg Rally, and often escorted her to the opera and theatre. The relationship quickly became the subject of scandal and gossip. The age gap between them with its undertones of incest was commented upon unfavourably, along with darker stories of unnatural love and perversion. Hitler was certainly, in modern terms a 'control freak', and Geli's natural desire to wear make-up, go out dancing, and enter romantic liaisons with other men drove him to paroxysms of jealous fury. Even the ever insatiable Goebbels fancied his chances with Geli. He met her on several occasions, was attracted, and according to his diary even made tentative arrangements to meet her in Berlin – though apparently nothing came of this.

Hitler's rage boiled over when he discovered that Geli was enjoying a long-term romance with Emil Maurice, his chauffeur, and hitherto a loyal follower who had shared his master's imprisonment after the Beer Hall Putsch, there taking down dictation of *Mein Kampf*. At first, Hitler tolerated the relationship for a year but put pressure on them both to end or at least delay consummation of the liaison in marriage. A jealous Hitler eventually broke up the budding affair, sacked Maurice, and forbade Geli from seeing him again.

Strangely, Maurice – unlike many of those who crossed Hitler – did not suffer fatal consequences for his impudence, apart from being permanently expelled from the inner circle. He became an SS officer, but when Himmler discovered that he had distant Jewish ancestry and wanted to drum him out of the SS ranks, Hitler personally intervened with an order declaring Maurice an 'honorary Aryan', saving his career and possibly his life. He survived the war to return to his original profession as a Munich watchmaker.

Apart from his possessiveness, which was obvious to all who observed the couple, we have definite evidence from three separate sources – Ernst and Helene Hanfstaengl, Otto Strasser, and an SA officer named Wilhelm Stocker – that Hitler's relationship with Geli not only became physical but went deeply into the darker side of sadomasochism. Admittedly, both Hanfstaengl and Strasser, at the time they testified to his perversion, had become embittered enemies of the man they had once served, and were speaking from the safety of exile during the Second World War. However, their accounts corroborate each other and fit with psychological assessments of Hitler's character made by professional psychiatrists.

Wilhelm Stocker claimed in an interview after the war that he had been an SA guard at Hitler's flat in the late 1920s who had taken advantage of Hitler's frequent absences to be one of several men to have an affair with the frisky and increasingly frustrated Geli. He told the interviewer:

> Hitler would have been furious if he had known that she was out with such men as a violin player from Augsburg or a ski instructor from Innsbruck. After she was satisfied that I wouldn't tell her uncle – and I had a personal reason for not telling him – she often confided in me. She admitted to me that at times Hitler made her do things in the privacy of her room that sickened her, but when I asked her why she didn't refuse to do them she just shrugged and said that she didn't want to lose him to some woman that would do what he wanted . . . She was a girl that needed attention and needed it often. And she definitely wanted to remain Hitler's favourite girlfriend. She was willing to do anything to retain that status. At the beginning of 1931

I think she was worried that there might be another woman in Hitler's life, because she mentioned to me several times that her uncle didn't seem to be as interested in her as he once was . . .

Another daring suitor who boldly paid court to Geli at this time was Otto Strasser, younger brother of Gregor Strasser, the Nazi head of organisation. Though married, Otto, hearing that Geli was free with her favours, invited her to a *Fasching* (carnival ball) in early 1931. Learning of the date on the day of the ball, an angry Hitler telephoned Strasser to forbid it. 'I don't allow her to go out with a married man,' he ordered. 'I'm not going to have any of your filthy Berlin tricks.' The Strasser brothers were rare examples of Nazis who were prepared to stand up to Hitler, and although the carnival date was scuppered, Geli insisted on her freedom to go out with him, and Otto bravely called at the Prinzregentenplatz.

Strasser told a post-war interviewer:

Geli seemed to have won the argument, but her eyes were red with weeping. His face stony, Hitler stood in the doorway as we left the house to climb into the waiting taxi. We spent a very pleasant, high-spirited evening. Geli seemed to enjoy having escaped from his supervision for once.

Towards the end of their date the couple climbed to the top of the eighteenth-century Chinese Tower in Munich's Englischer Garten park (later destroyed by Allied bombing). Here, Geli collapsed on to a bench, started to 'weep bitterly' and made her confession:

She told me that she really loved Hitler, but she couldn't bear it any longer. His jealousy wasn't the worst thing. He demanded things from her that were simply disgusting. She had never dreamed that such things could happen. When I asked her to tell me, she described things I had previously encountered in my reading of Krafft-Ebing's *Psychopathia Sexualis* when I was a student . . .

In a secret wartime report on Hitler's psychology, commissioned in 1943 from Freudian psychiatrist Dr Walter Langer by America's OSS secret service – the forerunner of the CIA – Strasser elaborated on what Geli had told him:

> Hitler made her undress . . . He would lie down on the floor. Then she would have to squat over his face, where he could examine her at close range and this made him very excited. When the excitement reached its peak, he demanded that she urinate on him and this gave him sexual pleasure. Geli said the whole performance was extremely disgusting to her and . . . it gave her no gratification.

Further confirmation of Hitler's S&M perversion and Geli's disgusted reaction to it comes from Ernst Hanfstaengl, the Harvard educated German–American musician who had been admitted to his inner circle with his wife Helene. As Hanfstaengl recounted in his memoir *Hitler: The Missing Years* (1957), the couple encountered Hitler and Geli on one of their outings to the theatre and afterwards had a meal and walked home together:

> Hitler . . . emphasised some threat against his opponents by cracking the heavy dog whip he still affected. I happened to catch a glimpse of Geli's face as he did it, and there was on it such a look of fear and contempt that I almost caught my breath. Whips as well, I thought, and really felt sorry for the girl. She had displayed no sign of affection for him in the restaurant and seemed bored, looking over her shoulder at other tables, and

I could not help feeling that her share of the relationship was under compulsion.

Hanfstaengl also attests that Geli had told one of her female friends that Hitler was 'a monster', adding, 'You'd never believe the things he makes me do.'

Unattributed rumours circulated that during his face-sitting sessions with Geli, Hitler had made pornographic drawings of her genitals, and that these had somehow found their way into the hands of blackmailers, along with a letter to her written in 1929 before she had moved into his flat in which he described masochistic and coprophiliac fantasies he had been having about her. The Nazi Party treasurer, Franz Xavier Schwarz, made successful efforts to buy back this material from the blackmailers using a racist Nazi Catholic priest, Father Bernhard Stempfle, as a go-between. His dangerous knowledge of Hitler's private life was the probable reason why Stempfle became one of the murdered victims of the 1934 Night of the Long Knives.

It is true that both Strasser and Hanfstaengl, by the time that they gave their accounts, were sworn enemies of Hitler who had both narrowly escaped his reach with their lives by fleeing the Reich, but it is surely more than coincidental that their stories fit what we know of the Führer's open displays of sadomasochistic characteristics. Whatever the truth of these reports, it is certainly clear that Geli was increasingly unhappy with the relationship and made ever more frantic efforts to escape it.

Rows between uncle and niece became louder and more frequent, and he forbade her from going out alone or seeing any man without his permission. By mid-1931 Geli was effectively a prisoner in the Prinzregentenplatz. Things came to a violent head in September 1931, when Geli was twenty-three. Hitler and Geli had a violent shouting match, ostensibly about her desire to return to her native

Austria to study music in Vienna, or, according to rumour, that she was conducting a new relationship with a Jewish student in the city. What happened next is shrouded in mystery. The official story is that Hitler left Munich on a speaking tour, and on reaching Nuremberg was told that his beloved niece was dead.

After Hitler's departure, it was said that Geli had retired to her room. Some hours later, although none of the household staff had heard a shot, she was found dead on the floor from a gunshot wound to her chest, apparently self-inflicted accidentally or deliberately with Hitler's own Walther pistol. Rumour ran riot. The socialist *Munich Post* newspaper reported that in addition to the fatal wound, Geli had a broken nose. An innocuous letter that she had been writing to a friend promising to come to Vienna was found on her desk, broken off in mid-sentence. The talk among his opponents was that Hitler had either murdered her himself in a frenzy of jealousy or had had her killed. No solid evidence has emerged to support such charges and most historians accept the official verdict of suicide. Strong suspicions continued to surround Geli's sudden death, however, and several of those in a position to know the truth were later conveniently murdered.

At all events, whether guilt stricken or remorseful about his fatally possessive and perverse behaviour, there is no doubt that Hitler was devastated by Geli's death. He broke off the speaking tour, went into seclusion, made a pilgrimage to visit her grave in Vienna, and even appeared to temporarily lose interest in politics. He turned Geli's room into a shrine to her memory, and ordered that fresh flowers be placed in it each year on the anniversary of her death. When he became Chancellor, he had her pictures displayed in the Berghof and the Reichschancellery, and told anyone who would listen that she had been the great love of his life.

For Geli, of course, all this extravagant mourning came too late. Speculation on the motive for her suicide – if such it was – continued unabated. The rumour mill overflowed: had she shot herself in a moment of despair at the prospect of being permanently imprisoned by her dominant uncle? Had she ended her life because of his perverse sexual practices? Had she been made pregnant by Hitler in an act of incest? Or was the fatal shot a protest against Hitler's own dalliances with other women – Mimi Reiter, or Eva Braun?

Geli's suspicion that Hitler had become involved with a rival was based on fact. In October 1929 Hitler had walked into the shop on Munich's Schellingstrasse run by his personal photographer Heinrich Hoffmann. The opportunistic Hoffmann had inveigled his way into Hitler's inner circle and won the right to be the sole snapper licensed to take photographs of the Führer. This profitable monopoly made him a rich man, and also gave him insights into Hitler's tangled inner life. On this occasion Hitler's attention was distracted by the legs of Hoffmann's young assistant in the shop, eighteen-year-old Eva Braun, who happened to be standing on a stepladder as he arrived.

Eva had all the qualifications that attracted Hitler: young, blonde, pretty, placid and pliable; she was naïve and so inexperienced in the ways of the world that at first she did not recognise the man with a 'funny moustache' who had come to see her employer. Hitler was introduced to her as 'Herr Wolf', and she was invited to join the two men for a snack of Bavarian beer and sausages. (Hitler only became a vegetarian after Geli's death.) He interest was obvious: Eva told her sister Gretl that '. . . he was devouring me with his eyes all the time.'

The parameters of the relationship were formed from the outset – Eva was sent out to buy their snack. Unlike Geli, she was prepared to be totally subservient to Hitler, with none of his niece's fiery and defiant independence of spirit. After their initial meeting, Hitler began to play cautious court to the innocent Eva in his usual manner: bringing her flowers and inviting her to the opera. He carefully calibrated the

Top: Count Galeazzo Ciano (far right), the Italian Foreign Minister, here depicted with his father-in-law Mussolini, Hitler, French Premier Edouard Daladier and British Prime Minister Neville Chamberlain at the Munich Conference, 1938.

Below left: German Foreign Minister Joachim von Ribbentrop, whose department's money may have funded Salon Kitty.

Below right: Heydrich's scar-faced successor, Ernst Kaltenbrunner, who lived next door to Salon Kitty at Giesebrechtstrasse 12. After the war, both he and Ribbentrop were tried at Nuremberg, convicted and hanged.

Above: The aerial view (above) shows the extent of the devastation suffered by Berlin during the war. All districts were threatened, including the area in which Kitty and her girls worked. Below right shows the damage to buildings in the business district of Berlin. Compared with much of the city, the damage here is relatively light.

Left: The highly decorated First World War naval hero Count Luckner, with the ID card (below) he found for the Jewish woman Rosalie Janson aka Frieda Schafer, allowing her to work in the kitchen at Salon Kitty and so survive the Holocaust.

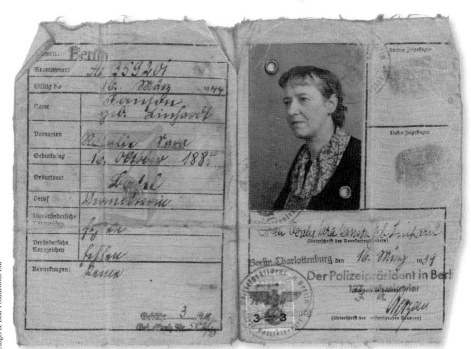

The comfortable and sophisticated setting of Salon Kitty's reception rooms (above, date unknown) little indicated the mass of microphones and wires aiding the spying, which was being monitored below stairs in the cellar rooms of Giesebrechtstrasse 11 (below left and right).

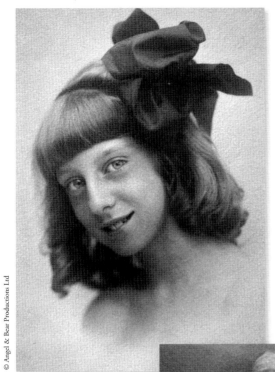

Kathleen Schmidt as a child.

Kathleen in her career as a dancer.

Right: After the war, Kathleen continued to run the salon and is pictured here in the early 1950s, sitting with her working girls in the brothel.

Below: Lisel Ackermann was a sex worker at Salon Kitty during the war. Here she is pictured in the 1970s with a poster for the film *Salon Kitty*.

Above: The cast of the film *Salon Kitty*.

Left: The actor in sweeping robes, Ingrid Thulin, played 'Kitty Kellermann' in the film.

Regardless of how well they are remembered, Kitty and Kathleen Schmidt certainly left a distinctive legacy. *Above*: A photo of Kitty, with her immaculately styled hair, and a young Kathleen, probably taken in Britain during the First World War. *Below*: Years later, after the end of the Second World War, a much older Kitty sits with Kathleen kneeling beside her.

new relationship to fit in with his ongoing liaison with Geli – only taking Eva to opera matinees and devoting his free evenings to Geli.

Psychologically, it is interesting that Mimi Reiter, Geli Raubal and Eva Braun were all about twenty years younger than Hitler. They fitted the pattern of young women whose characters he thought he could mould, and who would pose no challenge to his dominance. The difference between Eva and her predecessors is that she was prepared to accept this role uncritically, not seeking marriage like Mimi, or trying to escape the suffocating spell of Hitler like Geli. Eva's reward for her years of devotion was to wed Hitler just forty hours before their joint suicide. Like Mimi, however, she would make two half-hearted attempts at suicide in an effort to attract Hitler's attention when she thought he was neglecting her after he had become Germany's ruler.

After he had recovered from the initial shock of Geli's death, the relationship between Hitler and Eva became more intense. She was often invited to Berchtesgaden, where it was easier for them to associate away from prying eyes than in Munich. It is not clear exactly when the relationship became physical, but the likelihood is that this happened in 1932 after the first of Eva's suicide bids. With Geli's fate clearly in mind, Eva shot herself in the chest, but, and probably deliberately, only inflicted a minor flesh wound.

The bid had the desired effect of attracting Hitler's attention. He rushed to her bedside and lavished gifts upon her – including buying a house for his lover in a quiet Munich suburb. Like Mimi and Geli, Eva had little interest in politics and never joined the Nazi Party. After Hitler had become Chancellor, she became a semi-permanent fixture at the Berghof, where the couple had adjoining rooms. The relationship was kept secret from the German people, and Eva never accompanied Hitler in public.

Eva spent most of her time in Bavaria, and in May 1935, once more feeling neglected, she took an overdose of sleeping pills – but recovered. During Hitler's absences from the Berghof, Eva led a carefree lifestyle there, beyond the disapproving glare of her lover. Always sporty, she led swimming trips with friends to the nearby lakes, smoked, wore make-up, and took her friends aloft to the Eagle's Nest, the mountaintop eyrie constructed by Bormann as a fiftieth birthday present for Hitler. Maintaining her interest in photography, she took cine films, and much of the surviving footage of Hitler at his house was shot by Eva.

Within the inner circle, the relationship was an open secret to Hitler's intimates, and though she was excluded from important meetings, when he relaxed among his cronies Eva was a frequent presence. The relationship was ill-balanced in that Hitler did not have the passionate, obsessive interest in her that he showed to Mimi and Geli, which probably explains why the affair was of such long duration.

His liaison with Eva did not mean that Hitler lost all interest in other women. As we have seen, he had an intense attachment to Magda Goebbels, and in the late 1930s an aristocratic English young woman, Unity Mitford, a fanatical Nazi sympathiser, deliberately stalked Hitler at his Munich hangouts, and succeeded in worming her way into his circle, along with her sister Diana, the mistress and later wife of Britain's Fascist leader Sir Oswald Mosley. The Mosleys married in Berlin in October 1936, with Hitler and Goebbels as guests of honour at the ceremony. The Mitford sisters not only fitted Hitler's physical ideal of blonde Aryan womanhood, but were politically at one with him, too – although he deprecated their use of make-up.

Diana Mosley spent as much time stalking Hitler in Berlin seeking funds for Mosley's fascist movement as her sister did in Munich. She would receive late-night invitations to visit the Führer at the Chancellery, where, Diana told her stepson Nicholas Mosley, Hitler would amuse her by doing impressions of foreign leaders he had met, including Mussolini. The Führer's humour, she concluded, was 'a hoot'.

On the day that Britain went to war with Germany in September 1939, Unity shot herself in the head in Munich's Englischer Garten park – yet another of the suicide bids by women associated with Hitler. She survived but was hospitalised. Hitler paid for her treatment by the city's top surgeons and visited her in hospital that November just before Georg Elser's attempt on his life when the Bürgerbräu beer hall was bombed. The Führer arranged for her to be repatriated to England via Switzerland when she had partially recovered, but she eventually died as a result of her injuries in 1948.

Yet another suicide by a woman linked to Hitler had occurred in 1937. The woman concerned was a beautiful and successful film actress called Renate Müller, who had replaced the exiled Marlene Dietrich as the leading German goddess of the silver screen, appearing in a score of movies. She had first met Hitler by chance in 1932 when she was filming on location in northern Germany near the Danish coast. He had hung around the film set and that evening contrived to meet Müller at the house where she was staying.

According to the account which Renate told to her friend the film director Alfred Zeisler, who later repeated it in Walter Langer's wartime OSS report, Hitler's behaviour at their first encounter was strained and strange: 'He sat there, not moving at all, looking at me all the time, and then he'd take my hand in his and look some more. He talked all the time – just nonsense.'

After Hitler had become Chancellor, Renate received an invitation to attend a reception at the Reichschancellery. He ignored her until the end of the event when, with everyone departing, he took her arm and offered to show her around the building. More meetings followed, until one night Hitler became excited telling her about deep interrogation methods used by the Gestapo, comparing them to gruesome mediaeval tortures. He invited her to strip and removed his own clothes, but if Renate was expecting a conventional sexual encounter she was in for an unpleasant surprise.

She told Zeisler that after they had undressed the Führer lay naked on the floor and begged her to hit and kick him. She refused, but he insisted, saying that he was her slave and unworthy to be in the same room. Acceding to his pleas, Renate hit and kicked the prostrate Führer, and beat him with one of his whips, accompanying the action with screamed insults and obscene abuse. Hitler became excited under the blows, and masturbated to orgasm. They then got dressed, and he offered her a glass of wine. Finally, he kissed her hand with courtly Austrian manners, thanked her for a 'pleasant evening' and she was dismissed.

That was the last time that Renate met Hitler, but he evidently did not forget her. In 1936 she obtained permission to visit Britain, and while there spent time with a Jewish former lover, Frank Deutsch, who had fled from Nazi Germany. She also believed that she was being tailed by Gestapo agents who observed her meetings with Deutsch. On returning to Germany, she found her career was on the rocks. She was officially blacklisted, and heard that she was to be charged with 'race defilement' for fornicating with a Jew. Frightened and worried, she turned to drink and drugs and became, like Göring and Inga Ley, a morphine addict. She sought treatment in a Berlin sanatorium, and, while there, requested a meeting with Hitler, which was refused.

Renate's end was wrapped in as much mystery as Geli's fate. Her death in October 1937 was officially attributed to epilepsy, but according to other accounts she was either murdered by four SS or Gestapo agents who called at the sanatorium and threw her from a window, or jumped or slipped out herself when she saw them arrive to arrest her. Goebbels, who knew her well from her film career, sent a wreath to her funeral, but there were no floral tributes from the Führer.

Chapter Six

TWISTED LOVE

– How the Nazis used real and fake sex scandals
to achieve total power

On the chilly evening of 14 January 1930, Frau Elisabeth Salm, a thirty-year-old widow, left her flat at 62 Grosse Frankfurter Strasse, on Berlin's poverty-stricken eastern side, bent on serious business. Little did she suppose that her short trip would eventually lead her, after fifteen miserable years, to her death in a Nazi concentration camp.

Her mission was to sort out the troublesome young man she had sublet a room to the previous September, and who now shared her cramped apartment together with his girlfriend, an eighteen-year-old former prostitute named Erna Jaenicke. Her 22-year-old tenant was already notorious in the troubled Berlin of those times – his name was especially well known to the denizens of the drinking dive Der Bär ('The Bear' – Berlin's symbolic animal) in the Dragonerstrasse off Alexanderplatz, the headquarters of the local branch of the Communist Red Front Fighters' League – which was Frau Salm's destination that winter night. The tenant's name was Horst Wessel.

Wessel was born in Bielefeld, north-west Germany, on 9 October 1907, the elder son of a Lutheran pastor, Dr Ludwig Wessel. Germany's Lutheran Protestant Church had close ties to the Prussian state, which dominated northern and eastern Germany. Ever since its founder Martin Luther had himself sided with the ruling princes against the Great Peasants' Revolt in the sixteenth century, Lutheranism had been identified with a strong state, obedience to authority and German nationalism. Ludwig Wessel was firmly in that tradition – he had served as chaplain to Paul von Hindenburg, Germany's army commander in the First World War. Now the venerable Hindenburg was President of the Weimar Republic, and coming under increasing pressure to name the man he contemptuously called a 'Bohemian corporal', Adolf Hitler, as Chancellor to save Germany from the economic misery of the Great Depression, and the anarchic brawling that was disfiguring her city streets.

Firmly schooled by his father in the conservative nationalist tradition, when still a schoolboy, young Horst had joined the Bismarck Bund, the youth wing of the nationalist DNVP party. Finding the stuffy conservatism of the party too tame for his taste, Wessel moved on to the Viking Bund – the youth wing of the secretive Organisation Consul, a murderous terrorist group led by Captain Hermann Ehrhardt, one of the leading Freikorps Führers of the early 1920s. The Freikorps were the irregular military forces that had sprung up in the wake of the war to counter the threat of Communist revolution. Having brutally fulfilled that task, the more extreme Freikorps had taken to plotting the overthrow of the fragile Weimar Republic that had first called them into being.

Ehrhardt and his men had provided the military muscle for the Kapp Putsch in Berlin in March 1920 – a short-lived attempt to overthrow the Republic and install a right-wing dictatorship. After the coup collapsed, Ehrhardt had gone underground in Munich and set up Organisation Consul, or 'OC', with the aim of assassinating the Weimar politicians they blamed for losing the war and bringing down the monarchy. In a short but bloody campaign, OC succeeded in killing scores of the Republic's leading figures, most prominently

Matthias Erzberger, the Catholic politician whose chief crime in the eyes of the right was to have signed the 1918 Armistice ending the war. In 1922, young OC gunmen murdered the Republic's Jewish Foreign Minister, Walther Rathenau, in the wealthy Berlin suburb of Grünewald where he lived. While still a schoolboy, therefore, Horst Wessel had already aligned with those elements of the extreme right most violently opposed to Weimar democracy.

Wessel spent his student years at Berlin University's law faculty, mixing in the milieu of the 'combat leagues', the right-wing paramilitary units that had succeeded the Freikorps. He was also a member of the *Burschenschaften,* the traditional elitist student drinking and duelling fraternities that had arisen in the 1840s as the embodiment of liberal nationalism, but which had since morphed into all that was most reactionary in Germany's universities. Neither entirely satisfied young Wessel's restless quest for an ideology to match the political traumas amidst which he had grown up – war, civil strife, assassinations, ruinous inflation and economic misery. Then, in late 1926, he found what he was seeking.

The militarisation and violence of post-war German politics had persisted, and each of Germany's four largest political parties boasted a strong-armed paramilitary militia – private armies of toughs who repeatedly clashed in the beer halls, bars, and on the streets. The Nazi NSDAP had the brown-shirted SA; the Communist KPD had the Red Front Fighters' League; the Social Democratic SPD had the republican Reichsbanner; and the nationalist DNVP had the Stahlhelm (Steel Helmet), an organisation of First World War veterans. Without hesitation, Wessel joined the SA.

'The Bismarck Bund – that was fun and games,' he explained in an autobiographical sketch. 'Viking, that was adventure, stirring up putsches, playing at soldiers. The NSDAP on the other hand was [my] political awakening. They had an ideology.'

With ferocious energy and blind fervour, Wessel threw himself into his new commitment. His dedication was rewarded with a swift rise within the ranks of the SA. Significantly, his father died in the year that he joined the Brownshirts, and he underlined his break with his 'bourgeois' origins by moving out of his parental home in the ironically named Judenstrasse (Jews' Street) in a bid to identify with Berlin's proletariat. That same year, 1926, Joseph Goebbels – the man who would make Horst Wessel into the archetypal Nazi martyr – had arrived in Berlin to take up the job of Gauleiter with the task of turning the 'red' city 'brown'.

Wessel – like the early Goebbels, Ernst Röhm and the Strasser brothers – was one of the radical Nazis who took the word 'socialist' in the party's name seriously. 'The parties of the Right . . . called us National Bolsheviks or National Marxists because of our socialist posture . . .' Wessel wrote.

> They were correct, for the National Socialists in general had more sympathy for the [Communist] Red Front Fighters' League than for the [Conservative] Stahlhelm . . . In the Red camp there were just as many, perhaps even more, fanatical idealists ripe for martyrdom than on the other side. Added to that was the whole shocking realisation of the unbelievable delusion and abuse of the entire working class. And that's how I became a socialist.

Aware that the son of a middle-class pastor might lack true proletarian credentials, Wessel refused to practise law and earned his living as a casual labourer and cab driver. He was determined to live in the same conditions as the men of Sturm 5, the branch of the Berlin SA that he swiftly rose to command. Wessel relished a dangerous challenge. In basing himself in the working-class Friedrichshain quarter, a Communist bastion, with a population of some 350,000, he was provocatively pushing his head into the red lion's jaws.

The constant and often deadly brawls between the Nazis and Communists in late 1920s Berlin had, despite their bitter strife, bred a grudging mutual respect born of their common working-class origins and their shared totalitarian ideologies. Both wore similar uniforms and aped each other's organisation, propaganda, music and militarist mindset. Both despised the 'bourgeois' parliamentarianism of Weimar, and sometimes even co-operated to attack their common Social Democratic enemies.

Berlin had been a 'red citadel' since at least January 1919 when the Freikorps had bloodily suppressed a Spartacist revolt in the east of the city, and murdered the Communists' leaders, Karl Liebknecht and Rosa Luxemburg. The large working-class quarters in the east such as 'red' Wedding and Friedrichshain, with their ill-lit, swarming tenement blocks, smoking factories, and dingy drinking dens, were Communist strongholds. Any attempt by the Nazis to break this iron grip was fiercely and violently resisted.

Even in Weimar Germany's most prosperous and 'peaceful' period between 1924–1930, around ninety Communists, thirty Nazis, twenty-six Stahlhelm nationalists, and eighteen Reichsbanner socialists were killed in clashes with their political opponents. Far left and extreme right infiltrated and heckled each other's meetings, attacked each other's marches, disrupted each other's funerals and routinely trashed the bars in which their rivals met. And all the time another battle – one of hearts, minds and loyalties – was being waged as the two ideologies struggled to win over and convert Communists to Nazis and vice versa.

Horst Wessel packed a lot of activity into the three short years between joining the Nazis in December 1926 and his death in February 1930. In the year 1929 alone he delivered more than fifty public speeches – gaining a reputation second only to Goebbels as the Nazis' leading orator in Berlin. In 1928, Goebbels had entrusted him with a six-month mission to Vienna – where he had spent a semester in his university days – to report on the state of the Austrian Nazis. Back in Berlin, as the militant leader of Sturm 5, he built his branch to an impressive membership of 250. Imitating the Communists, he appropriated Die Möwe (The Seagull) and Das Keglerheim bars on the Petersburger Strasse as his Sturm's HQ. As part of his propaganda effort, Wessel equipped his men with a Communist-style wind band, Schalmeienkapelle, and wrote the words for some of the songs they played – including the rousing anthem that would make him so posthumously notorious.

In September 1929, Wessel led members of his branch to proudly parade at the annual Nazi Party rally in Nuremberg. Soon after returning from Nuremberg, he was passing the Café Mexico near the Alexanderplatz when his attention was attracted by a violent quarrel between one of the young streetwalkers who haunted the area and a client who had turned nasty. The girl was just one of the hundreds of prostitutes who swarmed the streets of east Berlin, and was known professionally as 'Lucie of the Alexanderplatz'. Her real name was Erna Jänicke, and after rescuing her from her assailant, Wessel fell violently in love. He took her to live with him in the room he had just rented from Frau Salm, and apparently persuaded Erna to drop her profession. However, neither Wessel's mother or sister, nor his Nazi bosses, approved his choice of mate, and, worryingly for the party, his new domestic bliss seemed to lead to a decline in Wessel's previously fervent political commitment.

Goebbels despatched Wessel's best friend Richard Fiedler – later, after surviving the Night of the Long Knives, a leading SS officer – to see Wessel in an attempt to bring him back to the path of Nazi righteousness and persuade him to give up his unfortunate new relationship. Wessel responded furiously that Erna was a true proletarian daughter of the *Volk*, and that aspersions on her unfortunate former way of life was merely petit-bourgeois prejudice. Fiedler – the leader of the neighbouring Sturm 6 of the SA – retreated with a flea in his ear.

A personal tragedy at the end of 1929 was another incident causing Wessel to rethink his way of life. That Christmas, his younger brother Werner, an equally fervent member of the Berlin SA, went skiing in the Harz mountains, got lost in a snowstorm, and died of exposure. Wessel went to identify and collect his brother's body and fell into a deep depression. Goebbels eulogised the dead young man at a propagandist funeral, little thinking that he would be doing the same thing for Werner's elder brother within a few weeks. There were rumours that Wessel at this time was considering throwing up his budding but dangerous political career, relocating to a provincial university where he would be less notorious, and resuming his legal studies. But before he could make any such move, fate – and Elisabeth Salm – took a hand.

By New Year 1930, Frau Salm's issues with her troublesome young tenants had reached a crisis point. Apart from their political differences, Wessel's rent was in arrears, and he was refusing to pay rent for his live-in girlfriend. Frau Salm – who was a tenant herself – was afraid that she would lose her lodgings if Erna resumed her prostitution and used the place for immoral purposes. The two women shared the kitchen in the tiny attic apartment, and the resulting rows were frequent. Thoroughly exasperated, Frau Salm decided that Wessel and Erna needed to be taught a lesson and set off for Der Bär. The Communists, rather than the police, she decided, were the ones to give Wessel and his whore the punishment they deserved.

She knew the men of the 2 Bereitschaft (Readiness Squad) of the Red Front Fighters' League, the Communist equivalent of Horst Wessel's Nazi Sturm 5 of the SA, and they knew her. Her recently deceased husband had been a Communist militant, and she shared his political leanings, so Wessel was hardly her ideal tenant anyway. Given the intimacy in which Communists and Nazis lived cheek by jowl in working-class Berlin, such domestic arrangements were not unusual. Despite a dispute over Frau Salm's insistence on giving her late husband a Christian, rather than a Marxist, funeral, the boys of the Bereitschaft were more than happy to listen to her tale of woe.

At the bar, Salm outlined her problem to Erwin Rückert, the 26-year-old leader of the 2 Bereitschaft. Learning that Wessel was alone in her apartment, apart from Erna and a friend of hers, Rückert swiftly summoned reinforcements from the neighbouring 3 Bereitschaft. Rückert's deputy was a giant 6-foot-5-inch 31-year-old thug and career criminal named 'Ali' (Albrecht) Höhler. As much an underworld figure as he was a Communist, Höhler had a criminal record as long as his heavily tattooed arm. He had no fewer than sixteen convictions for offences ranging from burglary and perjury to pimping, including a two-and-a-half-year prison stretch for living off a prostitute's immoral earnings. Rückert and Höhler gathered a squad of a dozen Bereitschaft members and set off for Frau Salm's flat to administer what one of them, Max Jambrowski, assured Frau Salm would be a good 'proletarian drubbing'. Höhler tooled himself up with a loaded pistol.

The Communists did not really need Frau Salm's tenancy problems as an excuse to attack Horst Wessel, as he was already only too well known to them. As the leading Nazi activist in their east Berlin manor, he had become an ever more painful thorn in their flesh. His success in turning former Red Front fighters into Nazi Stormtroopers turned the knife in the wound. Wessel's activities had recently culminated in him leading a brazen assault on the KPD's HQ in Friedrichshain, the Hoppe Inn, in which four Communists had been seriously hurt. Enraged, the party newspaper *Der Rote Fahne* (*The Red Flag*) coined a new slogan for its militants: 'Beat the fascists wherever you find them'. 'Wherever', as Horst Wessel was about to discover, included his own home.

To underline their determination to wreak revenge on Wessel, the Communists had recently issued a 'wanted' poster with a drawing of

Wessel brandishing a pistol and dagger while standing over a prostrate worker. 'Red Workers!' the poster proclaimed. 'Remember his face! Storm leader, worker murderer!' – before helpfully adding Wessel's address. Unfortunately, the poster mistakenly printed the address as Kleine (rather than Grosse) Frankfurter Strasse 62. Now, thanks to Frau Salm, the Communists had the right address. Had he known of their impending arrival, Wessel would have had few illusions about the fate awaiting him.

Upon arrival, the Communists posted three sentries: a painter named 'Sally' Epstein, a baker called Hans Ziegler, and a third man named Peter Stoll, at the door of the apartment block to ensure that no one entered or left. Then, four of them – Rückert, Höhler, Jambrowski, and Joseph Kandulski – climbed the stairs to Frau Salm's flat. Wessel himself answered the door. Immediately – according to Höhler's later account – the SA man reached for his pocket. Thinking that he was about to draw a pistol, Höhler produced his own weapon and shot Wessel in the mouth at point blank range, yelling, 'You know what this is for!' The bullet tore out Wessel's front teeth and tongue and bore deep into his palate, lodging too near his brain to extricate. The murder squad turned and fled into the night.

Erna did her best to help her grievously wounded lover, but SA men summoned to the flat turned away the assistance of a local doctor because he was Jewish. It was more than an hour before acceptable Nazi medical help arrived in the shape of Dr Leonardo Conti, an ideological soulmate of Wessel's who had known him since his days in the Bismarck Bund. Later in his career, Conti became head of the Nazi Doctors' Association and an SS-Obergruppenführer. As such, he was the driving force behind the Nazi T4 programme to murder the physically and mentally disabled by involuntary euthanasia, and pioneered the gassing of victims later used in the Holocaust. Conti hanged himself in his Nuremberg jail cell in October 1945 while awaiting trial for his crimes.

Conti had his patient conveyed to the local St Joseph's Hospital in Friedrichshain where he lingered in agony for forty days. While he lay there, Goebbels turned the sordid shooting into one of his propaganda triumphs. In speeches and articles for *Der Angriff* Goebbels portrayed the stricken SA leader as a fallen Christlike martyr, slain by 'subhuman beasts' and 'a pack of murder-crazed degenerate Communist bandits'. Just as he had recognised Wessel's worth to the Nazi cause in life, so Goebbels orchestrated his protracted passing from the world to extract as much mileage for the movement as possible. He issued dramatic daily communiques from Wessel's bedside as the dying man slowly sank. He interviewed Wessel's mother, painting a mawkish picture of the thuggish Horst as the perfect son. He invented wholly unrealistic word pictures of his martyr, and made up quotes from a man whose missing tongue had rendered him speechless:

There he lies, sitting up on his pillows, his face ripped apart. But you still recognise him immediately. Those eyes are the same: big, fixed, grey-blue. With difficulty he lifts his hand and gives it to me saying, 'We must keep going!'

Building up the dying Wessel to quasi-Messiah status as the Nazi movement's most talented and tragic martyr was undoubtedly Goebbels' greatest propaganda coup as Gauleiter of the capital. It reached its culmination when Wessel finally died of blood poisoning on 23 February. Goebbels turned the martyr's funeral into a magnificent piece of street theatre. Bitterly disappointed that Hitler himself declined to attend – citing 'reasons of personal security' – the propaganda chief filled in for the Führer as chief mourner. He was accompanied by Hermann Göring, and – lending an unlikely touch of royal class to the proletarian proceedings – Prince August-Wilhelm, known as 'Auwi', fourth son of the fallen Kaiser Wilhelm II. Auwi had enthusiastically joined the Nazis and would become a brownshirt-wearing member of the SA himself a few weeks after the funeral. As we shall see, he would even lend his august presence to the murder squad who avenged the killing of Wessel.

The funeral cortège – limited by the police to ten vehicles – was watched by an estimated 30,000-strong crowd. The Nazis braved brickbats and insults flung by Communists as they wound their way from the Wessel family home in Jüdenstrasse to the St Nikolai cemetery, in his father's old parish, where Ludwig and Werner Wessel were already buried. The cemetery wall had been freshly daubed with the words: 'A final Heil Hitler to the pimp Horst Wessel!' reflecting the official Communist line that Wessel's murder was merely a quarrel between two pimps over the favours of Erna Jänicke, and had no political context.

The obituary penned by Goebbels in *Der Angriff* went completely over the top in reconstructing Wessel's squalid lifestyle into the gospel of a latter-day Jesus Christ:

He went forth as a preacher in the wilderness, harvesting hate rather than gratitude, and only persecution instead of recognition . . . They laughed at him, mocked him, spat at him, wherever he came among them, and turned their backs on him with abhorrence . . . In the end he was prepared to forsake his mother and his parental home, going among those who mocked and spat at him . . . Beyond, in a proletarian quarter, high above in an attic room above a block of flats he created an austere young man's existence. A Christian socialist! One who through his deeds cries: 'Come to me, I will redeem you!' . . . Five weeks long he lay in agony, close to death . . . He did not complain . . .
And in the end, tired and wracked with pain, he gave up the ghost. They bore him to the grave . . . those he sought to save threw stones at the dead . . . he drank the pain-filled chalice down to the dregs . . . The deceased who is with us, raises his

weary hand and points into the dim distance: Advance over the graves! At the end lies Germany!

The cherry on the propagandist cake that Goebbels had cooked around the fallen SA man was three verses of doggerel that Wessel had written for his Sturm's *Schalmeienkapelle* – musical groups which took their name from a wind instrument known as schmalmei or shawm – and set to an old marching tune. This song, called from its opening line 'Die Fahnen hoch' ('The flags are high') was retitled by Goebbels 'Das Horst-Wessel-Lied' and received its premiere sung by a massed choir at the Berlin Sports Palast. After the Nazi seizure of power, it became the ubiquitous second anthem of the Reich along with 'Deutschland über alles'. The song's lyrics took swipes at both the Communist Red Front and the 'Reaction', reflecting the dead man's socialist sympathies.

The song wasn't the only prominent facet of the cult surrounding Horst Wessel, which reached astronomically absurd proportions under the Third Reich. In Berlin itself, Friedrichshain, the quarter where he had made his home, was named after him, as was the hospital where he had died. Karl Liebknecht House, the huge KPD headquarters on Alexanderplatz, was renamed the Horst Wessel House after the KPD was banned and evicted. Streets and squares throughout the Reich were rebaptised with the martyr's name, along with a steel-hulled square-rigged naval training ship and an armoured division of the Waffen SS. No fewer than nineteen hagiographies, along with novels and plays, appeared based on Wessel's life, as well as a big screen movie lightly fictionalising him as 'Hans Westmar', an ideal SA man.

Near Wessel's birthplace in Bielefeld, a vast stone monument to his memory was erected on the supposed site of the battle of the Teutoburg Forest where, in AD 9, the Germanic tribes under a chieftain named Arminius had annihilated a Roman legion under Publius Quinctilius Varus, ending any attempt by Rome to penetrate further into Germany. Thus, ironically, the Christlike pastor's son repeatedly eulogised by Goebbels was converted to symbolise the ideal Germanic soldier who had saved Germany for paganism. In the end, even its author tired of the cult he had created: in 1942 Goebbels forbade any further canonisation of his martyr and limited commemorations to Wessel's birthday in October.

After the Second World War, Wessel's apotheosis turned to oblivion. The Teutoburg memorial was blown up by Allied forces and the streets and squares named in his honour reverted to their original names. In East Berlin, the Communist authorities bulldozed the street where he had lived and changed Grosse Frankfurter Strasse to Karl Marx Allee. They destroyed his grave memorial and changed Horst Wessel House on Alexanderplatz back to Karl Liebknecht House. (Today, it is the HQ of the far-left Die Linke Party, successor to East Germany's ruling SED.) In Germany as a whole, singing of the 'Horst-Wessel-Lied' was banned. From being Nazi Germany's foremost martyr, Wessel became a forgotten man.

The immediate consequences of Wessel's murder in the aftermath of his killing were deadly for all those who had played even the smallest part in it. Acting swiftly on the night that he was shot, the Communists had established their party line: that the shooting had no political content and was merely the result of a quarrel between two pimps – Höhler and Wessel – for the affections of a common prostitute. There may have been a grain of truth in this story, as Höhler had probably known Erna Jänicke before she met Wessel in their respective roles of prostitute and pimp; and she identified him as the killer at his subsequent trial. However, the tale ignores the fact that the Communists had long hunted Wessel and organised a squad to give the SA leader his 'proletarian drubbing'.

On the night of the shooting, Max Jambrowski, the KPD official who had promised Frau Salm that her tenant would receive the drubbing he deserved, and acting on the orders of the KPD propaganda chief, Hans Neumann, warned all members of the murder squad at Der Bär that anyone who told the truth about the affair would share Wessel's fate. Frau Salm was summoned to Karl Liebknecht House and ordered to follow the same line: the assassination attempt had been down to a quarrel between two criminals and nothing more.

As for the killer himself: 'Ali' Höhler's existence was a major embarrassment to the party and a standing contradiction of its 'line'. So, he became the scapegoat. The party's financial aid outfit, Rote Hilfe (Red Aid), spirited him out of Germany to the Czech capital Prague. Once he was there, however, they dropped Höhler like a hot brick, absconding with the money intended to support him. Almost starving, Höhler made his way back to his Berlin haunts and was arrested on 3 February. Bitter at the KPD's betrayal of him, when he appeared in court charged with Wessel's murder, he contradicted the party line, admitted that he had been part of the squad sent to punish Wessel, and pleaded self-defence as his motive for the murder. Höhler was sentenced to six years for the killing. Frau Salm and the other members of the murder squad got lighter jail terms. The lenient sentences enraged the Nazis, and when they took power they had their revenge.

Two of those who had stood guard outside Wessel's apartment block, 'Sally' Epstein and Hans Ziegler – probably because Epstein was Jewish – were retried and sentenced to death. Hitler personally rejected their appeals, and they were beheaded by guillotine in Berlin's Plötzensee jail in 1935. None of the other squad members survived the war. The squad leader Erwin Rückert and Joseph Kandulski, who had accompanied Höhler to Wessel's door, died in Austria's Mauthausen concentration camp. Max Jambrowski similarly perished in Buchenwald. Elisabeth Salm died of typhus in Bergen-Belsen camp at the end of the war, aged forty-four.

As for Höhler, in September 1933, during a staged transfer

between two Berlin prisons, he was abducted by a squad of specially selected high-ranking Nazis. Among the squad's members were Karl Ernst, the Berlin leader of the SA, Rudolf Diels, a police official and protégé of Göring, who was briefly the boss of the newly created Gestapo before Himmler took charge of the organisation, and none other than 'Auwi' – Prince August-Wilhelm of Prussia. Also included in the murder gang was Richard Fiedler, Horst Wessel's closest friend. The squad took Höhler for a ride out to the deserted pine forests east of Berlin. He was well aware of the fate awaiting him. When the car stopped deep in the woods Diels asked Höhler if he knew what was going to happen to him. 'One of you is going to bump me off,' the doomed man replied. They were his last words. A few weeks later, Höhler's remains were found by a passing forester. Erna Jänicke – said to have married another SA Stormtrooper – vanished into historical obscurity.

If Erna Jänicke had been the unwitting cause of one of the Nazis' greatest propaganda triumphs during the party's rise to power, another young woman of easy virtue, also known as Erna, was to be the equally unwitting agent in a scandal that cemented Hitler's hold over the Wehrmacht in the run-up to the Second World War.

Sometime in 1937, Luise Margarethe Gruhn, commonly known as Erna or Eva, had met the towering sixty-year-old Field Marshal Werner Blomberg, War Minister in the Hitler government, and, as Commander of the Wehrmacht, Nazi Germany's most powerful military man. Exactly how the ill-matched pair first encountered one another is unclear. One account claims that the lonely widower was on holiday and was introduced to her by the hotel manager where he was staying. Another story says they met while the field marshal was taking a walk in a Berlin park, and yet another tale alleges he picked her up in a Berlin nightspot.

Whatever the circumstances, Blomberg, who had an eye for the ladies, swiftly made the buxom blonde his mistress and soon decided that he wanted to marry her. His friends and his five grown-up children were appalled – Gruhn was thirty-five years younger than the besotted Blomberg; she was humbly born, worked as a lowly stenographer for the Reich's Egg Marketing Board, and rumours were already rife that she was a 'woman with a past'. But the field marshal remained adamant.

Blomberg had been one of the main movers in the machinations that had brought the Nazis to power. A bitter personal enemy of his military rival General Kurt von Schleicher, briefly the last Chancellor of the Weimar Republic, he had been appointed Defence Minister by President Hindenburg in Hitler's first coalition government, with the idea that, although sympathetic to the Nazis, he was a safe pair of conservative hands who would curb the Nazis' excesses. Instead, the pliable general lived up to his nickname, Der Gummilöwe ('the Rubber Lion'). A fierce warrior with Germany's highest military medal, the Pour le Mérite, twinkling at his throat, Blomberg was a moral coward who did little to control or thwart the Nazis' relentless pursuit of total power, untrammelled by law or the stern values that his Prussian military caste embodied and were sworn to uphold.

The one moment when Blomberg did exert pressure on Hitler was on the eve of the Night of the Long Knives in the summer of 1934. The Wehrmacht was increasingly disturbed by the threat posed by the brawling SA Brownshirts to their monopoly as sole arms bearers of the state. The SA's Chief of Staff, Ernst Röhm, made little secret of his ambition to absorb the 'grey' army with his 'brown' cohorts and transform the Wehrmacht into a real 'people's army' as part of a radical National Socialist 'second revolution'. As the Brownshirts numbered some four million to the army's 100,000 this was a threat that could not be ignored. Moreover, the SA were alienating the middle and upper classes with their rowdy and violent behaviour and the open homosexuality of Röhm and his closest cronies, and while they had been Hitler's most useful weapon in his struggle for power, they had no clear purpose now that power was won.

The Rubber Lion exerted his influence with the ageing President Hindenburg to warn Hitler that unless he acted against the SA, then the Wehrmacht would take control and institute a military dictatorship. Thus prompted, Hitler acted swiftly. Always the opportunist, he not only thoroughly purged the leadership of the SA, but simultaneously struck at a long list of other enemies too.

In a bloody summer weekend of unbridled state violence at the end of June 1934 that became known as the Night of the Long Knives, the SS and Gestapo murdered between eighty-five and 200 of Hitler's real and supposed enemies. Shockingly, the victims not only included the SA leaders, but three close conservative associates of Vice-Chancellor Franz von Papen and two Reichswehr generals – Kurt von Schleicher himself, along with his wife, and his right-hand man General Ferdinand von Bredow. Blomberg – who was among those who had foreknowledge of the purge – had delivered up Röhm to his killers by expelling him from the League of German Officers just before the murders, and the army had supplied the weapons to the Gestapo and SS gunmen with which the killings were carried out. By washing his hands of the crime, Blomberg had only succeeded in indelibly staining them with blood. The purge revealed to the world – if it had not already noticed – the criminal nature of the Nazi regime.

Blomberg was well rewarded for his complicity in the 'Blood Purge'. In 1935 he was made War Minister and given the newly created title of Commander-in-Chief of the Armed Forces; the following year he was made a field marshal, and in 1937 he was enrolled in the Nazi Party by Hitler and given the party's coveted Golden Badge. But these were empty baubles. The real power lay with Hitler, who on the death of President Hindenburg soon after the purge in August 1934, had combined the posts of head of government as Chancellor and head of state as President in the new title of 'Führer': the supreme leader of Germany. In addition, all members of the armed forces were compelled to swear a personal oath of loyalty to Hitler. From that point on, the Rubber Lion had become an empty, powerless vassal – the obedient slave of a man many of his fellow officers despised.

Blomberg's star began to wane as he came to realise that Hitler was bent on war. His nerves were first tested in March 1936 when Hitler occupied the Rhineland with a handful of troops – rightly anticipating that Britain and France would not raise a finger to stop him marching into 'Germany's backyard'. Four months later, Hitler decided to support General Franco's insurrection against the Spanish Republic. German planes ferried Franco's Army of Africa to the Spanish mainland to spearhead the revolt, and a German air force, the 'Condor Legion', became Franco's air arm. The bombing of the ancient Basque capital of Guernica was seen by the Nazis as a dry run rehearsal for the future wars they were planning.

On 5 November 1937, Hitler summoned Blomberg and the chiefs of the Luftwaffe and the Kriegsmarine to a top-secret meeting. The service chiefs could hardly believe their ears when the Führer announced his plans for the coming year. He intended, he said, to conquer and dismember Czechoslovakia. Hitler harboured a racial hatred for the Czechs from his Austrian youth, and wiping the hated state from the map would also boost the Reich's military might with the acquisition of the giant Skoda armaments works. Blomberg and his colleagues were appalled. They feared that such a takeover would unleash a war with Britain and France, and possibly Russia, for which the Reich was not ready. Hitler dismissed their fears with contempt. Blomberg, he said, was behaving like a 'hysterical woman'. From this time on, the Rubber Lion's card was marked.

A few weeks later, a 'highly excited' Blomberg set out for a week's winter sports holiday at the Thuringian resort of Oberhof. His companion on the ski slopes was none other than Erna Gruhn; and the vacation hardened his desire to marry his 24-year-old mistress. From Oberhof he travelled to Munich to deliver the funeral oration for Erich Ludendorff, Germany's First World War overlord who had been the figurehead of Hitler's botched 1923 Beer Hall Putsch. (Ludendorff had died in grumpy retirement after scoring a derisory 1.1 per cent share of the vote in the 1925 presidential elections as the Nazis' candidate against his old chief Hindenburg.) While he was in Munich, Blomberg took the opportunity to have a quiet word with a fellow mourner, the head of the Luftwaffe and Hitler's right-hand man, Hermann Göring.

Blomberg explained that he wished to marry Fräulein Gruhn but was doubtful whether the Führer and his fellow members of the officer corps would regard the young woman as a suitable match for Germany's top soldier. Erna, Blomberg admitted sheepishly but vaguely, was not necessarily a young lady of spotless virtue, and she came from a less than ideal background. (Erna's mother was a laundress, but on the side also ran a Berlin massage parlour that was a front for a brothel where Erna had grown up.)

Göring laughed away Blomberg's fears. There was no place for such outmoded snobbery in the new and egalitarian Germany that was the Third Reich. Fräulein Gruhn was doubtless a good daughter of the *Volk* and the field marshal had every right to wed her. Why, he added, the Führer and he himself would be honoured to attend the wedding. There was another problem, Blomberg admitted. A young man was also wooing his bride-to-be. Göring promised to take care of the difficulty and arranged to send the field marshal's rival on a long-term assignment to distant Argentina. Emboldened and relieved, Blomberg approached Hitler himself on the same day. He formally requested the Führer's permission to wed a socially inferior woman young enough to be his daughter. Hitler not only gave his consent to the marriage but promised that he and Göring would attend the ceremony as witnesses.

Having won the Führer's blessing, Blomberg, an old man in a hurry, did not hang about. Barely a fortnight later, on 12 January 1938, he and Erna tied the knot in the presence of Hitler and Göring. After Propaganda Minister Joseph Goebbels, conscious of the negative publicity and gossip that such a mismatch might attract, forbade all mention of the wedding in the German media, the newlyweds left for Leipzig on the first stage of an intended Italian honeymoon.

Hardly had they departed when rumours duly began to fly. Despite Goebbels' publicity blackout, word of the marriage spread, and a series of anonymous phone calls were made to senior officers and Nazi officials, some from giggling girls, who congratulated them on accepting one of their companions from Berlin's prostitution milieu into the Wehrmacht's highest ranks. The wife of a police official named Curt Hellmuth Müller mentioned the swirling rumours to her husband. The name Erna Gruhn rang a distant bell in Müller's memory, and the next day he checked his files.

Sure enough, with the ink hardly dry on Blomberg's wedding certificate, a clutch of pornographic photos tumbled out showing the field marshal's bride when she was eighteen performing oral sex on a shaven-haired Czech Jew named Heinrich Löwinger. Erna had a police record for prostitution, and she and Löwinger – who had been her lover and pimp – had also been prosecuted for selling the pornographic pictures.

Suitably aghast, Müller passed the explosive dossier up the bureaucratic chain of command until it reached the desk of the chief of the Berlin Police, Count Wolf-Heinrich von Helldorff. An aristocrat who had fought in the Freikorps, Helldorff had become a high-ranking member of the SA while pursuing a parallel career in Berlin's police. Notoriously corrupt, he had introduced fiercely anti-Semitic policies in the capital, extracting large sums from wealthy

Jews in bribes to allow them to emigrate. Like his colleague Arthur Nebe, head of the city's Kripo, Helldorff was destined to switch sides late in the day and to be executed as one of the plotters in the failed attempt to assassinate Hitler in July 1944.

Now Helldorff was faced with a dilemma. Strictly speaking, he should have passed the dossier to his superior, Heinrich Himmler, head of the SS. But, knowing that the Reichsführer would use the scandalous material to further weaken his own aristocratic officer caste, Helldorff chose to take the dossier to a former Freikorps colleague, General Wilhelm Keitel, head of the Wehrmachtsamt and effectively the manager of Blomberg's office. Despite the fact that his eldest son Karl was about to marry Blomberg's youngest daughter Dorothea, and that he owed his position to the field marshal, Keitel did not agree to Helldorff's suggestion that the dossier should be destroyed and forgotten. Like his boss, a moral coward, Keitel proposed instead that they take the explosive file to Hermann Göring.

The Reichsmarschall was delighted to hear of Erna Gruhn's past misdemeanours, even though he had acted as a portly Cupid in facilitating the Blomberg marriage. His own ambition was to command all Germany's armed forces in addition to his present post as head of the Luftwaffe. He saw the scandal as a heaven-sent opportunity to get rid of Blomberg and fulfil that ambition. Göring lost no time in rushing to Berchtesgaden to show Hitler the material at his rural retreat. Hitler, mindful of Blomberg's past services in smoothing his path to total power, was reluctant to take action, but Göring insisted. The army, he averred, would not stand having its head married to a whore. Blomberg had to go.

The ever-perceptive Goebbels recognised the gravity of the crisis, noting in his diary:

Blomberg must go. The only way out for a man of honour is the pistol. The Führer was a witness at the [marriage] ceremony;

it is unthinkable. The worst crisis for the regime since the Röhm affair. I am completely distraught. The Führer is as grey as a corpse.

Without further ado, Hitler summoned Blomberg back from his Italian honeymoon and acquainted him – (if Blomberg did not already know) – with the unsavoury details of his bride's murky past. Blomberg stubbornly refused the Führer's demand to immediately divorce Erna, so Hitler insisted on his resignation. It had now struck Hitler that the scandal presented him with an ideal opportunity to cement his hold over the army and get rid of the men who had proved so reluctant to support his plans to go to war. The Führer sugared the pill: he told Blomberg that the scandal would be hushed up, and that he would retain his field marshal's rank and the pension that went with it. Moreover, he added that when – not if – war came, Blomberg would be recalled and given command of Germany's army once more. This was a promise that would not be honoured.

In a second interview, Hitler asked Blomberg's advice about his successor. Not knowing of Göring's part in his downfall, the disgraced field marshal suggested him as a suitable replacement. Hitler dismissed the idea with something close to contempt – the Reichsmarschall, he said, was far too lazy. In that case, Blomberg, obsequious to the last, ventured: how about Hitler himself? This idea, even if he had not already decided upon it, was music to the Führer's ears. And if that happened, he asked, who should transmit his orders to the army? Blomberg shrugged. 'Who ran your office?' Hitler demanded. Blomberg – again not knowing of Keitel's role in his disgrace – named him, adding however that he didn't think that Keitel had a first-class mind. 'That's exactly the man that I'm looking for!' a delighted Führer exclaimed.

And so, the deed was done. Within a week Hitler, who had never held a military rank higher than corporal, had named himself

Supreme Commander of the Armed Forces. And to head up the newly created *Oberkommando der Wehrmacht* (OKW) the colourless but subservient Keitel was promoted far beyond his limited abilities as he had the qualities that Hitler prized beyond all others: loyalty and obedience. Not for nothing was the new OKW chief nicknamed *Nickesel* ('nodding donkey') or *Lakeitel* ('lackey'). He would stay by Hitler's side until the end.

Blomberg and the bride who had ruined his career resumed their rudely interrupted honeymoon. To keep them well out of the way until the scandal had blown over, the honeymoon turned into an extended world tour that took them as far as Ceylon (today's Sri Lanka) and Java in the East Indies (today's Indonesia). While they were still in Italy, Admiral Erich Raeder, the Commander of the Navy, who was noted for his extreme puritanism, went to the lengths of sending Blomberg's naval adjutant, a junior officer named Lieutenant von Wangenheim, to Italy in hot pursuit of the honeymooners. His mission was to persuade Blomberg that it was his duty to divorce his bride to save the honour of the officer caste. The lieutenant chased the Blombergs to the idyllic island of Capri. Here, he exceeded his brief and insisted that the field marshal should fall on his sword and commit suicide for the disgrace that he had brought on the Armed Forces High Command. Wangenheim actually tried to force a pistol into the Rubber Lion's hand to shoot himself when he declined to do the decent thing!

On their eventual return to Germany, the Blombergs retired to the remote lakeside Bavarian resort of Bad Wiessee. The town, piquantly enough, had been the scene of a dramatic confrontation during the Night of the Long Knives – which Blomberg had done so much to bring about. For it was here that Hitler had stormed into the Pension Hanselbauer to arrest Ernst Röhm and the SA leaders who had gathered there. Blomberg took no part in the Second World War. He was arrested at the war's end and abandoned by his faithless Erna.

Taken to Nuremberg to give evidence at the war crimes tribunal, he was diagnosed with rectal cancer and went into a sad decline, refusing food and literally starving himself to death in March 1946 before he could take the witness stand. Erna went back to Berlin where she died in 1978, living alone and forgotten in a bedsit.

It had occurred to Hitler that he could kill two birds with one stone not only by dismissing Blomberg, but by simultaneously firing the Rubber Lion's more obstructive and obdurate deputy, the Commander of the Army, General Werner von Fritsch. The army chief was a typical soldier of the old school down to the monocle he wore in his left eye. The epitome of the Prussian military caste whom Hitler had always mistrusted, Fritsch was an austere bachelor devoted to his profession, and a notable drag on the Führer's desire to dominate and direct the armed forces. As a distinctly non-political professional, Fritsch had already expressed his opposition to the Führer's plans to absorb Austria and then dismember Czechoslovakia, thus risking a premature European war.

The weapon to destroy the stubborn Commander-in-Chief was handed to Hitler by Heinrich Himmler and Reinhard Heydrich, who, as with Röhm's SA in 1934, wanted to replace the Wehrmacht with their own SS as Germany's key arms bearers. In 1936, Heydrich's agents had discovered that a retired cavalry officer with a similar name to the C-in-C, Rittmeister (Baron) von Frisch, had been observed during a brief homosexual encounter with a rent boy, Martin Weingartner, known as 'Bavarian Joe', close to the Potsdam-Wannsee railway station. A gang led by a professional criminal, Otto Schmidt, had observed the tryst and subsequently blackmailed Frisch. Heydrich had compiled a report on the episode, falsely naming General Fritsch as the officer concerned, and taken it directly to Hitler. The Führer had refused to listen to the allegations at the time and ordered Heydrich to destroy the evidence. Instead, ignoring Hitler's order, Heydrich had filed the report away for possible future use.

Now, sensing an opportunity to destroy both Blomberg and Fritsch and deal a devastating blow to the whole officer corps of the Wehrmacht at the same time, Heydrich decided that the right hour had come. Slyly, he showed the 1936 report to Reichsmarschall Göring, knowing that with his ambitions to take over as Commander of the whole armed forces, Göring would show it in turn to Hitler. Göring duly took Heydrich's report with him to Berchtesgaden along with the evidence of Frau Blomberg's notorious past on 25 January 1938. At first, Hitler still seemed disinclined to believe Heydrich's 'evidence', but when Blomberg, smarting at the way he was being treated by the officer caste over his marriage, told the Führer that his deputy was 'not a ladies' man' and that Fritsch might well indeed have 'succumbed to weakness', Hitler authorised further secret investigation of the C-in-C's alleged misconduct.

Himmler and Heydrich had made frantic but unavailing efforts to stand up the false charges against Fritsch, investigating every garrison town where the general had ever been stationed, and even sending Heydrich's 'expert' in combating homosexuality, Joseph Meisinger, to Egypt – where the general had holidayed in 1937 – in search of incriminating evidence. Nothing was found. The only witness left in their locker was the lying blackmailer Otto Schmidt.

Defying Hitler's order to keep the matter quiet, Colonel Friedrich Hossbach, the Führer's adjutant, hastened to warn Fritsch of the claims against him. The general was horrified, denounced the charges as 'a pile of stinking lies' and gave Hossbach his word of honour that he was entirely innocent. Hossbach returned to Hitler and persuaded him to give Fritsch an opportunity to clear his name. Meanwhile, Himmler and Heydrich, uneasily aware that their frame-up of von Fritsch could backfire disastrously if it was exposed, had hauled Otto Schmidt out of a concentration camp where he had been sent for a long list of offences including theft and forgery as well as blackmail. Subjected to the usual Gestapo pressures, the wretched Schmidt was 'persuaded' to identify Fritsch as the man he had seen with the rent boy, rather than the real culprit – the hapless Rittmeister von Frisch – whom Schmidt had been blackmailing since 1935.

Himmler attended Hitler's confrontation with General von Fritsch at the Berlin Reichschancellery. He brought with him Otto Schmidt, dirty, dishevelled, and bearing all the signs of the rough treatment he had recently received. Fritsch – taciturn at the best of times – was so outraged by the sudden appearance of this disreputable character with his pack of lies that he was rendered utterly speechless. Hitler took his silence for an admission of guilt and sent him on indefinite leave, effectively suspending him from duty. The decisive power struggle between the army and Himmler-Heydrich's SS/SD/Gestapo apparatus was now at hand.

In the last days of January 1938, the atmosphere in Berlin was similar to what it had been in the tense time four years previously, just before the Röhm 'Blood Purge'. The city was awash with rumours that the army was about to seize power in a military putsch. Hitler abruptly cancelled a meeting of Nazi bigwigs that was due to celebrate the fifth anniversary of his coming to power. The putsch rumours were not entirely unfounded: Ludwig Beck, Fritsch's deputy as his Chief of Staff, tried to interest his dismissed boss in the possibility, only to be told by Fritsch that German generals did not mutiny against their superiors. That decision was to eventually cost both men their lives.

Fritsch's failure to do anything concrete in his own defence beyond indignant spluttering, was widely shared in the officer corps. Beck himself seems to have had second thoughts about a putsch. When another general, Franz Halder, stormed into his office demanding to be told what was going on, Beck remained silent. Why didn't he, insisted Halder, organise a raid on the Gestapo HQ in Prinz-Albrecht-Strasse, which was surely the vipers' nest from where all the poison was emanating? 'Mutiny and revolution,' responded Beck, who would belatedly commit both on 20 July 1944, 'are not words in the lexicon of a German officer.' The indecision and procrastination that was to become the hallmark of anti-Hitler officers, were already exercising their malign and paralysing influence. Beck was destined to be shot dead after the failure of the July 1944 plot, while Halder ended the war in a concentration camp.

In stark contrast to his generals' inaction, and as so often when faced with a crisis, Hitler acted boldly, rapidly and ruthlessly. Within days, he had completed his coup against both the High Command and the remaining conservatives in his Cabinet who were acting as a brake to his hungry ambitions. It was announced that Blomberg and Fritsch had retired for 'reasons of health'. Ever the opportunist, Hitler took the chance at the same time to send many other members of their caste into premature retirement. Sixteen senior generals belonging to the instinctively anti-Nazi Prussian officer corps – including von Rundstedt, von Leeb, von Kluge, von Kleist, von Witzleben and Ludwig Beck – were sacked, and forty-four more junior officers regarded as opposed to or lukewarm towards Nazism were shifted to unimportant posts, though several of the generals would be recalled to command on the outbreak of the war.

At the same moment – 4 February 1938 – Hitler called his cabinet into session for what proved to be their last meeting. He announced to his startled ministers: 'From now on I take over personally the command of the whole armed forces.' Hitler did not stop there. He also sacked Konstantin von Neurath, a professional diplomat, as Foreign Minister, replacing him with his acolyte Joachim von Ribbentrop. Hjalmar Schacht, the 'economics wizard' who had masterminded the economic policies of the early Third Reich, was also out – because he disapproved of Hitler's plans for rearmament. He was replaced by a colourless bureaucrat, Walther Funk, from Goebbels' Propaganda Ministry. Also fired were Ulrich von Hassell and Herbert von Dirksen, two conservative diplomats respectively occupying the key posts of ambassadors to Germany's future wartime allies, Italy and Japan.

Because it involved no actual bloodshed, the Blomberg–Fritsch affair and the purge that accompanied it has received less attention from historians than the lurid massacre that was the Night of the Long Knives. But the events of January/February 1938 were arguably at least as important as those of the earlier purge. At a stroke, Hitler had decapitated the armed forces and dispensed with those civilians still forming a roadblock on his road to war. From this moment, there was no legal means of opposing his will and the imposition of a criminal dictatorship policed by the sinister duopoly of Himmler and Heydrich.

The army chiefs made only one feeble show of protest. Outrage at the 'fitting up' of von Fritsch was widespread among the army's remaining officer corps, and in March a military tribunal was convened to inquire into the whole affair. Although the tribunal was presided over by Göring, both Otto Schmidt and Rittmeister von Frisch appeared as witnesses, having been temporarily prised from the tender hands of the Gestapo. Schmidt admitted that he might have confused Frisch with von Fritsch, and the baron agreed that he was the man who had met 'Bavarian Joe' for gay sex and had been paying the price in the form of blackmail money to Schmidt ever since. The true depths of the perfidy of Himmler and Heydrich were exposed, and von Fritsch was only narrowly dissuaded from challenging the SS-Reichsführer to a duel. (Later, both Schmidt and Baron Frisch were quietly murdered, for dead men tell no tales.)

The inquiry totally exonerated the former Commander-in-Chief, but it was too late: he had lost his job. Humiliatingly, he was reinstated in the army, but only as Commander of an artillery regiment. In December 1938, Fritsch met Ulrich von Hassell, the diplomat who had also been dismissed as Ambassador in Rome. When von Hassell tried to draw Fritsch into the anti-Nazi conspiracies that would eventually cost him his life, the general refused. Fatalistically, according to the diplomat's diary, he added: 'This man, Hitler, is Germany's destiny for good and for evil. If he now goes over the edge, he will drag us all down with him. There is nothing we can do.'

Within a year of uttering these prophetic words, Fritsch himself was dead. Given command of a corps in the invasion of Poland that touched off the Second World War in September 1939, the general, either carelessly or deliberately, exposed himself to enemy fire and was hit in the thigh. Within minutes he had bled to death. Those who knew him were convinced that he no longer wished to live.

The exposure of the dirty tricks practised by Himmler and Heydrich in framing Fritsch was a dangerous moment for them, and for their project of building the SS/SD/Gestapo into an all-powerful police state within a state in Hitler's Reich. Two factors saved them and ensured their victory in the power struggle for supremacy with the army: another political crisis culminating in the *Anschluss* – the absorption of Austria into the Reich – and the fatal dithering and pusillanimity of the officer corps themselves.

The tribunal inquiring into the Fritsch case coincided with Hitler's occupation of his native Austria – a foreign policy objective of uniting all the German peoples into a single Reich that he had long cherished. The Nazis had already tried to seize the small country with their usual gangster methods in the bloody summer of 1934 when, weeks after the Röhm Purge, Austrian Nazis, sponsored and supported from Germany, mounted a botched putsch in Vienna. They murdered the authoritarian Austrian Chancellor, Engelbert Dollfuss, but the putsch ignominiously failed. Since then, Dollfuss's successor, Kurt Schuschnigg, had fought an uphill battle against Nazi pressure, including terrorism and economic sanctions, to maintain his country's independence. When Schuschnigg announced a referendum on the issue, Hitler mobilised the Wehrmacht and occupied the country to a delirious reception from cheering crowds.

The Anschluss – or union – between the two states was accompanied by the usual adornments of Nazi rule – mass arrests of thousands of Jews and political opponents; the suicide of hundreds; and open anti-Semitic atrocities in the streets, where Jews were forced on their hands and knees to scrub out anti-Nazi slogans watched by jeering onlookers. The oppression was personally supervised by Himmler and Heydrich who arrived in Vienna several hours before Hitler's triumphal entry into the city. The Anschluss also served as the perfect excuse to bury the Blomberg–Fritsch scandal. From now on, the sinister duopoly would do things their way.

Chapter Seven

THE RIVALS

– Heydrich, Canaris and the competing
Nazi police and intelligence agencies

On 14 June 1931, Reinhard Heydrich, a 27-year-old newly un-employed naval lieutenant, caught a train from his home town of Halle to Munich. He was unsure of his reception at his destination or even whether the man he had come to see, Heinrich Himmler, would agree to meet him. He need not have worried, for the partnership between the two men that was born that day would create an apparatus of terror, surveillance, repression and mass murder that would leave Germany and much of Europe in ruins.

Heydrich was born on 7 May 1904. His father, Bruno Heydrich, was a singer and composer of sub-Wagnerian operas who had founded the Halle Conservatoire where Reinhard's mother, Elisabeth, worked as a piano teacher. Always something of a loner, young Reinhard was not popular at school – partly owing to the Heydrichs being Catholic converts in Halle's overwhelmingly Prussian Protestant society, and partly due to a rumour that a family name, 'Suss', meant that the Heydrichs were of Jewish descent. In the anti-Semitic atmosphere of Wilhelmine Germany, this was a slur that bit deeply into the young boy's psyche. Heydrich was naturally aloof anyway, and his unusual physical appearance – with wide feminine hips, beaky nose, close-set eyes and a high voice – drew the taunts of his male schoolmates and increased his isolation.

Heydrich inherited his parents' musical talents and interests and became an accomplished violinist. His other chief interest was in becoming a naval officer. By a strange twist of fate, a major influence over this ambition was a family friend of the Heydrichs, Count Felix von Luckner, a legendary naval hero of the First World War, whose adventures and exploits had won him the nickname *Der Seeteufel* ('The Sea Devil'). Von Luckner's life was later to strangely entwine with that of Heydrich when the Sea Devil became a denizen of Salon Kitty.

Growing up in the pre-war era of rising international tensions and a naval arms race between Germany and Britain, Reinhard Heydrich held the prevailing nationalist and militarist views of his class and family. Too young to fight in the Great War, Reinhard followed the fortunes of the conflict with passionate interest, and shared in the widespread shock and dismay when the war ended in Germany's defeat, plunging the country into chaos and revolution.

In February 1919 the revolutionary wave, spreading inland from the northern ports where mutiny in the High Seas Fleet had sparked the turmoil, reached Halle. Mass demonstrations and strikes by workers paralysed the city, and one of the first Freikorps raised to put down the revolutionaries, led by General Georg Maercker, moved to retake the city. As Maercker's men marched into Halle, they were bitterly resisted by the revolutionaries and had to barricade themselves into a school where they endured a veritable siege. For two days a full-scale civil war raged in the city, with artillery and machine-gun fire sweeping the streets. Eventually, after proclaiming Martial Law, Maercker restored order, but the cost had been high: thirty revolutionaries and seven Freikorps men had been killed.

A year later, in March 1920, violence returned to Halle during the abortive Kapp Putsch – a short-lived right-wing attempt to overthrow

Weimar spearheaded by the naval Freikorps of Captain Hermann Ehrhardt. Reacting to the putsch, the industrial workers again seized Halle – leading to more street fighting in the city between the Freikorps and Communists even bloodier than the first bout. Dozens were killed on both sides before order was eventually restored.

These terrifying scenes of civil strife and anarchy were witnessed by the Heydrich family, and the experience could only have reinforced fifteen-year-old Reinhard's nationalist views – especially as some of the leading original revolutionaries had been mutinous sailors from his beloved navy. When order was restored after the original fighting, the teenager joined the civil defence militia set up by Maercker to maintain control over the city. Heydrich later claimed that he had acted as a messenger for Maercker's Freikorps during the fighting, though there is no other evidence to support the claim, nor to back his subsequent boasts that he had also joined two right-wing racist societies which aimed to reverse the results of the war, purge the country of Jews and Bolsheviks, and restore Germany to greatness.

Whatever the truth of his later claims of early involvement in extreme right-wing *völkischer* politics, the experience of seeing at first hand a total breakdown of law and order accompanied by savage violence in the streets where he had grown up can only have reinforced the hardline nationalist views of Heydrich and his family and confirmed their horror of Bolshevism. For the moment, however, his main focus was concentrated on his career: his burning ambition to join the navy.

The need for young Reinhard to get a job was becoming acute. The economic chaos that had followed the war had seen a steep decline in the fortunes of his parents' conservatoire. Middle-class families now no longer had the spare cash to give their children singing or dancing lessons, and enrolments for the conservatoire nosedived. Bruno Heydrich failed to get a state subsidy for his creation, and its future looked bleak. If his parents had hoped that Reinhard would inherit the conservatoire as a thriving concern, such hopes now lay in ashes. In the spring of 1922, having passed his school-leaving Abitur exam with flying colours, Reinhard arrived as a naval cadet at the port of Kiel.

Heydrich was no more popular in the navy than he had been at school. Though keen on sports such as swimming, rowing and fencing – at which he would reach championship standards – he remained somewhat aloof. His fellow cadets found him smug and arrogant, and his habit of practising daily on his violin attracted ridicule from his Philistine comrades. His high voice and equine features won him the nickname 'the Nanny Goat'. Dislike of him was also fed by the rumours of his Jewish descent that had followed him from Halle. Nor did he display any interest in the right-wing politics that permeated the naval corps.

Despite the fact that the navy was considered the most conservative of the three armed services, and naval officers – shamed by the fact that the 1918 revolution had first broken out in the fleet – had taken a prominent role in the Freikorps' repression of the revolution, the Kapp Putsch, and the later assassination of the Weimar politicians Matthias Erzberger and Walther Rathenau, Heydrich displayed no apparent interest in such events. Nonetheless, despite his outsider status, and the bullying it provoked, he progressed satisfactorily if not spectacularly in his chosen career. In the summer of 1923, he was posted to the training cruiser SMS *Berlin*, commanded by the man whose life would become inextricably tangled with his own: Captain Wilhelm Canaris.

Canaris, the son of a wealthy industrialist from the Ruhr, born on New Year's Day 1887, was of an older generation than Heydrich, and had a distinguished record in the First World War. Believing that he was descended from Constantin Kanaris, a naval hero of the Greek War of Independence, Canaris had joined the Kaiser's navy, the *Kaiserliche Marine*, in 1905. Despite his small stature, and introspective nature, Canaris proved a natural sailor, skilled in navigation and devoted to the service. Highly intelligent, Canaris was a fluent linguist, speaking six languages, including English and Spanish. He had displayed a fascination for secrets and espionage from an early age, earning the nickname 'the Peeper' for his excessive curiosity. While still at school he had experimented with invisible inks and using false names, and once in the navy a specialisation in intelligence came naturally.

The outbreak of war in 1914 found Canaris serving as intelligence officer aboard the light cruiser *Dresden*. While the rest of the squadron was annihilated by the Royal Navy in the Battle of the Falkland Islands in December 1914, the *Dresden* survived, and Canaris's navigational skills helped steer the ship to safety in neutral Chile, where he and the rest of the crew were interned after scuttling their ship. Eager to get back to the war, and using his fluency in Spanish, Canaris escaped with the help of German expatriates and made his way back to Europe.

Returned to Germany, Canaris was sent to neutral Spain on his first spying mission – organising the observation of enemy shipping and the supplying of U-boats in the Mediterranean. His espionage abilities attracted the unwelcome attention of British agents, and it became necessary for Canaris to make a hasty exit. His naval superiors now had a high regard for Canaris's skills, and organised a special exfiltration by U-boat. Once safely back home, he was awarded the Iron Cross 1st Class.

Canaris's U-boat voyage had so impressed him that he applied for a transfer to the submarine service. After two months' training – during which he met his future wife Erika Waag – he was given command of three U-boats in swift succession in the Mediterranean. Once again, he proved a success, evading determined Allied pursuit, sinking several merchant ships, and taking their skippers prisoner.

Ordered home as Germany collapsed in November 1918, Canaris returned to Kiel to find the port engulfed by revolution. There was no question of where the loyalties of the deeply conservative and nationalist officer lay. Along with the rest of the navy's officer caste,

Canaris now devoted his considerable energies and his experience in espionage to reversing the revolution. He attached himself as naval adjutant to Gustav Noske, a right-wing Social Democrat and the strong man of the new and precarious Weimar regime. Noske was rapidly forming the Freikorps paramilitary forces to resist the subversion of the Spartacist Communists who were vying with the Social Democrat government in Berlin for control of a country dissolving into anarchy and chaos.

Canaris was closely involved in covering up the Freikorps' murders of the two Spartacist leaders, Karl Liebknecht and Rosa Luxemburg, after they had attempted to stage a Communist revolution in Berlin in January 1919. He coached the naval officers who had carried out the crimes in their false cover stories. When – despite his efforts – Kurt Vogel, the officer who had shot Luxemburg, was jailed, Canaris, using the fake name of 'Lieutenant Lindemann', visited the Moabit prison, sprung Vogel from jail, and smuggled him to safety across the Dutch border.

This, then, was the man who Heydrich encountered when he joined the *Berlin* for training at sea. Although apparently polar opposites in appearance and character – Heydrich was tall, blond, boastful, vain and lecherous, while Canaris was small, cautious, quiet, professional and sly – they had much in common. Both were musical, which made them outsiders among their heartier messroom shipmates. Both were introspective, yet supremely confident in their own abilities, and both were ambitious for their own and Germany's future. Already deeply enmeshed in secret intelligence activities, Canaris fired his young protégé's incipient interest in the same field, encouraging him to specialise in signals and communications.

Canaris was drawn to the lonely young cadet, and during their time together on the *Berlin* made himself Heydrich's mentor. Discovering his protégé's ability as a violinist, Canaris regularly invited him to his home in Kiel where his wife Erika held musical evenings with her own string quartet – Heydrich played the violin alongside Erika, while Canaris, clad in a chef's hat and apron, cooked his favourite Spanish recipes for his guests. The two men soon separated as their naval careers took them in different directions, but the bond formed aboard the *Berlin* would last for the rest of Heydrich's life.

Heydrich's voracious sexual appetite got him into trouble at his next posting – a voyage on the *Schleswig-Holstein*, flagship of the North Sea Fleet, to the Mediterranean when he caused a scene when the wife of a British naval officer declined his invitation to dance; he also visited bars and brothels in Spain and Portugal. Having completed his training, he was promoted to the rank of lieutenant and made the ship's radio officer. Other facets of Heydrich's character that came increasingly to the fore as he rose in rank were his arrogance, his hungry ambition and his disdain for others.

Stationed onshore in Kiel, Heydrich had plenty of free time, which he largely devoted to sports and social activities. In December 1930, at a ball, he met and was instantly attracted to a bright and blonde nineteen-year-old named Lina von Osten, the daughter of an old but impoverished family from the island of Fehmarn. After a whirlwind courtship, within three weeks the young couple were engaged. There was just one problem: Heydrich had already promised to marry another young woman.

A lovestruck Heydrich made no secret of his engagement to Lina, and one of the recipients of the announcement of their betrothal was a young woman from Berlin whom Heydrich had met some six months before. The couple had visited each other in Kiel and Berlin, and had had sex – even after he had met Lina – and the young lady considered herself compromised. Upon receipt of the news of her lover's engagement she collapsed. The identity of Heydrich's lover has never been revealed, but one thing is certain: her family had influential connections in the navy.

The aggrieved young woman's father, who knew Grand Admiral Erich Raeder, Commander of the Navy, made an official complaint to the admiral and a court of honour was convened to investigate the affair. Although a breach of promise did not automatically warrant dismissal for a naval officer, the navy's conservative code of conduct for its officers was strict, and Heydrich's behaviour had clearly fallen well short of what was expected from an officer and gentleman. More importantly, Heydrich's arrogant attitude at the hearing alienated and annoyed the three-man tribunal of his fellow officers and sealed his fate. Instead of taking responsibility for his indiscretion, Heydrich denied that he had promised to marry his lover and unconvincingly tried to blame her for initiating their sexual relationship.

The tribunal's unfavourable report was passed to Raeder who deemed Heydrich to be 'unworthy' of continuing in the navy and decreed his instant dismissal. It was a shattering blow to the vain young man's pride, and grim news for his future prospects. In 1931, Germany was deep in the toils of the Great Depression triggered by the Wall Street Crash of October 1929. Unemployment was climbing towards six million, and a jobless former naval officer with a black mark to his name and few obvious qualifications beyond his own burning ambition was in dire straits. Although Heydrich was entitled to a generous two years' severance pay, it was the loss of his high social status as an officer that hit him most. He took his dismissal very hard, and after an appeal against his dismissal was turned down by President Hindenburg himself, he locked himself in his room and wept bitter tears of frustration and rage.

Heydrich owed his professional survival to his fiancée Lina von Osten and his own family. Scornfully rejecting a demeaning offer to become a yachting instructor, Heydrich turned in his trouble to the forceful young woman to whom he had plighted his troth. Lina could have been forgiven for breaking off her engagement because of the scandal. Instead, she stood by her man and came up with an idea:

Heydrich, she suggested, should scout out the possibilities of a new career in the rising Nazi Party.

Up to this point, Heydrich had shown scant interest in politics and had even made scornful remarks about the 'Bohemian corporal' Hitler and the 'cripple' Goebbels. In contrast, Lina was already a keen supporter of National Socialism. Her brother Hans had joined the Nazi Party and the SA in 1929, and she herself had attended a Nazi rally and heard Hitler speak. In addition, she was a virulent anti-Semite, who blamed the Jews for Germany's economic woes and the impoverishment of middle-class families like her own and Heydrich's.

The financial situation of his parents had continued to deteriorate while Heydrich had been in the navy, as he discovered when he and Lina went to Halle to inform them of Heydrich's plight and ask for their help. Bruno Heydrich had suffered a stroke, and his conservatoire had continued to decline in the economic blizzard and was now facing bankruptcy. In despair, Heydrich's mother Elisabeth turned to his godmother, Baroness Elise von Eberstein, for assistance. The baroness's son, Kurt von Eberstein, was a seasoned and senior Nazi and SA officer, who had joined the party in the mid-1920s. In close contact with the Nazi leadership in Munich, he advised an initially reluctant Heydrich to inquire about job opportunities within the swelling party apparatus.

Lina too backed up Eberstein's advice, and so Heydrich wrote his fateful job application to Himmler. He knew little about Nazi ideology, had not read *Mein Kampf*, and was wary of the SA's well-deserved reputation as a bunch of low-class, ill-disciplined street brawlers. What motivated Heydrich, both now and in the future, was not the Nazi Party's programme, but his desire to be part of an elite, a uniformed caste that would be some sort of substitute for the position he had so ignominiously lost. Increasingly, too, it was a lust for power that drove him on.

On 1 June 1931, Heydrich joined the Nazi Party. A fortnight later, on 14 June, he travelled from Halle to Munich. He had almost cancelled the journey after Eberstein sent him a message that Himmler had a cold and could not see him. But Lina urged him to go anyway, and he took the train. He was met by Eberstein who drove him to meet Himmler at the SS chief's country property at Waldtrudering outside Munich, where the Reichsführer had unsuccessfully attempted to run a chicken farm.

Himmler was impressed by the young man's tall Aryan appearance and, according to legend, gave Heydrich half an hour in which to sketch out how he would run an intelligence service for the party. Informed only by his enthusiastic reading of pulp spy fiction, his brief experience of signals in the navy, and his own inordinate ambition, Heydrich completed the task on time to Himmler's satisfaction. He was immediately offered the job, and just as quickly accepted. The partnership of terror that would form the core of the Nazi state was born.

Before taking up his new duties, Heydrich had to prove his credentials as a tough and committed Nazi, not afraid to get his hands dirty. He was sent to Hamburg, the traditional left-wing port city where an election battle was in progress. Here, with the enthusiasm of a convert, he apparently threw himself into the clashes with communists and socialists that were the everyday reality of life in the cities in the last days of Weimar – taking part in Nazi raids on opposition clubs and bars, he acquired the first of his many nicknames, 'the blond beast'.

A month after joining the party, Heydrich was inducted into the SS itself. The *Schutzstaffel* (Protection Squad) had, as its name implies, its origins in 1925 as a bodyguard unit of tried and tested thugs assigned to guard Hitler himself and keep order as stewards at Nazi Party rallies. Hitler never fully trusted the much larger party paramilitary militia, the SA, which, under the capable and ambitious leadership of Ernst Röhm, enjoyed a semi-detached and often fractious relationship with the party.

The SS really got off the ground and assumed the form by which it became known and feared when Himmler took over the leadership as SS-Reichsführer in 1929. Himmler's ambitions for the SS knew few bounds, and as a super bureaucrat unrivalled for his skills at the manoeuvres for power within the party, he grew the organisation into an ideologically committed elite, dressing its members in the sinister black uniforms designed to instil fear into friend and foe alike. He built the SS into a racially 'pure' and secretive vanguard of Nazism, with its own ethos and agenda. Within three years, Himmler had vastly expanded the SS from fewer than 300 members to more than 10,000 when Heydrich joined. Although it was still only one tenth of the size of the SA, the seeds of its growing power had been firmly planted.

As every SS member had to prove their family's unsullied Germanic origins back to the eighteenth century, Heydrich's own ancestry was investigated to discover whether the rumours of Jewish blood that had dogged him since his schooldays had any truth. The subsequent report gave the new recruit a clean bill of Aryan racial health, and by August 1931 Heydrich had moved to Munich and was installed in a tiny office with a single typewriter shared with a colleague in the party's central headquarters, the Brown House.

Heydrich's original cramped and primitive working conditions may have seemed unpromising but had distinct advantages for his ambitions. Starting from scratch, at first working alone and answerable only to his boss, Heydrich could mould his new creation in his own image. His task assigned by Himmler was to build an intelligence and counter-intelligence department within the SS, to keep a watchful eye not only on the party's political enemies – Communists, Social Democrats and Catholic conservatives – but also on their own members. With the party's membership lists on hand in the Brown House, Heydrich began to compile his own comprehensive card index of files, noting the habits, opinions and weaknesses of people he deemed of interest. And that meant almost everyone. In addition, within weeks he had begun to establish a network of spies, narks and informers ready and willing to snitch on their enemies and colleagues.

From the beginning, Heydrich worked long hours late into the evening and his labours soon bore fruit. By November he had moved his office to his own lodgings in Munich's Türkenstrasse and acquired three subordinates. At the same time he had inserted fifty spies – under the thin disguise of 'liaison officers' – into every branch of the SS throughout Germany with a brief to watch out for anti-Nazi infiltrators. It is an indication of Heydrich's mistrustful nature that he was at first more concerned to sniff out spies within the Nazi Party's ranks than to plant his own agents in the opposition.

The job fitted Heydrich as perfectly as his own newly tailored black uniform. His own nature – suspicious, cynical, malign, trusting no one and immune to the usual human feelings of kindness, compassion and generosity – made him an ideal spymaster. In December, when Heydrich married Lina to the strains of the Nazi 'Horst-Wessel-Lied' anthem, Himmler signalled his pleasure with his new subordinate by promoting him to *Sturmbannführer* – the SS equivalent of major.

Heydrich had joined the Nazis at precisely the right time for the fulfilment of his unbridled ambitions. In 1932, unemployment had risen to more than six million, the Reichschancellor Heinrich Brüning had resorted to governing by decree, and the frequent elections were disfigured by murderous street battles between the Nazis and Communists, which left hundreds dead and thousands injured. As the political manoeuvres in Berlin that would lead to Hitler's appointment as Chancellor in January 1933 reached their climax, and the Weimar Republic agonised in its death throes, Heydrich continued to strengthen and expand his organisation – now officially named the *Sicherheitsdienst* (Security Service) or SD.

By the middle of 1932, the SD had more than thirty full-time employees, and hundreds of agents reporting to its Munich office throughout Germany. Modelling it on the much admired British Secret Service, MI6/SIS, Heydrich even reportedly signed his memos 'C' in green ink in imitation of his British counterpart. He defined its task as '. . . to gather, evaluate and verify substantive material on the objectives, methods and plans of internal enemies; and to report on potential wrongdoers within our own ranks'.

When Hitler was appointed as Chancellor, Himmler and Heydrich moved quickly to gain control of the police and security apparatus in Bavaria. Himmler was made Police President and immediately named Heydrich as Commissioner of the state's Political Police. This vastly extended his power base, giving him a springboard to gain control of the political police in most of Germany's other states – with the temporary exception of the largest of them, Prussia.

With exquisite irony, Heydrich now found himself in charge of a force that for the past decade had been battling the Nazis – along with other extreme right- and left-wing groups – in Bavaria. His main man in absorbing his new employees was a professional police official, Heinrich Müller, who had headed the Bavarian Political Police before the Nazi takeover. Though a fierce anti-Communist, Müller did not join the Nazi Party until 1939. Heydrich was prepared to use this apolitical official because of his ruthless efficiency and his intimate knowledge of the Nazis' left-wing enemies. Their partnership would endure until Heydrich's death, by which time Müller was in charge of the Gestapo, and would become one of the main executors of the Holocaust.

Bavaria became the model for the systematic and disciplined SS state repression that would be rolled out across the whole Reich. Hitler's assumption of power had been followed by a wave of horrific repression, at first directed against the Communists and Social Democrats who had been battling the SA in the streets. Now the Brownshirts took a bloody revenge. They became auxiliaries of the official police. Armed with these powers, thousands of KPD militants and SPD activists were arrested and taken to so-called 'wild concentration camps' set up in disused factories, barracks and cellars where they were beaten, brutalised and often murdered.

Such disorderly violence by their SA rivals offended the discipline and order that formed the ethos the SS embodied. Naturally, Himmler and Heydrich had no objections to violence per se: indeed, institutionalised violence was the foundation of their struggle against Jews, Bolsheviks, Christians and anyone else perceived as enemies of the new order. But they intended that the repression should be carried out efficiently and systematically. In pursuit of this aim, the SS took over control of a former munitions works at Dachau, just outside Munich, which they converted into the Reich's first 'correctly' organised concentration camp.

At first, most of the inmates at Dachau were not Jews but the Nazis' leftist and Catholic political opponents. Thousands of them were subjected to a brutal regime of dawn-to-dark hard labour and an inadequate diet, interspersed by brutal beatings and tortures administered by the SS guards. Those lucky enough to be released were forbidden to speak about their experiences, thus spreading a stain of fear about what went on in the camp into the general population. It was but a foretaste of the fog of terror that was to come.

The main obstacle standing in the path of Himmler and Heydrich's aim to totally dominate the Third Reich's police, security and spying agencies was the existence of the largest and most populous German state: Prussia. The most dominant state since it had led the drive for German unification and the creation of the Kaiser's Reich under Otto von Bismarck, Prussia had possessed its own political police since the 1848 liberal revolutions that had briefly engulfed Europe in that year. With the largest Socialist and Communist Parties in continental Europe to keep under observation, the Prussian Political Police had continued under Weimar, and by 1930, this agency,

Department I, had about a thousand officers, mainly drawn from the ordinary Criminal Police (Kripo).

When the Nazis came to power, the Prime Minister of Prussia was Hitler's leading lieutenant, Hermann Göring. Göring appointed a career bureaucrat from the Interior Ministry, Rudolf Diels, to head a new political police force – the *Geheime Staatspolizei* (Secret State Police) – better known under its feared acronym as the Gestapo. Though a ruthless opportunist happy to use violence when necessary – as seen in him leading the squad that murdered Horst Wessel's assassin Ali Höhler – Diels was not a reliable Nazi and became a pawn in the power struggle between Göring and Himmler for control of Prussia's police – including the infant Gestapo.

Infighting was endemic among the Nazis' leading paladins, and Himmler and Heydrich were past masters at such poisonous office politics. For them, Göring represented the conservative wing of the party, ready to compromise with 'reactionary' circles, and, though ruthlessly anti-Semitic, more interested in his own greedy sybaritic pleasures than he was in their single-minded pursuit of power. After targeting and removing Göring's protégé Diels, they finally won their struggle with the Reichsmarschall in April 1934 in the run-up to the Night of the Long Knives.

Göring, Himmler and Heydrich formed a tactical alliance to get rid of their mutual enemy: the SA Chief of Staff Ernst Röhm and curb the dangerously anarchic antics of his Brownshirts. Hitler was reluctant to part political company with his old party comrade to whom he owed so much, but pressure from the army, affronted by Röhm's ambitions to absorb them in a people's army composed from the SA's ill-disciplined ranks, pushed him over the edge into ordering the purge. Eliminating the SA perfectly suited the SS project to become the real motor of Nazi power.

After Göring had been persuaded to hand control of the Prussian Political Police to Himmler, Heydrich lost no time in asserting his personal power. He moved to Berlin and set up his headquarters in the Prinz-Albrecht-Strasse along with the youthful team of acolytes he had selected in Bavaria who owed him their personal loyalty. Heydrich's style was to rule by fear. Almost all descriptions of him by survivors who knew him remark on his cold, cynical and cruel nature, his hunger for work and detail, and the dire implications for all those not prepared to subscribe to his own brand of ruthless amoral efficiency.

The foot soldiers who executed his orders and spread the webs of terror across the Reich expanded exponentially. Within three years the Gestapo's original 1,000 officers had grown to 7,000. They were informed by an army of spies and stooges – many of them former political opponents of the Nazis hoping to buy their freedom or curry favour with the new order by informing on their old comrades. These narks were backed up by the system of *Blockleiter*: wardens acting as concierges in the blocks of flats in the cities where most Germans lived. These snoops – usually Nazi Party members or sympathisers – were volunteers who kept an eye on their neighbours, listened out for those tuning in to foreign radio stations, and reported anyone who was behaving suspiciously or making anti-Nazi remarks or jokes.

By 1935, then, with astonishing speed, the template for the totalitarian police state that Nazi Germany would become under the control of Himmler and Heydrich had been firmly established. On 1 January of that year, Wilhelm Canaris was appointed chief of the Abwehr, Germany's foreign military intelligence and counter-intelligence service – the equivalent of Britain's MI6/SIS: the fateful paths of the 'little admiral' and his former naval protégé were about to cross again.

In the years since Canaris had enjoyed his musical evenings in Kiel with Heydrich and first introduced him to the world of intelligence, the career of the younger man had been transformed out of all recognition, while that of Canaris had largely marked time. He had been employed on abortive missions in Japan and Spain to set up contracts for the clandestine building of ships – part of Germany's military expansion that had been explicitly forbidden under the Treaty of Versailles.

Frustrated, like most of the officer caste, by the chaos and instability of the democratic Weimar Republic, and always a fervent nationalist, Canaris had enthusiastically backed the rising Nazi Party. As captain of the old battleship SMS *Schlesien* he even gave lectures supporting Hitler as the only hope of combatting Communism, and returning Germany to orderly central government, with a strong military that would restore the nation to its former great power status.

The personal relationship between the two former shipmates on board SMS *Berlin* was crucial to the development of the Nazis' intelligence and spying communities, both domestically and abroad. On the surface the relationship that had begun ten years before was a friendly one. Not only did the two men share their naval background, but they were also near neighbours with adjoining gardens in the leafy lakeside Berlin suburb of Schlachtensee where both men owned villas. They were thus able to renew the musical evenings with their respective wives and indulge their mutual passion for horse riding. After the war, Lina Heydrich described the relationship between Canaris and her husband as 'paternal'.

Beneath this companionable naval camaraderie, however, both men were mistrustful. Heydrich already had the phones of the Abwehr at its headquarters on Berlin's Tirpitzufer tapped, and had a wary professional respect for his mentor, describing him to subordinates as 'a wily old fox'. The shrewd little admiral, for his part, accurately described Heydrich in his private diary as 'a brutal fanatic with whom it will be difficult to have an open and friendly co-operation'. In public, however, in his first speech to Abwehr officers, Canaris called for 'comradely co-operation with the Gestapo'. If Heydrich's hidden microphones picked up these words, he would have been well pleased.

Despite his secret doubts, within a few weeks of the admiral's appointment to head the Abwehr, on 17 January, he and Heydrich were photographed dining together with a convivial party at Horchers, one of Berlin's most fashionable restaurants, and a favourite haunt of Göring and other Nazi leaders. (Heydrich himself is reputed to have placed hidden microphones in the vases of flowers on the restaurant's tables.) The party's occasion may have been a celebration of the agreement made on the same day between the two men – known as the Ten Commandments – delineating the division of labour between their respective agencies.

Essentially, the Ten Commandments stipulated that the SD would be responsible for internal security while the Abwehr would look after foreign intelligence. Increasingly, however, as his ambitions and power grew, Heydrich trespassed on the Abwehr's territory. By the time of his death in 1942, having united and centralised all of the Reich's intelligence and security under his command with the creation of the *Reichssicherheitshauptamt* (RSHA), Heydrich was on the point of driving his tanks over Canaris's immaculate lawns and absorbing the Abwehr completely.

The Third Reich's intelligence community was what Canaris's British biographer Richard Bassett rightly calls a 'vipers' nest' of no fewer than seven competing agencies. As well as the Abwehr and the SD, the Wehrmacht had its own intelligence section nominally commanded by General Wilhelm Keitel, head of Hitler's OKW. On the Eastern Front, this was run by the brilliant Reinhard Gehlen, who after the war would head West Germany's foreign intelligence service, the BND. In addition, four of the leading Nazi exponents – Göring, Foreign Minister Joachim von Ribbentrop, the party ideologue Alfred Rosenberg and Hitler's secretary and gatekeeper Martin Bormann – all had their own private intelligence services too. But the two cleverest and most effective snakes in the vipers' nest were Heydrich and Canaris.

At first, and for several years, the cordial collaboration between the two former sailors continued. The Abwehr played their part in some of Heydrich's dirty tricks operations – such as supplying uniforms for the 'false flag' fake Polish attack on the Gleiwitz radio station that triggered the attack on Poland and the Second World War. When Canaris was first appointed, his predecessor as Abwehr chief, Conrad Patzig, had solemnly warned him about the machinations of Heydrich and his acolytes. 'Don't worry,' Canaris responded, 'I can take care of those young men.'

The admiral was bolstered in his confidence by initially enjoying the trust of Hitler himself. Records show that in his first three months in the job, Canaris had no fewer than seventeen private meetings with Hitler. Early in 1936, he assured the Führer that, thanks to his contacts in Britain, he was certain that London would not react unfavourably to the Führer's plan to occupy the demilitarised Rhineland – the first step in Hitler's escalating programme of expansion that would eventually lead to war. Thus encouraged, Hitler moved his plan to reoccupy the Rhineland forward to March 1936. When – as Canaris had predicted – there was not a peep of protest from either Britain or France, Hitler's trust in the Abwehr chief was reinforced.

Despite, as a German nationalist, approving the move into the Rhineland, the admiral's disillusionment with other aspects of Nazi rule was increasing, and he embarked on the dangerous double game that would eventually lead to his destruction. To all outward appearances, Canaris carried out his work with his customary smooth efficiency. Behind the scenes, though, he had started on a very different course. He filled the ranks of the Abwehr with men such as his de facto deputy, Colonel Hans Oster; his legal expert Hans von Dohnanyi; and the Protestant theologian Dietrich Bonhoeffer – all of whom had perceived the evil nature of National Socialism at an early date and were convinced and principled opponents of the regime. Within a short time, the Abwehr was an active, if covert, centre of opposition, and most of the conspiracies that would be launched against Hitler in the coming years had the hidden and unspoken approval of the 'wily old fox' who headed the organisation.

Cautiously and cleverly, with his habitual cunning and love of intrigue, Canaris used the legitimate foreign espionage activities of the Abwehr as cover to establish contact with the ruling classes in Germany's potential enemies and warn them of the danger that Hitler, with his programme of aggression and expansion, presented. Various envoys were despatched to London and other foreign capitals in the years leading up to the war to carry such warnings.

As part of his double game, while Canaris's left hand was increasingly dabbling in anti-Nazi conspiracy, his right hand was continuing to pursue orthodox intelligence activities on Germany's behalf. Like Heydrich at the SD, he massively expanded the Abwehr's staff, from 150 when he took over to more than a thousand operatives within three years. Like Heydrich, he was a workaholic who often slept on a camp bed in his office. His marriage, though giving him two daughters, was not very happy or close and he was dedicated to his work.

Emboldened by his bloodless occupation of the Rhineland in March 1936, Hitler's next foreign policy success was not of his own making but was fortuitously presented to him in July of that same year. A group of Spanish generals, led by Francisco Franco, appalled by increasing anarchy and what they saw as the rising threat of Communism, staged a military coup against the country's left-wing Republican government. Resisted by the organised militias of the working class, the coup was only partially successful. Franco's Army of Africa was trapped in Spain's North African colonies and needed to cross rapidly to the Spanish mainland to save the coup.

Franco's envoys met Hitler while he was at the annual Richard Wagner Festival in Bayreuth and appealed to him for help. With civil war spreading across Spain, and ever the opportunist, the Führer saw a potential opportunity to try out his expanding Luftwaffe in real combat and install an ideologically friendly government in Madrid. He duly supplied the aircraft that ferried the rebel army to Spain and created an air arm – the Condor Legion – to help Franco win the war.

Canaris's extensive experiences in Spain during the First World War and later had made him the regime's Spanish expert, and he strongly supported intervening on Franco's side, persuading Hitler of the strategic advantages of such a move. The Abwehr's far-flung network of agents throughout Europe, and a personal rapport that the admiral struck up with Franco during his frequent visits to Nationalist Spain during the conflict, were decisive factors in increasing his credit with the Führer, especially as the support that Nazi Germany and Fascist Italy gave to Franco were crucial in his eventual victory.

At the same time, as part of his double game, Canaris advised the Generalissimo to avoid too close an alliance with Hitler. The two men were ideological soulmates, both being nationalist conservatives, but not sharing the racist and anti-Semitic agendas of the Nazis. By the time that Franco finally took Madrid and proclaimed victory in the spring of 1939, the war clouds were gathering across Europe, and Hitler's appetite for conflict had been sharpened by his acquisition of his native Austria and his dismemberment of Czechoslovakia.

While Canaris had been busy in Spain, Himmler and Heydrich had been hard at work consolidating their control of the population in the Reich. Once in charge of Germany's police and internal security establishment, the diabolic duo turned their attention to implementing their radical plans to change German society and remodel it on National Socialist lines. Their first targets had been the Nazis' principal political enemies – Communists and Socialists – and the leading officials and activists of the KPD and SPD either fled into exile or were the first to populate the concentration camps that were proliferating across the Reich.

Having neutered and silenced the political opposition, they then turned their attention to the Nazis' spiritual and racial enemies and those deemed unfit to survive: the Jews, Roma, Jehovah's Witnesses, the physically and mentally handicapped and the Christian churches. Himmler's long-term plan was to eliminate Christianity entirely, replacing the 'weak' and 'meek' religion with its Jewish roots with a return to pagan Teutonic religion, complete with its Nordic gods, arcane mysticism and runic symbolism. Although Heydrich officially left the Catholic Church, proclaiming himself to be the preferred SS term *gottgläubig* ('believing in God'), he was never truly interested in the racial/religious manias that so obsessed his boss. The pragmatic pursuit of total power was what intrigued and motivated him.

In March 1938 Hitler carried out his long-cherished plan to unite his native Austrian homeland with the Reich in which he now reigned supreme. The Anschluss came about after years of escalating intimidation, bullying and violence – including the assassination of the Austrian Chancellor Engelbert Dollfuss in an abortive Nazi putsch in 1934. Dollfuss's successor Kurt von Schuschnigg was summoned by Hitler to the Berghof in February 1938 and browbeaten into accepting Nazis into his cabinet. Three weeks after his return to Vienna, however, Schuschnigg announced a referendum on the question of whether Austria should continue as an independent state.

A furious Führer immediately ordered the Wehrmacht across the Austrian border, where they were welcomed by ecstatic crowds. But even before Hitler and his troops had arrived in Vienna, Himmler and Heydrich had flown into the Austrian capital. They took over the Hotel Regina and convened a meeting with Ernst Kaltenbrunner, head of the Austrian SS, and leading police officials. Previously prepared plans for repression were immediately put into action. Twenty-five thousand opponents of the Nazis – Communists, Socialists and anti-Nazi German exiles – were detained and shipped to concentration camps. A new and particularly brutal camp was set up in Austria at Mauthausen, and measures were enacted to confiscate property and businesses from the country's 200,000-strong Jewish community.

Kaltenbrunner, who would succeed Heydrich as head of the RSHA after his assassination in 1942, would also play a part in the Salon Kitty story as he owned the neighbouring house in the Giesebrechtstrasse.

Austria had traditionally strong anti-Semitic elements, and in the immediate aftermath of the Anschluss, the bigotry was let off the leash and exposed to a horrified world. As well as forcing Jews to scrub anti-Nazi slogans off the streets with buckets of water that had been laced with acid, elderly Jewish women were made to climb into the trees of Vienna's Prater Park and ordered to sing like birds; and others were coerced into cleaning toilets with their sacred prayer bands. Such public atrocities, and the unfavourable international publicity that they attracted, were displeasing to Heydrich, who insisted that persecution of Austria's Jews should be carried out in a 'rational' and 'orderly' way, with the emphasis placed at first on stealing Jewish economic assets. The horrors of the Holocaust would follow as night follows day.

Canaris, too, was swiftly on the scene in Vienna, together with a team of Abwehr agents. His motivation, as so often, was twofold: offensive and defensive. He was anxious to absorb the Austrian intelligence service into the Abwehr before Heydrich could get his territorial hands on it. He also wanted to take control of the spy service's extensive archives, again, before Heydrich could lay eyes on them. The admiral was worried that scrutiny of the Austrian archives would reveal his own contacts with intelligence chiefs in central and Eastern Europe that could be interpreted as potentially treasonous.

By the time of the Anschluss, Canaris's disillusion with the methods and character of his former protégé had turned to definite disgust. One key element in his awakening was a manoeuvre that Heydrich had practised in his ever-growing effort to exponentially extend his empire. According to post-war reports by survivors, Heydrich had innocently asked Canaris for examples of the signatures of leading Soviet generals, so that he could append them to forged documents in order to frame the commanders in Stalin's eyes, and so trigger a purge of the Red Army's High Command and thus weaken the Soviet forces ahead of the great battle with Russia that Hitler was already planning. Another report alleges that Heydrich's men broke into the Abwehr HQ in order to steal the signatures. It is certainly unlikely that Canaris would have handed them over voluntarily as he would have seen this as Heydrich trespassing on his turf, thus transgressing the Ten Commandments deal between them that divvied up their responsibilities for foreign intelligence and internal security respectively.

If the story is to be believed, Heydrich duly forged the signatures of the generals – including that of Marshal Tukhachevsky, the Soviet Union's leading soldier – and passed papers implicating the generals in a plot to stage a coup and overthrow Stalin to the Vojenské Zpravodajství, the Czech military intelligence service, who duly passed them on to Moscow. It is certain that in June 1937, Stalin had Tukhachevsky and seven other leading generals arrested, accused of treason and espionage, tortured and shot – the beginning of his purge of the Red Army's hierarchy that would eventually see a staggering 35,000 officers executed – including 90 per cent of the General Staff.

When Canaris heard of the purge he was allegedly horrified by the bloodshed and the massacre of men who may have been Russian Communists but who were fellow members of the officer caste. Putting two and two together, he went to Heydrich and asked if he had had any hand in tricking Stalin into launching the murderous purge. When Heydrich admitted to his share of responsibility Canaris was reported by colleagues to have been in a state of 'deep spiritual shock'. At a meeting with Conrad Patzig, his predecessor as head of the Abwehr, he expressed his feelings in no uncertain terms: 'From top to bottom they are all criminals who will bring Germany down.' If he felt that way, Patzig asked, how could he remain as the Abwehr's chief? Canaris replied: 'It is my destiny. If I go, Heydrich will take over and then we are all lost. I must sacrifice myself.'

CHAPTER EIGHT

SPIES IN THE HOUSE OF LOVE

– Converting a brothel into a spy centre

As the main man tasked by Heydrich with setting up and running Salon Kitty, Walter Schellenberg is tantalisingly elusive, and typically sparse with concrete information about the spy brothel in his self-serving post-war memoirs, posthumously published in 1956. He devotes only a couple of pages to the enterprise. Schellenberg was writing against the clock in 1950, as he was already ill with the liver cancer that would kill him in 1952. His motive – as well as providing an income for his widow – was to present his role as one of the surviving top officials in the Nazi intelligence services in as favourable a light as possible, minimising his part in atrocities, and not hesitating to paint his Nazi superiors – particularly Himmler and Heydrich – as the villains of the piece, especially as they were both conveniently dead.

Nevertheless, as the distinguished British historian and Hitler biographer Alan Bullock writes in his introduction to the English translation of the book, despite these caveats:

Schellenberg, with all his faults (and they are plain enough to need no underlining), had two rare qualities as a writer of memoirs. For the most part he limits himself to describing events of which he has first-hand knowledge, and he is comparatively free from that passion for tortuous self-justification which disfigures so many German memoirs of these years. What drove him to write was the desire to recapture, not to disown, the sensations of power and importance. It is this lack of self-consciousness, damning as a revelation of character, which makes him the more valuable as a historical witness.

It is entirely possible that Heydrich picked Schellenberg for the Salon Kitty job precisely because he suspected his subordinate of having an affair with his own wife and assigned him the task for reasons of warped revenge. Certainly, Schellenberg suspected this: 'Unknown to me, however, he was using the new relationship between his wife and me to set a trap.' Schellenberg relates that Heydrich would invite him round to his home for cosy evenings playing bridge in what Heydrich called with sickening sentimentality 'the dear intimacy of the family circle'.

According to Schellenberg, on the very next evening after these convivial occasions, he would get a call from his boss with his voice making a 'suggestive leer', proposing a very different type of entertainment: 'This evening we must go out together – in mufti. We'll have dinner together and then . . . "go places."' During dinner, writes Schellenberg, Heydrich's conversation would become ever more obscene, and then, 'He would try to make me drunk as we prowled from bar to bar.' According to Schellenberg, however, he stoutly resisted his chief's temptations, made his excuses not to join Heydrich on a brothel crawl, and went faithfully home to his new wife.

Be that as it may, Schellenberg says that it was on one such convivial evening that Heydrich came up with the idea of turning a brothel into an espionage centre. His account states that Heydrich's original plan was for the SD to spy on VIP visitors from abroad and

> . . . set up an establishment where . . . they could be 'entertained' in a discreet atmosphere and where they would be offered seductive feminine companionship. In such an atmosphere the most rigid diplomat might be induced to unbend and reveal useful information.

Heydrich evidently gave further thought on how best to develop the scheme, for shortly afterwards he summoned Schellenberg to his office to give him the official order to set up the 'establishment'. For, as Schellenberg puts it: 'the increasing number of visiting foreign diplomats and their entourages made some such place almost a social necessity. The establishment was to be called Salon Kitty.'

Schellenberg is vague as to the details of how he set to work. He merely states that 'a large house was rented in a fashionable district of Berlin. The furnishing and decoration were supervised by a leading architect.' Once a suitably comfortable ambience had been created, the SD's eavesdropping technicians, already skilled in bugging operations, went to work. At least three SD technicians, sworn to secrecy not to reveal what they (over)heard, were on permanent duty in the basement to monitor the operation. Kitty Schmidt, whom Schellenberg does not identify, calling her the 'ostensible owner' of the brothel, 'was provided with the necessary domestic and catering staff for the establishment to be able to offer the best service, food, and drink'.

With a shudder of bourgeois distaste, Schellenberg claimed that he declined the mucky job of actually recruiting the twenty spy 'hostesses' who would staff the brothel: 'I refused to have anything to do with this. As I pointed out to Heydrich my department supplied only the most valuable of women agents and I could not afford to assign them to such work.' Instead, he alleges, the dirty work was given to Arthur Nebe, chief of the Kripo.

Nebe was a logical choice because he had already had plenty of experience of dealing with Berlin's sexual underworld. Besides, by the time Schellenberg wrote his memoir, Nebe too, like Himmler and Heydrich, was safely dead. Having taken a prominent part in commanding one of the *Einsatzgruppen* – the extermination squads that had murdered thousands of Polish Jews in the early stages of the Holocaust – the amoral Nebe, like Canaris, had tried to ensure his future by getting involved with the anti-Hitler conspirators planning the July 1944 plot to assassinate the Führer, and had been executed for his pains.

Intriguingly, Schellenberg alleges that Nebe cast his net wide in his search for suitable hostesses:

From all the great cities of Europe he recruited the most highly qualified and cultivated ladies of the demi-monde, and, I regret to say that quite a few ladies from the upper crust of German society were only too willing to serve their country in this matter.

It can be assumed that these *Belle de Jour*-style amateurs were dedicated Nazis willing to do the party's bidding and combine pleasure with their duty as loyal citizens of the Reich. Doubtless Nebe also recruited professional prostitutes prepared or compelled to mix their usual duties with espionage.

According to Peter Norden's 1970 book *Madam Kitty*, Schellenberg appointed one of his underlings named Untersturmführer Karl Schwarz as his executive officer to assist him in the task of converting an ordinary high-class brothel into a sophisticated espionage centre and listening post. Bearing in mind that Norden described his book as a 'documentary novel', we think it possible that 'Schwarz' was a fictitious persona invented by Norden to cover up the actual involvement of Alfred Naujocks in the project.

The first post-war reference to Salon Kitty in a published book came in 1952 (the year of Schellenberg's death) in the memoirs of Heinrich Himmler's masseur Felix Kersten. The masseur recounts being invited to visit the brothel by Heydrich, who boasted of being able to hear the unguarded comments of the 'gentlemen' visiting the salon.

The German journalist and author Klaus Harpprecht had an interview with Kitty Schmidt shortly before her death in 1954 in which she admitted the existence of listening bugs in her salon. All nine of the establishment's 'love rooms' were fitted with tiny microphones. Naturally, said Kitty, according to Harpprecht, all the young ladies working there were aware of the bugs but were under strict orders not to share that knowledge with their clients. Whether or not this is true, we cannot be sure. A main plotline in Tinto Brass's controversial *Salon Kitty* movie of 1976, relies on one of the girls *not* knowing about the microphones.

In an article for *Stern* magazine, in 1959, the journalists Michael Löhde and Wolfgang Horbach went into more technical detail in describing the setting up of the eavesdropping operation. They wrote that in obedience to Heydrich's orders, and under the technical direction of Alfred Naujocks, long cables linked to the microphones were hidden under carpets, behind picture frames and in cupboards. Some fifty microphones were in turn concealed in lampshades, behind paintings, under tables and in vases of flowers, not only in the bedrooms but also in the reception area and lobby of Giesebrechtstrasse 11. In addition, hidden cameras were also placed in almost all the rooms. A changing cast of between two and five SD officials were on permanent duty in the cellar beneath the house to monitor the recordings.

The overheard conversations were recorded on large wax discs some fifty centimetres wide. When such a disc was 'full' it was dated and numbered and despatched straight to the SS/SD Gestapo headquarters in Prinz-Albrecht-Strasse. Peter Norden estimated that as many as 3,000 discs were sent every month. In the two and a half years that the monitoring operation continued, he writes, around 70–80,000 discs were made.

Norden further claims that after each sexual encounter, the woman concerned had to make a full report of her conversation with her client to her SD handlers, which was compared to the recordings to check they were fully accurate. The spies in the cellar, according to Norden, were members of the technical and signals branch of the Waffen-SS, under the supervision of an officer from Heydrich's newly created umbrella intelligence organisation, the RSHA.

Heydrich's rival intelligence chief, Admiral Wilhelm Canaris, head of the Abwehr, was distinctly dubious about the value of the intelligence gleaned from the Salon Kitty operation. When informed of Heydrich's set-up at the salon, he told one of his agents:

> Firstly, I couldn't agree to send an Abwehr officer to a brothel, and secondly, I cannot imagine that a diplomat, while enjoying horizontal sex with a girl, would break off to discuss his country's military plans, and then renew horizontal relations.

The one-time janitor at Giesebrechtstrasse 11, Walter Loll, was strictly forbidden – for reasons he was not given – to enter the house's cellar during the war years. His stepson Eberhard Rick, in an interview with the authors in 2016, said: 'He would always tell us that he was not allowed to go near there.' Another witness, Karin Zickerick, whose grandparents lived at Giesebrechtstrasse 11, and who she would frequently visit as a young girl, told us:

I remember once when I was sick. It was a very cold winter, the upper floors of the house had been damaged by a bomb, and the heating system was naturally no longer functioning. My grandfather made up a bed in the cellar for me, and I slept there for a couple of weeks. It was at least warm down there. I didn't see any listening equipment. But there were many cellars below the building and it's certainly possible that one of them was closed to us.

It is equally likely that the listening operation had been wound up and the equipment removed by the time of Karin's stay in the cellar.

During building maintenance work at Giesebrechtstrasse 11 in the 1960s, some strange and suspicious cables and containers were found in the cellars that were linked to the house's third storey. Eberhard Rick, who succeeded his stepfather Walter Loll as janitor in 1968, said that the cables were hidden inside the gas pipes that ran down to the cellar.

After the war, for entirely understandable reasons, it proved difficult to identify any of the ladies of the night who worked for the Nazis at Salon Kitty. We do, however, have the testimony from two survivors. One was a then 27-year-old woman called Liesel Ackermann who lived in Berlin's Schöneberg district. Throughout the war, from 1940 to 1945, Liesel worked at Salon Kitty as a call girl-style prostitute, being summoned to the brothel whenever a client had chosen her from the establishment's picture album. When not required at the salon, Liesel also worked on a casual basis at other Berlin brothels. In an interview in 1976 with the German news magazine *Der Spiegel*, Liesel claimed that the police had given her the choice of working at Salon Kitty or being employed at a factory making tank tracks for the Wehrmacht.

Describing her work after the war, Liesel said that she would be called to the Giesebrechtstrasse by telephone. Upon arrival she would dine and drink Sekt – the German version of Champagne – with the client in what she called a 'cultivated atmosphere'. 'Then,' she said discreetly, 'came the other thing.' Asked if she remembered the identity of her clients, Liesel recalled that one was the Italian Foreign Minister and Mussolini's son-in-law, Count Gian Galeazzo Ciano, who she described as a 'tender cavalier' who kept his black socks on even when they were in bed.

Ciano was a notable ladies' man who, as we have seen, as a young diplomat in China had allegedly enjoyed an affair with Mrs Wallis Simpson, the later Duchess of Windsor, and the cause of King Edward VIII's abdication in 1936. He continued his career as a prize philanderer despite his marriage to Mussolini's equally promiscuous elder daughter, Edda. On his appointment as Foreign Minister in 1936, he was widely assumed to be his father-in-law's favoured successor. Young, handsome and intelligent, Ciano was widely despised because of his vanity and arrogance.

His position and his closeness to Mussolini made Ciano a subject of interest to German intelligence, although many leading Germans shared Hitler's opinion of him as a 'repulsive kid'. One of the main objectives of Nazi foreign policy in the late 1930s was to cement Italy as their main ally in the European war that Hitler was planning. The two dictatorships shared their Fascist ideology, with its associated ruthlessness and propensity for violence. Ciano, however, was widely regarded as an unreliable partner. Although he admired the Nazis for their efficiency, he disliked the German national character, and became increasingly concerned that Italy, as Germany's junior partner, would be dragged into a conflict for which she was unprepared and could not hope to win.

Ciano graduated from merely grumbling about the alliance with Germany in his famous private diaries to actually working against the Axis. He even went so far as to warn Belgium in May 1940 that

Hitler was about to attack her. When, the following month, Mussolini declared war against Britain and France, the Foreign Minister wrote in his diary: 'I am sad, very sad . . . God help Italy.' As Ciano had foreseen, Italy's participation in the conflict proved disastrous. Her armies were defeated in the Balkans and North Africa, forcing Hitler to come to their rescue, and diverting the Wehrmacht from their main effort on the Eastern Front.

There is every reason, therefore, to believe that Ciano was indeed lured to Salon Kitty in the hope that he would be trapped into making indiscreet and damaging remarks that could be used against him. The Nazis were well aware that Ciano was both a secret enemy of theirs and an incorrigible womaniser. Before one of his several visits to Berlin, he had telegraphed ahead to the Italian consul-general in the city, Giuseppe Renzetti, with the imperious command: 'Provide women.' Women, including Liesel Ackermann, were duly 'provided'.

We don't know for sure whether Ciano's post-coital conversations with Liesel and other women he encountered in Berlin played a part in his eventual disgrace and downfall, but it is clear that the Nazis became increasingly distrustful of his steadily more overt opposition to the war. They applied pressure to Mussolini, and in 1943 he sacked his son-in-law as Foreign Minister, demoting him to Envoy to the Vatican's Holy See. On 24 July of that year, after the Allied invasion of Sicily, Ciano was one of the majority on the Fascist Grand Council in Rome who effectively voted to depose the Duce and return power to King Victor Emmanuel III.

The following day, Mussolini was arrested after an audience with the King. He was confined on two islands and then sent to a remote mountain hotel high in the Appenines. Hitler ordered German glider-borne commandos to stage a daring rescue mission and set the Duce up as the puppet ruler of a new Fascist state in northern Italy, which was still controlled by the Wehrmacht. Following the fall of Fascism in Rome, Ciano unwisely sought refuge in Germany with his family.

He was treated with contempt as a traitor and returned to the custody of his father-in-law. After a show trial in Verona in January 1944, he and four other members of the Grand Council who had voted against Mussolini were, on Hitler's insistence, summarily shot. The victims were tied to chairs with their backs to the firing squad to shame them.

Another client 'entertained' by Liesel Ackermann was General Friedrich 'Fritz' Fromm. A prominent Wehrmacht commander, Fromm was head of the army's armaments department until 1944 when he was appointed as Chief of the Reserve Home Army based at the Bendlerblock in Berlin. This force was intended to guard Germany's home front against possible insurrection and unrest, particularly by the large numbers of foreign slave workers who had been imported into the Reich to make up the labour shortfall caused by the absence of male Germans on the fighting fronts.

Fromm's subordinates, General Friedrich Olbricht and Colonel Count Claus von Stauffenberg, both convinced anti-Nazis, covertly altered an existing plan, codenamed 'Operation Valkyrie', to counter a possible rebellion by the foreign workers. Their scheme, 'Valkyrie II', was to use the Wehrmacht to seize control of the capital and other cities occupied by the Reich, including Paris and Prague, in a putsch carried out in conjunction with their assassination of Hitler. The idea was to arrest and neutralise loyalist Nazi units – primarily the SS – and set up a government to end Nazi rule and negotiate peace with the Allies.

Fromm was undoubtedly aware of the conspiracy being hatched under his nose, but he carefully held himself aloof. He, like Canaris, Helldorf and Nebe, was playing a double game. By ignoring the plotters' plans, he hoped to take advantage of them and keep his prominent position if the assassination plot succeeded. At the same time, by not taking an active part in the plot, he could claim not to have been involved if the assassination and putsch misfired – as it did.

When Stauffenberg's bomb exploded but failed to kill Hitler on

20 July 1944, Fromm quickly denounced the conspirators as traitors, and was briefly arrested by them. Released by pro-Nazi loyalist officers in the Bendlerblock, he held an impromptu drumhead court martial of Stauffenberg, Olbricht and the other leading plotters, and had them instantly shot in the Bendlerblock's courtyard. General Ludwig Beck, the army Chief of Staff who had resigned after the Fritsch–Blomberg affair in 1938, and who had been named by the plotters as their head of state if Hitler had died, was allowed by his old comrade Fromm to attempt a botched suicide before he too was shot.

Fromm's cowardly and clumsy attempt to exculpate himself from the consequences of the conspiracy failed miserably. When after the executions he went to see Goebbels to claim credit for crushing the conspiracy, the Propaganda Minister remarked acidly, 'You seem to have been in a damned hurry to get your witnesses below ground.' As the orders for Valkyrie II had gone out under Fromm's signature, which had been forged by the plotters, the Nazis were highly suspicious – their suspicions confirmed by the rapidity with which Fromm had ordered the permanent silencing of his inconvenient witnesses. The general was stripped of his rank, expelled from the army, accused of cowardice, and shot by firing squad in March 1945.

A third customer prominent in the Reich to have enjoyed Liesel's favours at Salon Kitty was Hans von Tschammer und Osten, the head of the Nazi state sports organisation within the Interior Ministry. Because organised sports played such a major role in National Socialist ideology, von Tschammer was far more important in the Reich than a mere civil servant. An early party member, he joined the SA and had a prominent role in preparing the 1936 Olympic Games in Berlin as a showcase for the 'new Germany'. He also played a leading part in transforming the Reich's sporting associations into military training outfits and organising war games in preparation for the coming conflict. Despite his enthusiasm for sport, the diminutive and balding von Tschammer was far from an athletic figure in person. Liesel had vivid memories of his physical deficiencies: 'He was so small!' she told *Der Spiegel*, '. . . and he had a crippled hand.' Von Tschammer did not survive the Reich, dying in 1943 from pneumonia.

A session with Liesel or her colleagues in Salon Kitty cost their clients 200 Reichsmarks – more than 800 euros in today's values. According to her recollections, the use of condoms was a compulsory condition of coition. Most of the 'gentlemen' visitors were respectable and dignified in their behaviour, she claimed, except for one occasion when a client, totally naked apart from wearing a dog collar and lead, attempted to crawl around the brothel on his hands and knees.

One of Liesel's regulars at the salon was a Count Hochberg, an officer and very much a gentleman as a wealthy member of the princely German–Polish Hochberg von Pless family. Liesel would be called to the Giesebrechtstrasse every Wednesday at noon for their encounters. According to her, the count became so besotted with her charms that he wanted to marry her. Describing her suitor as 'a little fat man with a red face', Liesel declined. Hochberg trusted Liesel enough to discuss political questions with her and expressed his feelings of guilt at having as a Gestapo member authorised and signed the death warrant of a Polish worker for the 'crime' of having a sexual relationship with a German woman.

A second surviving former prostitute who worked at the establishment in Giesebrechtstrasse under the Third Reich was interviewed anonymously in 2004 for a German TV documentary, *Salon Kitty*. This woman was working as a secretary in an electric motor factory when she was recruited as a sex worker towards the end of the war. By then Heydrich was dead, the salon had been badly damaged in an Allied bombing raid, and the SD's monitoring operation had apparently been recently wound up – though memories of it among the staff were still fresh. This anonymous surviving witness, by then in her eighties, remembered that the women who worked with her in the salon wore elegant cocktail dresses, and had been schooled in the ways of high society and the means of winkling secrets from their clients. Before beginning work at the salon, she said, she and her colleagues were asked about their attitude to Hitler and his rule, and she was sure that the regime made plenty of money from the wealthy clients. As for the bugging operation: 'There were listening devices in the house, I am one hundred per cent sure about that.'

Schellenberg is elusively discreet in his memoirs as to the content of the information picked up in Salon Kitty via the hidden microphones and the careless pillow talk imparted to the working girls. He does write that the bugging operation 'Certainly brought results – the most surprising information was yielded by some of the guests.' He adds that the information mainly concerned diplomatic secrets 'which Heydrich, with his usual astuteness, would use against Ribbentrop and his Foreign Ministry'.

Schellenberg also confirms that Count Ciano was one of these VIP clients who unwittingly divulged secrets. Mystified as to where the information was coming from, Ciano's counterpart, the German Foreign Minister von Ribbentrop – who had his own intelligence agency, the Ribbentrop Bureau – made futile efforts to find out, but the SD evaded all his inquiries so successfully that he was not even able to discover who owned the brothel. Ironically, Ribbentrop himself was one of Salon Kitty's VIP clients – without guessing that the source of secrets was the building that he himself frequented.

Schellenberg also reveals that Heydrich himself was a keen client of the brothel, disguising his visits there as 'tours of inspection'. 'On these occasions,' Schellenberg writes, 'I was given special orders to turn off the listening and recording apparatus.' According to his memoirs, Schellenberg's boss used this command as a trick to trap him in a 'characteristic intrigue'. To guard his own back, Schellenberg had taken the precaution of keeping Heydrich's boss Himmler fully informed of the Salon Kitty operation. Himmler, in his turn, kept a watching brief on his ambitious underling.

After one of his visits to the bordello, an angry Heydrich called Schellenberg into his office to complain that in spite of his 'strict orders' Schellenberg had failed to turn off the listening devices. 'I don't know how Himmler has got hold of the information, but he says that in spite of my orders you had the listening apparatus on when I visited "Salon Kitty",' Schellenberg reports Heydrich as saying. However, Schellenberg continues, the intrigue misfired because 'I immediately got sworn statements, which I put before Heydrich, from the entire technical staff, showing that I had carried out his orders.'

Having failed to entrap his subordinate in an act of direct insubordination, Heydrich tried a more drastic attempt to damage him. The background was a conference of SS and police leaders on the Baltic island of Fehmarn, where Lina Heydrich hailed from, and where the couple had a summer holiday villa. Following the conference, Heydrich flew himself back to Berlin in his personal plane while Schellenberg, who had a free day in hand, remained on Fehmarn as Lina's house guest. She invited Schellenberg to drive to the Plöner See, a large lake and beauty spot, where they enjoyed coffee and a discussion about music, art and literature. According to Schellenberg, they then drove back. This seemingly harmless excursion was to have dramatic consequences.

Four days later, Schellenberg was told by the sinister Heinrich 'Gestapo' Müller that Heydrich wanted him to accompany them on another round of Berlin nightspots dressed 'in mufti'. Schellenberg assumed that the outing would be yet another of their drinking and wenching evenings, and accepted the invitation 'without a thought'. Then, however, doubts crept in: 'As is often the case with people who continually feel their lives to be in danger, I was superstitious and had a rather uncomfortable premonition about the evening.'

Schellenberg's 'superstitions' were soon borne out. The evening began well enough, with Heydrich 'at his most charming'. Oddly, the SD chief did not want to hear, as he usually did, Schellenberg's latest intelligence reports and rumours, and said that for once they wouldn't speak of professional matters at all. After dining at an expensive restaurant, the trio made their way to a dim bar near the Alexanderplatz – before the war, Berlin's most notorious red-light district. 'I noticed . . .' Schellenberg commented primly for a secret service chief '. . . that the barman looked a most sinister individual.' He continued:

Müller ordered the drinks and handed me mine. Our conversation was casual, mainly about Heydrich's private plane, until suddenly Müller said to me, 'Well, how was it at the Plöner Lake? Did you have a good time?' I looked at Heydrich: his face was very pale. I quickly pulled myself together and asked him if he wanted to know about my excursion with his wife.

In a 'cold, sibilant voice', Schellenberg goes on, Heydrich said: 'You have just drunk some poison. It could kill you within six hours. If you tell me the complete and absolute truth, I'll give you an antidote – but I want the truth.' Though claiming that he did not believe a word of Heydrich's weird threat, putting it down to one of his boss's 'grisly jokes', Schellenberg still felt badly rattled.

I felt the tension within me expanding till it seemed as though my heart was ready to burst. But I had nothing to hide, and speaking as calmly as I could I told him truthfully about the events of that afternoon.

As though playing the 'good cop, bad cop' routine, it was 'Gestapo' Müller who quizzed him most intensively about Schellenberg's story, pointing out that his account had left out a walk he had taken with Lina after their coffee: 'Why did you hide that? You must have realised that you were being watched the whole time.' After Schellenberg had stuttered out an explanation, Heydrich 'sat motionless and withdrawn for several minutes'. Then: 'At last he looked at me with glittering eyes and said, "Well, I suppose I must believe you, but you will give me your word of honour that you won't attempt this sort of escapade again."'

Nettled by his boss's aggressive attitude, Schellenberg says that he hotly defended his honour: 'A word of honour secured in this way is just extortion. First, I must ask you to let me have the antidote.' Though claiming that he didn't believe in Heydrich's poison story, Schellenberg adds cautiously: 'It was always best to be on the safe side when dealing with Heydrich.' Schellenberg then appealed to Heydrich's own sense of honour as a former naval officer.

> Heydrich eyed me narrowly. He hated an appeal to his honour, but he nodded and I was given – somewhat to my surprise – a Dry Martini. Was it my imagination or did it taste peculiar? Certainly it seemed to have added an extra dash of bitters. I gave Heydrich my word of honour, then in view of what had passed between us I begged to be excused. But he wouldn't hear of it, and we had to continue the evening's merrymaking. Once more he had failed to entrap me.

Heydrich, however, usually got his man, and so it was to prove with Schellenberg. The means of entrapping him was via his new second marriage. As we have seen, Schellenberg had dumped his first, working-class wife in 1938 as her low social status was considered unsuitable for the rising Nazi star. But his second wife, a tall blonde woman named Irene Grosse-Schönepauck, though more socially acceptable, proved problematic for a different reason. On his engagement in 1940, as a prominent member of the SS, Schellenberg had to submit his fiancée's antecedents for examination in order to obtain an *Ariernachweis* – a certificate testifying to her Aryan racial 'purity'. The examination discovered that Irene's mother had suspiciously Polish racial origins.

Unwisely, Schellenberg took his problem to Heydrich, requesting his boss's help in getting Irene a clean bill of racial health from Himmler. Somewhat to his surprise, Heydrich agreed. Within four days, Himmler gave his official permission for the wedding to go ahead, and Heydrich returned his successful application to Schellenberg together with his best wishes. Schellenberg noticed that on the application form Himmler had marked Irene's lips and eyebrows on her photos with a green crayon, noting that they were 'exaggerated'!

Some six months later, Schellenberg was handed a top secret dossier from 'Gestapo' Müller containing the Gestapo report on his wife, based on a detailed surveillance of her family in Poland. The report revealed that Schellenberg's mother-in-law's sister was married to a Jewish mill owner. By this means – gaining knowledge that Schellenberg was distantly related, albeit by marriage, to a Jew – Heydrich had now got a hold over his talented underling. 'Now,' comments Schellenberg, 'he was satisfied and stopped all other efforts to entrap me.'

Obviously we have no independent way to check whether Schellenberg's stories of his treatment at Heydrich's hands are true, and it was clearly in his interests to distance himself from his former chief's vicious and murderous ways. However, the anecdotes fit well with Heydrich's known behaviour to even those closest to him. Taken together, Schellenberg's accounts ring true and give a vivid impression of the viper's nest that held even the most senior members of the Nazi terror apparatus in terrified thrall.

Chapter Nine

ON THE TRAIL OF KITTY SCHMIDT
– The quest for a woman of mystery

Owing to the lack of much primary source material, the life of the woman at the very centre of the story of Salon Kitty – Kitty Zammit Schmidt herself – can only be traced in outline, rather than told in detail. None of the usual materials used by biographers, such as exchanges of letters or diaries, exist. Nevertheless, our research has turned up enough previously unpublished source material to enable us to present an accurate sketch – rather than a fully documented account – of the course of Kitty's life. For example, thanks to a descendant, Irena Matei-Peraic, the wife of Kitty's grandson, we discovered in Slovenia in 2016 a veritable hoard of more than 500 family photographs and a revealing postcard written by Kitty. In addition, we have turned up a wealth of official documents such as birth certificates, death notices and changes of address.

In particular, in reconstructing an authentic picture of the life of the former brothel keeper, the memories and comments of her grandson Jochem Matei in various interviews have been of enormous value to us. Kitty's daughter Kathleen refused to co-operate in any way with previous authors, journalists and other media in an attempt to protect the privacy of her family. Kathleen's son Jochem Matei, by contrast, adopted a rather different attitude, even when in telling his stories about his grandmother a number of dramatic and even theatrical scenes were revealed. In addition to this, as the years went by, other accounts emerged from Kitty's friends, acquaintances and other witnesses in memoirs and interviews to fill out the picture.

Especially valuable to us were the childhood memories of Karin Zickerick, whose grandfather Fritz Hanslok was the janitor at Giesebrechtstrasse 11, and who observed with some surprise Kitty's comings and goings. Karin was the sole surviving eyewitness from the era of Salon Kitty that we were able to interview. In the following account we reconstruct the childhood and youth of Kitty – or 'Kätchen', as she was formally named. We then trace her progress to maturity, and her transformation to brothel madam, as well as our estimation of the probable role that she and her salon played under National Socialism.

Kätchen Emma Sophie Schmidt was born in Hamburg on 25 June 1882. She was the second eldest daughter of the salesman Johannes Andreas Theodor Schmidt and his wife Emma. Kitty grew up in the port city of Hamburg with her two elder siblings Elsa and Hans Ernst Ludwig, and her five younger siblings Gertrud Annita Emilie Elisabeth, Gertrud Catherina Marie, Lilli Ida Helene Ernestine, Walter Ernst Emil and Curt Francois Ludwig.

When she was just three years old Kitty suffered the first of the many blows that fate would deal her. Her younger sister Gertrud Annita died aged only nine months. When Kitty was seven, another younger sister, Lilli, also died in infancy at three and a half months. Kitty was twenty-six when her father died on Christmas Day 1908 aged sixty-four. Ten years later, in 1918, her brother Walter Ernst Emil died in a military field hospital in northern Italy – probably he was mortally wounded and taken prisoner while on active service in the First World War. Kitty's mother Emma Schmidt, by contrast, lived a long life, dying aged eighty in Hamburg on 14 November 1940 of stomach cancer. We know nothing of the relationship between Kitty and her parents. However, Kitty enjoyed close contact as an adult with at least two of her sisters, known to Jochem Matei as 'Aunt Elsa' and 'Aunt Trudel'. Elsa lived with Kitty in Berlin until her death in 1952.

Kitty grew up in Hamburg in an apartment at Holzdamm 37. One of her childhood playmates was the well-known German actor and singer Hans Albers (1891–1960). Albers became a leading star of stage and screen under the Weimar Republic, playing opposite Marlene Dietrich in the film *The Blue Angel*. According to Jochem Matei, in a TV interview in 1996, the young Hans wanted to marry Kitty. Interestingly, his actual lifelong partner was the Jewish actress Hansi Burg. When the Nazis came to power the couple tried to live a quiet life in rural Bavaria, but the regime's increasing anti-Semitism forced Hansi to flee to Switzerland in 1939, and from there she emigrated to Britain. The couple remained in covert contact, and the wealthy Albers was even able to send financial support to his lover in exile. They reunited after the war when Hansi returned to Germany in British uniform, and remained together until Albers' death, which was exacerbated by his alcoholism. Under the Third Reich, Albers was able to continue his acting career in non-political roles, and never lent public support to the Nazi regime. He died after suffering a haemorrhage on a theatre stage, and is buried in Hamburg.

According to Jochem Martei, early in the twentieth century, when she was in her early twenties, Kitty travelled to Britain to work as a piano teacher. While there, she met and married the love of her life, a Spaniard called Zammit. A Spanish diplomat named Jorge Zammit was appointed Vice-Consul in Cardiff in 1862, and it is likely that Kitty's lover was the son or nephew of this man. Sadly, we know nothing more of Zammit junior, beyond the fact that he later shot himself. The reasons for his suicide remain unknown.

On 15 October 1906, aged twenty-four, Kitty gave birth to her only child, a daughter named Kathleen, in Cardiff. At the time of the birth she was still single, and the child was registered as Kathleen Schmidt, though Kitty apparently married Zammit soon afterwards. As we don't know the exact date of Kitty's arrival in Britain, it is possible that she had already been made pregnant in Germany and was sent to Britain by her bourgeois family to hide the 'disgrace' of an unmarried woman expecting a child, and that Zammit was not Kathleen's biological father.

At all events, it is clear that Kitty's time in Britain was difficult. She was working as a governess as well as giving piano lessons while caring for her young daughter. Her grandson Jochem Martei recalled her saying that she was struggling financially, and even that Kathleen was sent to play down a Welsh coal mine. She was still in Britain when the First World War broke out in 1914. Anti-German prejudice was strong, with German-owned shops attacked by mobs and innocent Germans accused of being spies, and it is likely that Kitty and Kathleen suffered as a result in this toxic atmosphere. Kitty lost no time at the end of the war when travel became possible to go back to her native land. She was prompted to leave after her sister Elsa wrote a postcard encouraging Kitty to return to Germany with the words: 'Dear Kitty, Come with Kathleen to Berlin. The streets here are paved with gold.'

Kitty obediently followed this optimistic advice and journeyed to Berlin within weeks of the war ending. But far from the gold-paved streets described by her sister, she found a city in crisis and near civil war. The revolution that had caused the collapse of Imperial Germany and the flight of the Kaiser into exile had been followed by bitter political division and attempted revolts by Berlin's strong Spartacist Communist movement. After the leftist insurrections had been bloodily crushed in 1919 by the Freikorps units called into being by the new Social Democratic government, with hundreds killed, the Freikorps themselves attempted and failed to seize power in the Kapp Putsch of March 1920.

The political chaos was accompanied by deep social unrest. As depicted in the stark drawings of George Grosz, Berlin's streets were thronged by crippled and starving ex-soldiers and young women forced to earn a crust as sex workers. But amidst this near anarchy there were upsides and opportunities for ambitious and emancipated women like Kitty. Women, emboldened by the huge social changes wrought by the war, fought to assert themselves in a new order where they were no longer expected to stay quietly at home. Indeed, sheer economic necessity compelled them to find their places in a new world of work.

Many women asserted their new self-confident roles by wearing bold fashions and hairstyles. Symbols of liberated womanhood included cigarettes smoked in elegant long holders, shorter skirt lengths and bobbed hairstyles, long pearl necklaces, feather boas and decorated headbands. The nightlife of the 'Roaring Twenties' was variously portrayed as obscene, freewheeling and musical. In no other German city was this new liberated lifestyle practised more openly and frenetically than in Berlin. Alcohol and cigarettes fuelled the indulgence; Black Jack and Roulette were played at the gaming tables; and the Charleston, Shimmy and Foxtrot were tirelessly danced. What had once been regarded as mere vulgarity now strode the streets and cafés in proud demonstrations of a new feminism. One of the most prominent features of these new freedoms were open displays of female sexuality. It was in these years of the early Twenties, that Kitty Schmidt began to move into the world of Berlin nightlife that would lead her to grasp the business opportunities opening up in paid-for love.

Kitty was becoming one of the leading personalities in the ranks of these self-confident, strong, independent and dynamic women. Among her friends was the famous theatre and film actress

Hilde Hildebrand (1897–1976). Under the Third Reich, Hilde starred opposite Kitty's childhood friend Hans Albers in the film *Grosse Freiheit No. 7* (1944) known as *Port of Freedom* in English. A romantic musical comedy, set in the Reeperbahn red-light district of Hamburg where Kitty and Albers had grown up, and generously financed by Goebbels' Propaganda Ministry with 1.5 million Reichsmarks, the film was one of the escapist movies produced at the height of the war in an attempt to make the German people forget their mounting troubles. Despite having funded the film, however, Goebbels decided that the movie did not meet the exacting standards of National Socialist ideology and banned its distribution.

In 1918 or 1919 Kitty began to rent out rooms. Some of her tenants were 'working girls' for whom she felt a degree of responsibility to look after their welfare. At first Kitty lived with her thirteen-year-old daughter Kathleen at Berliner Strasse 10 in the Wilmersdorf district of the city. At some point in the decade between 1922 and 1932 she opened her first 'salon' as a business at her new home address – Budapester Strasse 27. In her official registration Kitty described herself as an 'artist'. But this first venture into the brothel business did not last long. Two years after opening her doors Kitty was forced to close the salon because she had failed to obtain a licence to sell alcohol on the premises.

Undaunted by this setback, in 1935 – after the advent of the Third Reich – Kitty moved upmarket to open a new salon on west Berlin's most exclusive boulevard at Kurfürstendamm 63. She thinly disguised the true nature of the establishment by describing her business as a *Fremdenheim* (hostel) on official documentation. Sometime in 1939 she moved the brothel round the corner from the 'Ku'damm' to its final home – Giesebrechtstrasse 11. At first, she only occupied a flat on the third storey of the substantial house on the quiet, leafy street with Kathleen. Later, she expanded the brothel to occupy both the ground floor and two apartments on the second floor. The rapid expansion of the brothel suggests that Kitty's business was proving extremely profitable. Indeed, she may have graduated from merely renting the building to buying it outright. Jochem Matei remembers being told by his mother Kathleen: 'Grandma paid a hundred thousand marks for this house. Therefore we must be very grateful to her that we can rent our rooms here so cheaply. Otherwise we would have to pay all the high maintenance costs ourselves.' Since 1939 was the year that Heydrich and the SD probably took over the running of Salon Kitty as an espionage centre, handing themselves a substantial slice of its profits, it is likely that they footed the bill for refurbishing the establishment.

Nineteen thirty-nine was also the year that, according to Peter Norden in his book, Kitty Schmidt made her abortive attempt to escape the Third Reich by trying to flee with a falsified passport to the Netherlands, with the aim of emigrating to Britain and opening a new business there. Norden also alleges that Kitty financed her escape attempt in advance by transferring large sums of money to England – at first legally, and later illegally by sending her working girls to London with banknotes sewn into their underwear. Apart from possible political motives, if Kitty really opened a bank account in Britain, the Wall Street Crash of 1929 and the subsequent depreciation of Germany's currency and the onset of the Great Depression made such a move an intelligent business decision. It is certain that, despite her previously unhappy experience of life in Britain, Kitty kept up contact with the country in the 1930s and travelled with her daughter to the land of Kathleen's birth. Sadly, a photograph of a smiling Kitty and Kathleen – by then in her twenties – dressed expensively, strolling along a seaside promenade in England, proved to have been taken on the North Sea island of Sylt.

Her newfound wealth enabled Kitty to maintain a high-society lifestyle and keep up with the latest modish fashions. Photos taken of her between the world wars suggest that she modelled herself on the popular film stars of the era. She particularly favoured the masculine suits made fashionable in the movies of Marlene Dietrich, and later sported the wide-brimmed hats worn by Greta Garbo. Karin Zickerick, who often visited her caretaker grandfather at Giesebrechtstrasse 11 as a child, remembers Kitty as a 'very strong woman, but very sympathetic and sweet . . . imposing, but not so as to inspire fear, absolutely not . . . actually, she was a very natural person, and I still recall that she always presented an impressive appearance.' Kitty's sister Elsa, who acted as housekeeper in the establishment, baking biscuits there, also recorded positive memories of her sibling.

Another neighbour, Evelyn Künneke (1921–2001), characterised Kitty as 'a composed, well cared for, very nice woman'. Evelyn Künneke moved into Giesebrechtstrasse 5, almost opposite Salon Kitty, in 1939, together with her father, the celebrated composer of operettas Eduard Künneke (1885–1953). An early Nazi Party member, Eduard Künneke was expelled from the party in 1934 after he was found to be of 'non-Aryan' (Jewish) descent. However, because his operettas, marches and film music were considered to be of propaganda value to the regime, he enjoyed the protection of Goebbels and remained unmolested to the end of the Reich. A plaque on his house in the Giesebrechtstrasse today commemorates his residence there.

Evelyn Künneke, who herself became a well-known singer and actress, recalled in a TV documentary on Salon Kitty in 1994 a friendly encounter when she was in her early twenties with the brothel's madam, during which Kitty tried to recruit her to the brothel's 'staff':

> During the war I had to bring a letter from someone – I no longer remember from who – to Frau Kitty Schmidt. She invited me in for a chat. Then she asked me if I might perhaps be interested in working in her establishment and earning good money. Unfortunately I said that I'd rather not. In those days I was still too dumb to accept.

A married couple, Hans and Magda Frintrop, who lived at Giesebrechtstrasse 10 from 1942, also only reported good things about their former neighbour. Magda Frintrop told another TV documentary in 2004: 'She was the ideal of a friendly older lady, always ready to help. Once my parents came early on a visit when I was out and before I was ready to receive them. Kitty said to them, "Oh, I'll take you. Come with me." So she took them in so that they didn't have to wait in the street. She was always friendly, I must say.'

Jochem Matei recalled her as 'very thrifty': a woman who despite her wealth would always prefer to take a bus rather than ride in a taxi.

> She didn't smoke. She always said: 'Why should I blow my money away into the air? That's just too dear for me. I'd rather save it.' Yes, Grandma was a very, very thrifty woman . . . She kept her money in a vase, or stuck it into her stockings just like Marlene Dietrich in *The Blue Angel*.

According to Matei, Kitty had only one weakness: she couldn't bear being alone. He said: 'She always had to have activity going on around her, and that's why she opened her salon in the Budapester Strasse, then on the Kurfürstendamm, and later in the Giesebrechtstrasse . . .'

A graphological analysis of the handwriting on a surviving postcard written by Kitty reveals her masterful character to be 'optimistic, temperamental and self-controlled'. The card, probably written during the war to an unknown woman she addresses as 'Uschylein' ('little Ursula') gives a glimpse of her busy social life and reads:

> Dear Uschylein! I was very pleased to get your letter, and happy that you had luck, but don't be so reckless with the clothes. It's boring here, but I actually feel very well, (and) play lots of tennis. The main thing is to earn money and I can save well here. What's Otto doing? Jean often calls me from Hamburg

in the evenings . . . He has fantastic engagements, earns lots of cash. Many warm greetings, your Kitty.

The 'Jean' referred to is probably Kitty's son-in-law, Jean-Florian Matei, Jochem's father, who met Kathleen in 1938 and died in December 1945.

We can discover quite a lot about Kitty from the few lines of this card. We learn that despite being aged around sixty, she is still healthy, sporty, and a keen regular tennis player. We understand that her brothel business is flourishing and profitable and – bearing out the testimony of her grandson Jochem – that she is indeed very thrifty. The postcard also lets us know that in all probability she had a close and warm relationship with her son-in-law Jean-Florian.

Nevertheless, and despite such clues, much about Kitty Schmidt's life and personality, and the circumstances of her death, remains murky and mysterious. In particular, we know next to nothing about her during the decade from the end of the Second World War to her passing, which her official death certificate tells us occurred early on 23 February 1954 in her flat at Giesebrechtstrasse 11 when Kitty was aged seventy-one. An office colleague of Kitty's named Otto Werrstein reported her demise at 6am on the day of her death. The death certificate lists the cause of her passing as a stroke or brain haemorrhage aggravated by heart disease and circulatory insufficiency.

Kitty's funeral and burial took place four days after her death, at 11am on 27 February 1954 in Berlin's Waldfriedhof cemetery on Heerstrasse. The ceremony was evidently a major event attended by many hundreds of her friends, colleagues and customers who had known her during her last years. In a report later that year a journalist speaks of 'thousands' of people following Kitty's coffin to her final resting place. A few days after the funeral, on 3 March 1954, *Der Spiegel* described Kitty thus:

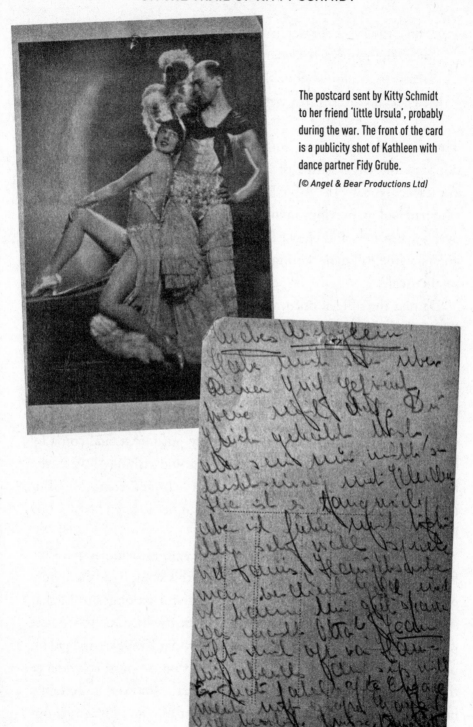

The postcard sent by Kitty Schmidt to her friend 'little Ursula', probably during the war. The front of the card is a publicity shot of Kathleen with dance partner Fidy Grube.

(© Angel & Bear Productions Ltd)

...since the 1920s she was in international, especially diplomatic, circles, the renowned owner of an establishment modelled on Parisian examples where chivalrous favoured foreign guests of the Federal Government were offered entertainment...

This discreet euphemism surely left *Der Spiegel's* readers in little doubt as to the real nature of the 'entertainment' offered to guests at Giesebrechtstrasse 11. After her mother's death, Kathleen Matei – who had had no previous involvement in running the brothel – took over the business and converted it into a hostel catering to 'artistic' guests, while still maintaining the brothel business on a discreet and smaller scale.

Despite the official documentation, in a 1995 interview, Jochem Matei vigorously denied both the cause and the location of his grandmother's death, which he claimed was not attributable to natural causes. According to Matei, Kitty had become seriously ill in November 1953. After suffering a stroke, she was admitted to her local hospital in Wilmersdorf – the Martin Luther Krankenhaus – where Jochem believes she was deliberately put into a fatal coma by her doctors. He remembers as a twelve-year-old visiting Kitty in the hospital: 'Both doctors said, "Come, Frau Schmidt, stand up!" But my granny couldn't stand, and they then put her to sleep because she had certain legal rights to her house.'

Jochem Matei privately named five people as being responsible for Kitty Schmidt's death. The authors of this book have the names of those he accused, but for legal reasons and lacking any further supporting evidence, we cannot make them public. Our own latest research has turned up no evidence to show that Kitty was the victim of a murder plot. Similarly, we have found no supporting evidence that Matei was cheated out of his inheritance. However, he certainly believed that there was a conspiracy to cheat him and his family out of their share in the valuable house. In an article in 1992, published in the *Berliner Morgenpost* newspaper, Matei wrote: 'I was cheated out of my inheritance. My grandmother once owned the whole house. Then financial interests got involved and my mother, who couldn't pay the legal costs, was talked into losing it all.' In the same year, 1992, Jochem Matei still retained links with the property and was listed as running a hostel for asylum seekers on the ground floor.

Unfortunately, we have found no official documentation to show who owned the property during Kitty's last years and at the time of her death. However, there are indications in statements from two witnesses from that time that suggest that at some point, she was indeed the actual legal owner and not merely its manager. Karin Zickerick, the daughter of the property's caretaker, told the authors in a 2017 interview: 'The house belonged to Kitty for a long time. As far as I know she bought it.' Berno von Cramm, who lived at Giesebrechtstrasse 11 for many years from 1965 to 1984 when Kathleen Matei was also living there and who became a good friend of the family, believes that Kathleen sold her mother's property rights to the house, but retained the right to live there during her lifetime. The likelihood that Kitty or her daughter sold the house is supported by the fact that a ground-plan of the property, published on 2 April 1954 – five weeks after Kitty's death – shows the owners of the house as being the furniture and property firm Hackenberger and Loll.

Precisely how Kitty Schmidt spent her final years after the capitulation of the Third Reich in 1945 is still obscure. Almost all the existing documentation on her and her salon – in films, documentaries, memoirs and press interviews – concentrates on the time before the end of the Second World War. Even the private interviews with Jochem Matei in the 1990s, conducted by his friend Manuel Stahl, shed little light on the post-war years. As Jochem was just twelve when his grandmother died, what scant knowledge he possessed is based on hearsay or remembered conversations with his mother Kathleen.

Among Kitty Schmidt's family archives is a coloured photograph of an oil painting showing Kitty in her prime. The picture clearly depicts her red hair and blue-green eyes. The location of the original painting is unknown after Jochem Matei sold it to a 'good family friend and customer'. In his book *Madam Kitty*, Peter Norden reproduced a black and white picture of another oil painting of the younger Kitty in a similar seated pose. The present whereabouts of this second picture, too, remains unknown. Kitty Schmidt has retreated without trace into the shadows from where she came.

CHAPTER TEN

KITTY SCHMIDT AND THE NAZIS

– Survivor, opportunist or collaborator?

Discrimination against and persecution of the Jews played a central role in the ideology and practice of National Socialism. Already in 1919 Hitler had announced that an 'anti-Semitism of feelings' must be replaced by an 'anti-Semitism of reason'. In his first surviving written political statement – a letter penned in September 1919, the same month that he enrolled in the German Workers' Party, predecessors of the Nazi NSDAP, when he was working as a spy for the German Reichswehr – Hitler wrote:

> Anti-Semitism as a political movement should not and cannot be manifested through momentary feelings, but rather through knowledge of actual facts . . . and therefore these consequences follow: Anti-Semitism based on measures arising from feelings finds expression in the form of Pogroms. (But) Anti-Semitism based on reason must lead to a Legal struggle and measures restricting the Rights of the Jews . . . its ultimate goal must be distancing from the Jews overall.

Jewish citizens in Nazi Germany were steadily deprived of their rights step by step. By means of laws and decrees they were put under ever increasing financial and economic pressure. From 1 January 1938, Jews were forbidden to work as salespeople and craft shop owners. In the same year systematic arrests were made of the 'workshy', 'asocials' and 'community aliens'. Reinhard Heydrich ordered every police station in the country to arrest at least two hundred males in these categories and send them to concentration camps. Thanks to this so-called 'June action', within a single week 10,000 people were detained, including 1,500 Jews.

Anti-Semitism climaxed on 9–10 November of that year in the 1938 *Reichskristallnacht* ('Night of Broken Glass') – so called because of the smashed windows of Jewish-owned stores that littered the streets after they had been trashed by Nazi mobs. During this pogrom across the Reich organised by the regime, 91 Jews were murdered, 30,000 sent to concentration camps, 267 synagogues were burned, 7,500 shops and businesses were looted, and 177 private homes were destroyed or damaged. Firefighters were ordered to stand aside while arsonists set fire to the synagogues. Surviving Jews were forced to pay for the damage to their own property and businesses.

On 24 January of the following year, Heydrich ordered the setting up of 'Emigration Centres' to organise and process the emigration of Jews from the Reich. Despite this, the problem of what to do with those Jews who remained still preoccupied the SD chief. After the Second World War had broken out, Heydrich told Foreign Minister von Ribbentrop in a letter of June 1940 that the war had ruled out the chance of ridding the Reich of its Jews through emigration alone. Ominously, he added: 'A territorial final solution (*Endlösung*) is therefore necessary.' Hitler had already used the sinister 'final solution' phrase in a speech to the Reichstag marking the anniversary of his accession to power on 30 January 1939, saying that Europe would never find tranquillity until a final solution had been found to 'clear up' the Jewish 'problem'.

On 31 July 1941, Hitler's chief lieutenant Hermann Göring activated Hitler's barely veiled threat when he wrote to Heydrich ordering him to put preparations for the 'Final Solution' into action – whether of a 'financial, organisational or administrative-technical nature'. The euphemistic bureaucratic phrases could not disguise the murderous intention behind the order. In obedience to Göring's command, on 1 September 1941, all people of Jewish descent were obliged to wear the notorious yellow star on the left breasts of their clothes in public, thus making it simpler for the Gestapo to detain and deport them.

Once war began, the already constrained existence of Germany's remaining Jews became more miserable still. Already subjected to vicious discrimination and persecution ranging from the petty – such as being forbidden to sit on the same park benches as 'Aryan' fellow citizens – to inhuman, including being banned from marrying or having sex with their fellow Germans, they were now, in the words of historian Roger Moorhouse:

. . . systematically expropriated, demonised and marginalised. Prohibited from state employment, and removed from most of the professions, the areas of legitimate activity open to them had dwindled to nothing. And new legislation now sought to remove what few comforts remained to them: radios were confiscated, and the keeping of pets was to be forbidden.

Among the 170,000 Jewish victims in Germany branded with the Yellow Star were Max and Gertrud Zuttermann, who, along with Fritz Hirschfeldt were deported to the east on 18 October 1941 and shortly afterwards murdered. Elsa Noah was deported on 17 July 1942 and murdered in March 1944. Frieda Loewy died in June 1942 'while attempting to escape'. All five of these people had one thing in common: they were Jewish near neighbours of Kitty Schmidt and lived in the very same building at Giesebrechtstrasse 11. From the twenty-two houses lining the short 355-metre street, a total of 116 Jewish men, women and children were sent to concentration camps and exterminated between 1941 and 1943.

Karin Zickerick, then just six years old, made daily visits after school to her grandparents in Giesebrechtstrasse 11. Her best friends there suddenly disappeared one day. She never saw them again. She remembers:

On the right hand side of the Garden House lived a film director who had a daughter who was the same age as me, and we often played together in the courtyard. As I came there one day someone told me, 'They have gone away.' I had also borrowed books from a lady who lived in the house at the back of the courtyard, and she had also gone. I never found out what happened to them.

As already mentioned, some of Kitty's neighbours held fond memories of her, variously describing her as a nice, sympathetic and open-minded woman. It is also clear that despite her Aryan-German 'purity' and her social and commercial involvement with top Nazi potentates during these years that were so cruel for non-Aryans, she was also on good terms with her Jewish neighbours.

On the other hand, though, she lived and ran a business in a house from which Jews were compulsorily deported to their deaths. To what extent such apparent contradictions posed moral and ethical problems for the 'Lady of the House' remains unknown. However, according to the former local doctor who treated the house's residents, Dr Hans-Oskar Schäfer, Kitty was a woman of integrity who was 'no Nazi and very friendly to the Jews'. Another relevant clue as to her true attitude

– though not coming directly from Kitty herself – may lie in a postwar photograph in a family album taken in the ground-floor flat in Giesebrechtstrasse 11. The photo shows a jubilant Kathleen Matei, Kitty's daughter, embracing an unknown and presumably Jewish middle-aged man. A handwritten caption around the photo in block capitals reads: 'Kitty helped this man flee to America. After the war he returned on a visit.' Two Jewish Stars of David have been drawn in the margin on the same page of the album.

In his book *Madam Kitty* Peter Norden writes that in the prewar years Kitty used her influence and money to help smuggle her Jewish friends, acquaintances and clients to safety in England. Norden writes: 'Kitty understood that Hitler had something against the Jews. What she didn't understand was what this had to do with her friends Herz, Levy and Cohen.' He continues: 'She celebrated the change of Government on 30th January 1933 [when Hitler was appointed Chancellor] together with Jews and SA leaders alike, as she made no distinction between people and didn't concern herself with politics.'

This picture of Kitty Schmidt as a politically naïve but fundamentally good-hearted woman steering the difficult path trodden by many Germans under the Third Reich, between her friendly feelings for her Jewish friends and fellow citizens and her own survival, rings true. Norden's story of her smuggling currency to England for her Jewish friends to set up a brothel business there for her cannot be simply dismissed out of hand either. The probability is firstly that Kitty did consider that a new brothel in Britain would be both a good business proposition and a way of using 'black' cash not declared to the German tax authorities. Secondly, she very likely retained good contacts in Britain dating from her previous long stay and marriage there as a young governess and piano teacher. We know that she went on holiday to Britain with Kathleen at least once in the 1930s, and she knew the land and its language well.

There is another fascinating source that suggests that Kitty went much further than most other Germans in helping persecuted Jews escape their terrible fates. If we are to believe the best-selling memoirs of Felix, Count von Luckner (1881–1966), he gave a Jewish woman made homeless in an air raid a false identity pass, and his friend Kitty Schmidt then hid her in the Giesebrechtstrasse 11, employing her as a helper in the brothel's kitchen, and thus saving her life. As we've seen, Von Luckner, known as the *Seeteufel* ('Sea Devil') was a well-known national hero in Germany for his incredible swashbuckling exploits at sea during the First World War. As Commander of a three-masted sailing ship, SMS *Seeadler* (*Sea Eagle*), von Luckner roamed the oceans for a whole year sinking Allied shipping, yet chivalrously saving their crews. After he was finally run to ground, von Luckner was interned in South America, but, like Wilhelm Canaris, at around the same time, escaped and took to the seas again in an open boat. He was eventually captured and spent the rest of the conflict as a prisoner of war in New Zealand.

Like Canaris and Kitty Schmidt herself, von Luckner played a double role under the Nazi regime. On the one hand, as a legendary national war hero, he was feted by the Nazis and accepted honours and financial rewards from their hands. He was cultivated by some of the leading Nazi paladins – including Reinhard Heydrich – and as a fellow former naval officer became a friend of the Heydrich family. On the other hand, the old seadog was not a Nazi, and never joined the party. Moreover, as a Freemason he became an object of suspicion to the regime who had banned the international Masonic movement for its loyalty to fellow Masons regardless of race or politics, and the aid that Freemasons gave to their Jewish members. Von Luckner's motives for co-operating with the regime were probably financial rather than ideological.

According to his post-war memoirs, during the Second World War von Luckner found the identity pass of a young 'Aryan' woman named Frieda Schäfer in the ruins of a bombed-out house on Berlin's Budapester Strasse – coincidentally or not the street where Kitty Schmidt had opened her first brothel in the 1920s. The pass described Frieda as a slim, dark-haired woman 1.65 cm (5'5") tall. Von Luckner claims he put the pass in his bag and shortly afterwards met a Jewish woman named Rosalie Janson living underground, who begged him to help save her. The woman said that she was being tracked and followed by the Nazi authorities and was on the run in fear of her life.

Von Luckner writes in his memoir that he decided to help the fugitive and had the idea of hiding her in plain sight in a flat in which most of the rooms had been 'confiscated by SS men'. He disguises the location of Rosalie's hiding place under the name 'The Lions' Den', and describes it as a 'large and beautiful apartment' run by a 'good acquaintance' of his. There is little doubt that this is the brothel at Giesebrechtstrasse 11, that his 'acquaintance' was Kitty Schmidt herself, and it also strongly suggests that the old seadog was a regular client at the bordello.

Von Luckner muses: 'Wasn't this kind of exclusive private establishment exactly the right hiding place for my fugitive? None of her pursuers would have the idea to search for the beautiful Jewess there.' Von Luckner took his idea and his fugitive to Kitty Schmidt who immediately accepted Rosalie into Giesebrechtstrasse 11. He claims the brothel madam welcomed the fugitive with the words 'We will work it out. The child can stay here. There's a spare bed, not particularly comfortable, it's true, but it will do. I have an apron for her to wear and she can stay here without fear. Felix has had the right idea . . .'

After her chance encounter with Count von Luckner, Rosalie Janson, the woman he had saved, lived for around three years hidden in Berlin. She thus escaped deportation to a concentration camp and almost certain death – the fate of most of the city's Jews – and survived the war. She emigrated to the United States in 1948 and confirmed von Luckner's story both in a TV broadcast and in letters to the count. In

April 1950 the pair were reunited at the St Paul's church in New York during one of the count's highly successful speaking tours of the US.

One year later, in 1951, in a letter to von Luckner, Rosalie thanked her saviour with the words:

> When I saw you again after all these years, and listened to your heartfelt lecture, I was plunged again into the torment, despair and deadly fear of being transported to Auschwitz. Then I fell into your arms and implored you to save my young life. You reached into your bag and gave me the Pass with the name Frieda Schäfer, a victim of a bombing raid, that you had just found lying in the street. An Omen that saved me. You were so kind, took me to the house of your wife at Limonenstrasse 3a, where Mrs Lindemann lived, and gave me protection and then a position in the Giesebrechtstrasse. Your words of comfort – that the Nazis would lose the war, and that I must be patient – gave me strength. God protect my saviour.

She signed the letter 'Frieda Schäfer, now Röschen Janson', and ended it with the words in English, 'God Bless You'. It is likely that von Luckner's concern for Rosalie continued long after the war. A letter from her exists in the count's archives in which she asks for his financial assistance after breaking both legs in a fall. This may possibly have been a suicide bid, as she was denied an insurance payout because her injuries were deemed self-inflicted.

Rosalie again confirmed her story in the US TV programme *This Is Your Life*, broadcast by NBC on 4 November 1959, in which von Luckner also appeared. Further confirmation has come from numerous Holocaust researchers and Jewish organisations, and Count von Luckner has been honoured as a 'righteous Gentile' with the planting of five trees in his memory in July 1966 in the Thomas Mann Forest in Israel. Because of his status as a national hero in Germany, von

Luckner is believed to have helped at least ten other Jews escape the Holocaust. The 'Mrs Lindemann' referred to in Rosalie's letter was a prominent cultural figure in Berlin: Dorothea Schneider-Lindemann, a friend of the count who also helped several Jews survive, including the actors Theo Lingen and Hilde Hildebrand.

There are admittedly several puzzles and apparent contradictions stemming from the episode that remain unexplained. Foremost among them is the question of Rosalie Janson's age. She was actually born in 1885, and was therefore approaching sixty when she encountered Count von Luckner, rather than being 'young' as she claimed in her letter. Another mystery is why she showed such gratitude to von Luckner but did not publicly thank her other rescuer – Kitty Schmidt. It's possible that she was ashamed of having worked as a humble kitchen helper in a brothel – whatever the extreme circumstances that compelled her to do so. It is also possible that she privately thanked Kitty in letters, since any papers left by the brothel madam disappeared after her death. All this must remain speculation, but the essential truth of Rosalie's story is incontestable.

Historically, the most crucial question regarding Kitty Schmidt is probably whether she was 'unwillingly' used by the Nazis for their espionage activities or whether she co-operated with them of her own free will. Whether she was in fact a victim or a collaborator with the National Socialist regime. The sparse literature on the subject of the Nazi spy brothel offers widely differing views.

Two journalists writing in *Stern* magazine have asserted that Kitty was quite prepared to go along with Heydrich's plan to use her brothel to spy on visiting foreign diplomats as well as leading Nazis. However, these writers place the main responsibility for the methods used – including the microphones – on Heydrich's account.

Peter Norden alleged that Kitty was acting under the orders of Walter Schellenberg who exerted maximum pressure and mistreatment – at first psychological, and finally physical – on her to allow her brothel to be converted into an espionage centre.

Count Felix von Luckner is clear that Kitty was never a willing tool voluntarily working to further the interests of the Nazis. In his post-war memoirs he writes: 'My acquaintance never did more than put a good face on an evil game.' He claims that Kitty once told him: 'Felix, when I make coffee for others, the water boils particularly quickly. Inside, I'm boiling too.' Von Luckner interpreted this gnomic utterance to mean that Kitty went along with the Nazis on the surface, while opposing them covertly.

As we have already seen, Kitty's friends, acquaintances and other eye-witnesses all attest to her friendly feelings towards the Jews and her rejection of Nazi racial ideology. But that she had no knowledge of the listening devices and other espionage methods that went on in her brothel is impossible to believe. It is possible that for business reasons she tolerated the Nazi presence in the brothel that brought her more clients. That is certainly what the local doctor in Giesebrechtstrasse, Hans-Oskar Schäfer, believed, when he told a 1994 TV documentary about Salon Kitty:

> Certainly, everyone who knew Kitty knew that she was no Nazi . . . I would say that she was careful as she was aware that she was under observation. She had a certain freedom to do as she liked as she was very useful to the state.

That Kitty practised at least passive co-operation with the regime is suggested by the fact that during the time when the Nazis were effectively running things in her salon, there is no official documentation in any archives of the real nature of the 'establishment' at Giesebrechtstrasse 11. Kitty herself was not even officially registered as a resident at the address. As the Berlin historian Joachim Kundler has stated:

In the Third Reich after 1933 she had patrons and protection coming not only from the RSHA security apparatus but also from the Foreign Ministry. That was her survival strategy. She did not rely on a single protector, but on a wide range of patrons, and these patrons were also sometimes her clients.

Kundler describes Kitty as a 'classical opportunist of that time' who manipulated the system to survive, but also to extend protection to Jews who lived in the same block.

So, opportunist, profiteer, collaborator or victim of National Socialism – what are we to make of Kitty Schmidt? This question cannot be simply or clearly answered. However, according to one of her former neighbours, the apothecary Jürgen Meyer-Wilmes, speaking in the 2004 documentary, Kitty 'at least consumed some Aryan ideas'.

The passage of time has revealed certain clues about Kitty's attitudes and behaviour. The city of Berlin, has, so to speak, passed a judgement on the woman who was once such a legendary citizen, and decided that it is preferable to draw a veil of oblivion over her rather than risk engaging with politically incorrect and difficult historical sensibilities. Kitty's grave in the Waldfriedhof in Heerstrasse has become overgrown and is likely to disappear in the coming years as she has no living relatives left in Germany to look after it. Because she is not listed as a 'prominent person' in the cemetery's register, she is not entitled to an 'honoured grave' to be maintained by the city of Berlin. The cemetery caretaker, Helmut Krauss, leaves her tomb off the tours of the cemetery's notable residents that he leads, not considering the former brothel madam as worthy of note. There is no plaque on Giesebrechtstrasse 11 to inform interested passers-by that this was the location of the once infamous 'Salon Kitty'.

It should be borne in mind that even if Kitty Schmidt were ever to emerge as a 'silent resistance fighter' against National Socialism and anti-Semitism, her reputation as a brothel madam and courtesan would still make giving her true justice and respect for her role difficult. Going right back to the New Testament story of Mary Magdalene, official attitudes to 'the world's oldest profession' have never been particularly kind. Moreover, Kitty Schmidt was a German – and not one of those Germans officially recognised as having mounted active resistance against Hitler, helped hunted Jews to hide, or who aided their flight. She was not one of those Germans who were persecuted and imprisoned for their opposition activities and could after the war wipe away the blemish of 'national guilt' and remove the suspicion of being collaborators and opportunists. Kitty had the privilege of being recognised as an 'Aryan' and belonging to the officially recognised German 'race'.

When war broke out, Kitty had a flourishing business and a daughter to protect. Not co-operating with the authorities who had a duty to shut down private brothels such as the one that she ran would not only have threatened her economic position, but might also have put her very life in danger. Leaving aside the question of how Kitty Schmidt was able to finance her first venture into the brothel business – a question that we cannot answer – and whether it was from her own earnings as a prostitute, the authorities had full knowledge of the real nature of her business. It would have been an easy matter for the Health Office or the police under the Nazi regime to declare her a prostitute or simply 'morally weak' and send her to a concentration camp as an 'asocial' criminal.

Notwithstanding any question of morality or guilt, it is quite obvious that Kitty Schmidt had much to lose if she had not co-operated and come to an arrangement during these perilous years living in a totalitarian society. Her strategy was to 'howl with the wolves' or run with the hares and hunt with the hounds, and thereby not only protect herself and her family, but make the best that she could from the precarious and dangerous situation in which she found herself.

CHAPTER ELEVEN

AFTERMATH

– The fate of Kitty Schmidt,
her brothel and her family

What happened to 'Salon Kitty' in the last days of the Second World War and after the arrival of the victorious Allies in the German capital? The sources for answering such questions are few and far between, and often we can only substitute solid facts with speculation in order to reconstruct the past. Much more is known about Kitty Schmidt's daughter Kathleen and her grandson Jochem. As mentioned earlier, a good deal of information came from Jochem Matei himself in interviews and documentaries before his death in 2009. Supporting his testimony, a number of photographs survive in the family's archives – especially from the late 1950s onwards.

The house at Giesebrechtstrasse 11, like many other buildings in Berlin, was badly damaged by a bomb in an Allied air raid in 1943. Such a substantial building had relatively good air raid protection in the form of a large subterranean cellar space, with passages to neighbouring buildings where residents could take shelter and, if necessary, flee. Presumably Kitty, her daughter Kathleen, and infant grandson Jochem – who was born in 1942 – often took advantage of this security to shelter in the cellar during the ever-intensifying Allied air offensive. Probably other family members, including Kitty's sisters Elsa and 'Aunt Trudel', also joined them in the shelter, along with other neighbours from the block. Fortunately the building sustained no further serious damage for the rest of the war, which effectively ended at the end of April 1945 when Soviet troops of the Red Army entered the ruined city.

Thanks to 63-year-old Kitty's intelligence, coupled with her strong will to live, and a good portion of sheer luck, she and her family had not only survived the war, but had managed to cling on to their living quarters. Surviving the difficult days of the immediate post-war period posed further challenges, but Kitty was doubtless able to count on the aid, as well as the silence and discretion, of a wide circle of friends and clients who had known her in her glory days as one of Berlin's foremost 'madams'.

There is anecdotal evidence from Jochem Matei (though he was a young child at the time) that the dubious reputation of Salon Kitty soon became known to the occupying Allied forces. According to Jochem in the year 1945:

One quiet Sunday Kitty and Kathleen were playing canasta in the salon when their game was interrupted by the doorbell ringing. 'I'll get it,' said Kathleen to her mother. She opened it and was confronted by a group of soldiers in US uniforms who asked her, 'Do you want American cigarettes?' [Kathleen replied] 'Yes, I do, for my husband Jean. He loves them, wait, I'll get the money.' Kathleen and Kitty were alarmed that a huge army truck stood in the street making a loud noise on a quiet Sunday. When Kathleen returned to the front door, she found herself staring into the muzzle of a gun. 'Hands up and do what I say,' the soldier told Kathleen in American slang. 'Where are your jewels, furs and cash?' 'In Room Five,' Kathleen answered, full of fear. 'Then let's go,' he replied in a harsh voice, and followed her inside. She took him into Room 5, Kitty's private bedroom, where the three-year-old Jochem lay. The soldier opened cupboards and grabbed handfuls of jewellery, fur coats and cash. 'Who is the lady of the House?' he demanded. 'My mother!' Kathleen cried, still fearful. Kitty stayed calm – as always – and did what the soldier wanted. 'Take the ring from your finger!' the soldier ordered. Kitty tried to obey but couldn't get the ring off. 'Take off that fucking jewellery or I'll cut off your hand with it,' said the soldier coldly. 'For God's sake,' screamed Kathleen. 'I'll get some soap!' After about five minutes the ring came off. The soldier made off with it, with the laughing threat 'That's enough for today. We'll be back. See you later.' Kitty and Kathleen, bathed in sweat, fell into each other's arms.

Whatever the truth of this melodramatic tale of violent looting, Kitty Schmidt kept her head and kept her brothel business going after the war, operating alongside a legitimate guest house at Giesebrechtstrasse 11, until her death in 1954. Among the visitors to the salon in the years 1948 and 1950 was the famous Jewish-French film director Claude Lanzmann, a French Resistance member and the sometime partner of feminist writer Simone de Beauvoir. Lanzmann, future creator of the influential nine-and-a-half-hour Holocaust documentary *Shoah* in 1985, admitted that he took full advantage of the sexual facilities on offer in the Giesebrechtstrasse. In a 2010 interview with *Stern* he described the visit as '. . . an ignition moment' of his time in Berlin, adding '. . . there were many pretty ladies there. I'm sorry. I was twenty-three!'

The nine years between the end of the war and Kitty's death offer few clues as to her salon's role during the war. But shortly before her demise she lifted the veil of her reserve a fraction and briefly broke her silence. The distinguished journalist and author Klaus Harpprecht, in his 2015 memoirs published a year before his death, described his intriguing personal encounter with the person he called the 'house lady' of the 'most luxurious, elegant and high-society brothel in the Reich's capital'. Harpprecht claims that he called at Giesebrechtstrasse 11 in 1954 to bring 'Kitty Schmitt' [sic] news of Walter Schellenberg, who had died in 1952, but whose memoirs – with their chapter on Salon Kitty – were about to appear in English.

As he waited for Kitty to appear, Harpprecht gives a vivid description of the interior of the brothel, which had retained the luxuriously intimate atmosphere of its wartime heyday:

> I was shown into a salon furnished with heavy, wine-red upholstered armchairs and sofas . . . on the walls with thick golden frames were copies of the Dutch Masters. Shaded lights. After a few minutes a lady in a flowing robe came in. 'Walterchen' (Little Walter), she murmured. 'Walterchen . . . what's he up to and where is he?' 'Sadly, he's dead,' I replied. 'Oh, God!' she said. 'Such a lovely man, and still so young. It's always the best who go . . . it's so sad. We must drink a glass of Champagne to his memory.'

Tactfully, Harpprecht told Kitty that Schellenberg's memoirs were about to appear in English with a 'respectful' chapter devoted to her and her 'institute'.

> She told me that in the cellar a listening apparatus had been installed manned by espionage experts. This was connected to tiny microphones in every room, which her young ladies naturally knew about . . . She knew the tastes of all her important clients including the 'Hausherren'. [Presumably those of the SD officers running the listening operation.]

If Harpprecht's account is to be believed – and he was a leading journalist with impeccable anti-Nazi credentials – it seems strange that Kitty had such fond memories of Schellenberg, the SS man who had, according to Peter Norden, brutally intimidated and bullied her into co-operation with the espionage operation. Perhaps she was just being careful and discreet.

Apart from this tantalising glimpse, Kitty took her other secrets with her to the grave. Discreet as always, she evidently had no enemies to denounce to the Allies as Nazi collaborators or minions of the SS. Instead, she made some new arrangements with the Allied authorities now ruling Berlin that allowed her to continue running her business. The Giesebrechtstrasse was in the British-controlled zone of the divided city. It is possible that the Allies used the brothel themselves in their own interests. Such an arrangement was claimed by Peter Norden:

> The Russians who had conquered Berlin, heard very soon about Salon Kitty and tried to use it for their own purposes. Similarly, the British and Americans did the same . . . but the SS had covered their traces well, and all these attempts came to nothing.

If the Allies did indeed have their own political plans for Salon Kitty, and may even have tried to set up their own spying operation in the establishment, this could explain why, in the immediate post-war years up to 1950 Kitty Schmidt was not listed in Berlin's telephone directory. It is likely that officers from the Russian, American, British and French occupation forces patronised the brothel. One surviving eyewitness, Karin Zickerick, who as a child often visited her grandparents who lived in Giesebrechtstrasse 11 during and after the war, recalls seeing 'men in uniform with many medals and beautiful hats' visiting the building. Karin also remembers seeing the many 'very beautiful' women constantly coming and going there, and hearing the 'klack, klack, klack' of their high heels.

In the immediate post-war era, and especially in the early 1950s, Kitty's daughter Kathleen, a passionate dancer, who had set up a dance school at Giesebrechtstrasse 11, took over more of the leading role in running the business and household from her ageing mother. Was Kathleen Matei going to follow in her mother's footsteps?

After her return with her mother from Britain in 1918 as a twelve-year-old child, Kathleen grew up in the rackety Weimar Berlin of the 1920s. A pretty girl, she soon developed an ambition to be an acrobatic dancer. Together with her friend and near-neighbour, the famous dancer Liselotte Köster-Stahl, she attended and trained at the ballet school run by the internationally renowned Russian ballerina and choreographer Tatjana Gsovsky in the Fasanenstrasse. In the late 1920s Kathleen formed a dancing partnership with the gay dancer Fidy Grube and performed with him and others at the Metropol Theatre.

In 1938, the 32-year-old Kathleen fell in love with the Romanian-born juggler and performance artist Jean-Florian Matei. Her lover was also internationally known, and had performed at venues all over Britain – between 1927 and 1938 giving no fewer than 400 performances in London alone. In June 1942 Kathleen gave birth to Jean-Florian's son Jochem Matei, and in October of the same year the couple married at the Standesamt (Registry Office) in Charlottenburg, the Berlin quarter where Giesebrechtstrasse is located. Kitty Schmidt evidently approved of the match, and gave the newlyweds and her grandson a flat on the third floor at Giesebrechtstrasse 11 with all mod cons, as Karin Zickerick remembers:

She [Kitty] gave them everything that was possible to give – an apartment, a ballet studio, and so on. It was a large flat with a big bed and carpets – furnished like something from a fairy story.

But the idyll did not last long. The war cast its long shadow over the happy young family and Jean-Florian was called away to northern Germany. It is unclear whether he was called up for military duties, or whether he was engaged on a theatrical tour, but he was still absent from Berlin when the war ended, and on Christmas Day 1945 he died suddenly in the port of Wilhelmshaven. The cause of death was registered as a lung infection. Because of the chaos of post-war Germany, and despite diligent inquiries, it has not been possible to establish any other details of Jean-Florian's demise.

Like her mother, Kathleen proved to be a great survivor. She converted the entrance hall of her flat into an acrobatic dance studio, equipped it with trapezes and opened her own dance school. Karin Zickerick, then ten years old, remembers going there for strenuous daily lessons. The school operated until Kitty Schmidt's death in 1954 when Kathleen closed it down in order to focus on running the guest house/brothel, which she called in honour of her late husband, the 'Pension Florian'.

The pension side of the business specialised in offering accommodation to performers, actors and artists in whose circles Kathleen had moved since the 1920s. Among the guests who stayed there in the 1950s were the famous writer Erich Kästner, author of the children's novel *Emil and the Detectives*, and the actors Berno von Cramm, Ernst Stankovski and Carl-Heinz Schroth. Other guests included the American opera singer Julia Migenes, the Dutch actor Johannes Heesters and the radio announcer Rolf Stiefel. Berno von Cramm stated in a 2018 interview that the pension was filled with the elegant furniture left over from the days when the premises was the location of Berlin's most infamous bordello. Alongside its function as a legitimate guest house for 'artistic' clients, the house continued to operate as a brothel for half a century until Kathleen's death in 1992, though on a smaller scale than in its heyday under the Third Reich.

Although the pension was now apparently 'respectable', as Cramm recalled, as if from force of habit, Kathleen continued to run her brothel in much the same manner as her mother.

> She [Kathleen] had officially given up the 'House of Joy' but there were still always visits from ladies. One room, Number 5, was not given to guests and was furnished as it had been in 1929, and this was the one to which the 'gentlemen' came. At first she kept this secret, but when you had lived there for three months you knew everything that was going on.

Karin Zickerick remembers peeping into this 'hidden room' which was almost filled with a huge bed.

According to Berno von Cramm, at first Kathleen could call on the services of around half a dozen 'regular' young women between the ages of eighteen and twenty-nine to provide 'love hours'.

> The girls were all very pretty, they didn't look 'tarty', one could well imagine going out with them. I only knew one of them well – there was also a blonde, a brunette, and a redhead. Kathleen knew the desires of her customers very well.

Contemporary photographs taken in the 1950s of Kathleen posing with her 'working girls' bear out Cramm's account.

Kathleen charged the customers a minimum fee of 100 Deutschmarks per hour (about 200 euros in today's values) for sex. She kept the phone numbers of the prostitutes she used in a secret book. Berno von Cramm describes a typical day in her life.

> Today I can still see Kathleen as she was then, always sitting in the kitchen. She came downstairs around noon or twelve-thirty, always neatly dressed. She worked on her finances in the

kitchen, writing everything down. Around two o'clock she'd go upstairs again to do her dance exercises. At twilight she came down again, having changed her dress and freshly showered, and then the clients would come. It was always the same. A bottle of Champagne went into the fridge and then the phone would ring. She would say: 'Hello. Yes. Good. Fine. When? Yes, good.' So it went. The customer would arrive and go into the 'special room'. About twenty minutes later the girl would arrive. The doorbell would ring, and Kathleen would spring up to meet her, and she'd be in the room in a jiffy. I never had a good look when they arrived, but would sometimes get a glimpse of dark or black hair . . .

One of the prostitutes who worked for Kathleen between 1975 and 1978, and who we encountered in the course of our research in Berlin, was Felicitas Schirow. Today in her early sixties, Felicitas is still a well-known activist for Prostitutes' Rights in Berlin. At that time Felicitas was eighteen years old and had been a working girl since she was sixteen, preferring the life to a humdrum nine to five job in an office or factory. She told us that during those years she was phoned around twenty times by Kathleen and summoned to Giesebrechtstrasse 11 to offer her services.

I would go into the 'Pension Florian', which was furnished in a typical old Berlin way. I remember the 'special room', which was on the left side of the entrance hall, was very small. There was a bed on the left, and on the right a small table and sofa, where one could have a chat beforehand. I also recall that there was a wash basin. All very old fashioned, like an old-style bordello during the war years. Nothing had changed since then and there was also red-gold wallpaper.

But it wasn't just the furnishings at Giesebrechtstrasse 11 that dated from the Second World War; so did some of Fräulein Schirow's clients who had been regulars there in the war years, and were now in their seventies:

> These were not poor people who went there; these were upstanding businessmen who had been going there since Kitty's time. The pension guests told me that it had been a Nazi brothel, and all Hitler's generals had been constantly going in and out. That is a fact, or so those guests freely told me.

The fees of 150–200 Deutschmarks paid by clients for sex were divided fifty-fifty between the working girls and Kathleen after she had done her totting up in the kitchen. Felicitas remembers Kathleen today as correct, but not particularly warm.

> She was always friendly and asked us what we wanted to drink, but she wasn't the type who you would take into your arms for a hug. But she was the sort of woman for whom you would always have overwhelming respect, and you could always have an open conversation with her. I'd describe our relationship as a 'businesslike friendship'.

Probably because Kathleen in her younger years had to learn the business of love for sale, she wanted to provide a more appropriate upbringing for her own adolescent son Jochem. In the conflict between feelings and reason, she developed what Jochem called her own version of 'schizophrenia', in which on the one hand she wanted to relinquish the business of selling love, while on the other hand being unable to completely give it up.

She knew when other people were making love. Then she was very happy, very euphoric when other people were there and something was going on in that room. Then it was as though she had taken morphine. It was a sort of spiritual peep-show.

As a boy, Jochem suffered the consequences of Giesebrechtstrasse 11's dubious reputation. He recalled that in his school playground some of his classmates wouldn't play with 'the boy from the brothel'. But during his childhood, Jochem only slowly came to the realisation that his home was also a brothel frequented by many young women. He recalled:

For me they were my 'Aunties' who took me to the cinema or the Christmas markets. They were all very kind to me, and acted as quasi substitute mothers. They were wonderful. If occasionally there was a [police] raid, they would come up to me in my room. I had a toy shop there and sold sweets. And the girls would come up to me completely naked. I didn't really understand why – I was just pleased that I could sell them my sweets. I was happy.

Eventually, Kathleen decided to remove her son from the atmosphere of the brothel, and, when he reached the age of sixteen, she sent him to a Swiss boarding school in St Gallen, then to a college in England. He then briefly studied in Paris, before attending an academy in Rambouillet outside the French capital. Jochem struggled with homesickness, and several guests at Giesebrechtstrasse 11 testified that he suffered greatly from the separation from his mother. One, the actor Ernst Stankovski, remembered: 'When he came home after two or three years abroad, he seemed superficially sophisticated, but somehow broken inside. As time went on, and during later visits, Jochem seemed to me to be in a terrible state.'

Back in Berlin, Jochem took a one-year course in hotel management at the airport 'Hotel Steinplatz'. Then, not enjoying office work, he studied music between 1963 and 1970. Because during these years he was still living off his mother and – even worse for him – he was well aware that her money came partly from the profits of prostitution, he found life very difficult.

> I suffered greatly from the fact that three-quarters of the money for my studies came from my mother's artistic guests at the pension, but one quarter came from Room No. 5 – the 'special room', and the visits of the friends of my grandmother.

Jochem's own early sexual experiences were with the 'pleasure girls' from the Pension Florian. In his mid-twenties Jochem – bravely defying his mother's opposition – had affairs with five of them. Their names were Lilly, Marina, Iris, Piroshka and Jeraline. He explained in retrospect: 'I was inclined to favour love as platonic rather than sexual.' Jochem numbed the inner pain caused by these unrequited loves by listening to the music of Elvis Presley, with alcohol, and by throwing frequent parties – for which the residence was well equipped. Among the guests were his friends the Wiere Brothers – Harry, Herbert and Sylvester – a well-known German comedy trio who forged a successful and durable career, first on stage and in film, and then in television between the 1920s and 1960s.

Reaching the age of twenty-eight, Jochem finally made an effort to free himself – at least financially – from his dependence on his mother. In 1970, on completion of his studies, he opened his own music school at Giesebrechtstrasse 11. By all accounts Jochem was a talented piano player, especially of Mozart. But – partly because he was still under Kathleen's roof – his relationship with his mother remained confused and tense. One of his close friends, Manuel Stahl, remembers: 'Jochem was always falling in love with the beautiful women who worked for his mother, or the artists who stayed overnight. The American actress and opera singer Julia Migenes, for example, was one such unfulfilled love from which he was long unable to free himself.'

In a guestbook in the Matei family archive, Julia Migenes wrote a note to Jochem dated 4 June 1980. It read: 'Never regret yesterday – life is in you today and you make your tomorrow.' A year before his death, in a letter to Julia dated 5 March 2008 that was returned by the German postal service, Jochem confirmed the deep bonds he felt for her: 'Dear Julia – Bye, Bye, Bye – I shall be seeing you. You are right what you or your husband did. I am sick and nothing can be done about it! God bless and so does Buddha. Jochem.'

Jochem's strained relationship with his sexuality eventually expressed itself bodily in skin rashes, and his inner conflicts in his dependence on alcohol. Berno von Cramm remembers a difficult phase in his life in his early thirties: 'He twice won the Lottery – once getting around 50,000 D-Marks. In four weeks it was all gone. Apart from this, he was a poor devil generally. But somehow I was fond of him. The business with women was terrible. Every woman used him, and then when the money was spent, they were off. Then he would stay upstairs listening to Elvis and never came down.'

Then, after so many setbacks in the lists of love, when he was forty-two, life looked up for Jochem. On 4 February he met a Slovenian-born woman named Irena Peraic during a visit to a sauna. In December of the same year the couple married in the local Standesamt (Registry Office). On the first anniversary of their meeting in 1986 they also wed in a church. The marriage appeared a happy one and Jochem and Irena stayed together for twenty-five years until his death in 2009.

Sadly, Jochem did not inherit the business abilities of his grandmother and mother. As time went on, more and more rooms in the Pension Florian emptied, either because the regular guests grew old and died, or because fewer international artists visited Berlin, or because of Jochem's unstable personality and excessive consumption of alcohol. Probably for similar reasons, the number of clients visiting 'Special Room No. 5' also went steadily downhill. In an attempt to stem the decline and rescue the business, Jochem opened the pension to foreign migrants.

Unfortunately, this only compounded the problems. Jochem's ever-increasing addiction to alcohol was not the only difficulty. In March 1992 he received notice from the house's management to quit the property after his neighbours complained of the noise, dirt and untidiness allegedly caused by his new guests. Eberhard Rick, the son-in-law of the house janitor, explained:

> No one had agreed that the pension should be turned into a sort of asylum home . . . He [Jochem] didn't look after these people, and let them do what they liked. We put up a Christmas tree in the entrance hall, which they simply took away because it didn't accord with their beliefs. Also, in a room that was supposed to be occupied by only two or three people, there were ten . . . that was bad.

In the midst of these mounting problems, on 23 August 1992, Kathleen Matei died. For all the difficulties in their relationship, the event was a crushing blow for Jochem, as he himself admitted. 'If Irena and my animals had not been there, I would not have survived my mother's death. I would have taken my own life.'

Kathleen's funeral took place on 10 September at the Waldfriedhof Heerstrasse – the same cemetery where her mother lay. Some thirty mourners attended to pay their last respects to the former ballet teacher. For the Giesebrechtstrasse residents the fact that around half the mourners were migrants who were staying in the pension at the time was somewhat strange. The local chemist Jürgen Meyer-Wilmes, who had been a neighbour of Kitty Schmidt, remarked:

For me . . . knowing as I did the whole story around Kitty Schmidt, this was peculiarly symbolic of how strongly the Aryan ideas [of the Nazis] had taken root. The fact that 80 per cent of the mourners at the burial were (foreign) asylum seekers was symbolic that this was the end of an era.

After the death of Kathleen in 1992 and their enforced departure from Giesebrechtstrasse 11, and the closure of the Pension Florian, Jochem and Irena Matei moved to the nearby Uhlandstrasse 33, and then to Wildenbruchstrasse 90 in the Neukölln quarter where Jochem died of unknown causes on 28 November 2009 aged 67. He was buried beside his mother and grandmother in the Waldfriedhof cemetery. His widow returned to live with her sister in her native Slovenia, where less than a year later she died of cancer on 15 January 2010. It was indeed the end of an era.

CHAPTER TWELVE

SALON KITSCH

– The 'establishment' in historical
literature and on screen

After the Second World War, Walter Schellenberg, the SS official who had done so much to transform Salon Kitty into an espionage centre, was the first person to mention the subject in print. Schellenberg had been arrested by the Allies in Denmark at the end of the war, and after interrogation had gone on trial in Nuremberg and received a prison sentence after testifying against some of his fellow Nazis. Suffering from the liver cancer that would kill him, he was released from jail on grounds of his ill health after two years. He had begun writing his memoirs in prison, and continued to do so in the sanatorium at Pallanza in northern Italy where he was being treated.

The original manuscript of more than a hundred handwritten pages – some of which is now held by the Institute of Contemporary History in Munich – was handed to the publisher Gita Petersen and the journalist Klaus Harpprecht by Schellenberg in the summer of 1951. Probably because it was written by a dying man, the manuscript was in a fragmentary, disorganised and often almost illegible state. It was written on hotel notepaper and menu cards, and sometimes consists of headings and brief notes on such subjects as Schellenberg's relationship with Reinhard Heydrich and Admiral Canaris, his activities as a leading functionary in the SD, and his alleged efforts to use captive Jews as a bargaining counter at the war's end. Harpprecht described the documents as being in a condition of 'indescribable chaos' and expressed his amazement that a man capable of such intellectual discipline, who had run many agents and a complex secret service department, could produce such a mess.

Before Petersen and Harpprecht could complete their editorial task of fashioning the memoirs into a publishable book, their work was interrupted by Schellenberg's death in Turin in March 1952 aged forty-two. Somehow, a version of the memoirs found its way from Switzerland to London, where the émigré Hungarian-Jewish publisher André Deutsch would eventually bring it out in an English translation in 1956 with an introduction by the distinguished British historian and Hitler biographer Alan Bullock. Before then, however, extracts had appeared in the German magazine *Quick* in September 1953 under the heading 'Die grosse Mörder-GmbH' ('Mass Murder Ltd'). Schellenberg was not identified as the author, with his name disguised as 'Colonel Z of the SD'.

A US version of the memoirs titled *The Labyrinth – the Memoirs of Hitler's Secret Service Chief* was published by Harper and Row in 1956. German editions of the book only finally appeared in 1959 and 1979. As already recounted, in the book Schellenberg gives his version of the birth of Salon Kitty, claiming that the original idea came from his boss, Heydrich, who asked him to implement the plan to 'find an elegant intimate setting staffed by beautiful women' where foreign VIPs as well as top Nazis could have their indiscreet conversations monitored and recorded.

Schellenberg, who writes that Heydrich's scheme did not greatly surprise him, says that he employed an intermediary to rent a suitable property – though he does not identify the premises. He then proceeded to convert the establishment into an espionage centre, erecting double walls and sophisticated bugging devices, together with the technicians to operate them. 'All the personnel from cleaning maids to waiters were from the secret services.' Schellenberg claims that the job of recruiting the working girls was sub-contracted to Arthur Nebe, the head of the Kriminalpolizei. Nebe found his recruits not only in the 'half world' of Berlin's vice scene, but from the ladies of 'so-called high society'.

Schellenberg claims that it was Heydrich who baptised the establishment with the name 'Salon Kitty'. He confirms that its clients included the Reich's Foreign Minister Joachim von Ribbentrop, and his Italian counterpart, Count Galeazzo Ciano – along with Heydrich himself. Schellenberg boasts that the salon was the best – albeit not the only – 'high-society spy centre' set up by the Nazis.

Although Walter Schellenberg was clearly an extremely important eyewitness, the information provided in a couple of pages of his memoirs about 'Salon Kitty' is unfortunately rather sparse. He writes more in a character sketch of his former boss Heydrich and the often bizarre ideas for espionage projects of the Nazi secret service under him. It is rather surprising that Schellenberg claims that the 'chat rooms' of Salon Kitty was the Number One success story of Nazi espionage. But the reader gets no clue about the 'valuable information' that the spymaster boasts the brothel furnished from Schellenberg's own account. What is also striking, is that – if all subsequent authors and our own research are to be believed – that it took so long for the Reich's security services to find, rent and use such a long-standing and well-established brothel for their own purposes.

Schellenberg's memoirs also pose the question of whether all – and if so which – of his personal descriptions and recollections represent the whole truth, or whether perhaps some of his retroactive memories are somewhat exaggerated or even mixed up with fantasies. The journalist and author Klaus Harpprecht, who met Schellenberg while he was writing the memoirs, certainly thought so, describing the document as containing . . .

> Outright lies and distortions. Cleverness and the desire for nuance drove him to serve up half-truths. His memories throughout the book are so disarming and filled with subjective honesty and a naive openness that one finds them almost shameless.

We know also from Harpprecht that in the post-war years Schellenberg lived on the advance fees for his memoirs. And he was well aware that sex, especially if combined with spying, sold well. As Schellenberg sickened and came under increasing financial pressure, he probably and understandably sought increasingly to present his story in such an interesting form – even with fictitious details – that they could become a marketable bestseller.

As we've seen, the first independent author to address the history of and rumours surrounding Salon Kitty was the journalist and writer Peter Norden – the pseudonym of Josef Gustav Walter Fritz (1922–1995). In 1973 he published his 'documentary novel' *Salon Kitty* (*Madam Kitty* in its English edition). Norden claimed that the book was the fruit of more than twenty years' research. It is evident that Schellenberg's sketchy 1950s memoirs encouraged Norden to dig deeper into the story. Immediately on publication, Norden's book became a huge commercial success, selling five million copies around the world. Although the book is now out of print, it is still relatively easy to find copies online or in second-hand bookshops.

Norden's family members are scarcely surprised that the writer spent so long researching his subject. The second of his three wives remembers her lively late husband as having an 'itch for whores', while the daughter of his first marriage similarly recalls that his primary preference was exploring the erotic 'half world'.

As with so many figures associated with Salon Kitty, concrete details of Norden's colourful life are sparse. Born in Hanover, he claimed to have studied Medicine, Law and Philosophy. During the Second World War he served for six years as a flier in the Luftwaffe. Later, he had a bewildering variety of occupations, working for short spells as a taxi driver, theatre stage manager, a waiter in a museum cafe, and as a tour guide, advertising copywriter, reporter, critic and editor before becoming an author. He published more than twenty books on a wide variety of subjects.

It is interesting that in his contemporary novel *Für eine Handvoll Zärtlichkeit* (*For a Handful of Tenderness*), published in 1986, Norden renews his relationship with Salon Kitty after it became the Pension Florian. At the centre of the story, Kitty Schmidt's daughter Kathleen Matei has a special importance for one of the fictional characters, Renate Koller, a pretty girl from Leipzig who flees from the GDR (Communist East Germany) and is possessed with the ambition to assume a leading position in the 'horizontal business'. In 1961 she therefore began to work for Kathleen as a prostitute.

Norden's novel, mixing truth with fiction, offers a heavy hint as to how the business in the salon at Giesebrechtstrasse 11 continued after Kitty Schmidt's death in a fictional scene recounting a conversation between Kathleen and Renate about the customs at the establishment:

This Kathleen Matei was not a brothel madam in the traditional sense. She was a lady with understanding of the problems of a patriarchal polygamous society and offered discreet help . . . 'We have here First Class clients,' said Frau Matei. 'One can say that it is the cream of Berlin Society. They come from all social circles; actors as well as directors, politicians, economists and film bosses . . . you [Renate] need not concern yourself with the financial side, I will deal with all that. You get fifty per cent of the fees. The other fifty per cent stays in the business to cover general outgoings. I like it when my ladies drink a half bottle of Champagne with their gentlemen so that Elvira [the house maid] earns something. We have reserved for you a lovely room, Number 5. You'll like it . . .

Later in the novel Renate falls in love with Miguel, a rich businessman from Guatemala. Kathleen ends their business relationship after which Renate, calling herself 'Kitty', goes on to open two successful brothels herself – one in Düsseldorf and one in Frankfurt. At the end of the novel she is a multi-millionaire, but falls into alcoholism. Despairing, she tries to cure herself of her addiction.

Peter Norden's documentary novel *Madam Kitty* is, as we have shown, a mixture of fact and fiction. His story begins with Kitty Schmidt's desperate attempt to flee abroad in June 1939 after she was asked by a police official called by Norden 'Reichskommissar Kuhn' to convert her brothel into a spy post. 'Kuhn' was probably a name invented by Norden to cover a real person. The novel broadly sticks to the story regarding Kitty's capture at the Dutch border and interrogation at the hands of the SS and Gestapo at their HQ in Prinz-Albrecht-Strasse; also her being persuaded to co-operate with her captors' scheme for her premises.

According to Norden's story, the spying scheme was highly successful. The salon was visited every day by around thirty clients, including leading members of the military and high-ranking foreign diplomats who gave away important information about the war in boastful or careless pillow talk. Like Schellenberg's account in his memoirs, Norden names the Reich's Foreign Minister Joachim von Ribbentrop and the Italian Foreign Minister Count Ciano among the VIP clients, along with 'Sepp' Dietrich, the chief of the crack SS-Leibstandarte, known as 'Hitler's bodyguard' The main suspense in Norden's novel is provided by a love story between a spy employed by the Secret Service called 'Rodger Wilson', alias 'Koltschew', and one of the young prostitutes recruited as an SD agent known as Gitta. Again, as with 'Kommissar Kuhn', these are names invented by Norden to cover the identities of real people. 'Rodger Wilson' gave his name in *Madam Kitty* as 'Baron von Itter' and was also known under the names 'Koltschew' and 'Lijubo'. He was said to work as the deputy press attaché in Romania's trade delegation.

Sadly, the affair between Gitta and her spy lover did not last long. He attempted to flee but ended up in Sachsenhausen concentration camp. Norden claims that Salon Kitty's function as a spy centre was almost as short. He says it ended in July 1942 when the building was heavily damaged in an Allied air raid – though most sources say the bombing happened in 1943. After that event, Walter Schellenberg lost interest in the project and abandoned it. Reinhard Heydrich, the original initiator of the plan was dead, having been ambushed and assassinated in Prague in May 1942 by British-trained Czech agents. That, briefly stated, is the content of Peter Norden's bestselling book.

Kitty Schmidt's family were less than pleased by Norden's research and revelations on the publication of his book in 1973. Kathleen Matei's son Jochem recalled that Norden offered his mother money if she granted him an interview – upon which she threw him out of the house.

Peter Norden came to my mother and said, 'Frau Matei, I'm offering you a lot of money. Please give me information, as we want to make a book and film about Salon Kitty.' My mother replied, 'Herr Norden please leave. I will not have my mother's name smeared.' As a result, Herr Norden left, saying as he went, 'Then I shall make my researches in my own way.' Soon after his visit this 'Salon Kitty' book appeared, in which he made up a whole heap of things.

Jochem Matei alleged that the family attempted to take legal action against Norden's 'untruths'. They consulted a lawyer named Dietrich Scheid. Jochem claimed that Scheid told him: 'Jochem, your grandmother was a historical personality and journalists have a fools' freedom, and press freedom, to say what they like about her. There's nothing that we can do against that.'

Peter Norden certainly did serve up some 'untruths' in his account. For example, he claims that Kitty Schmidt was born in the Berlin district of Wedding, whereas, as we have seen, her birth certificate states that she was born in Hamburg. Similarly, he writes that she trained as a hairdresser – a claim vehemently denied by Jochem Matei. Furthermore, Norden alleged both in the book and in an interview with the German film director Rosa von Praunheim that the conversations of the female agents with their guests were recorded on the wax discs which were collected by the RSHA – the umbrella organisation of the Nazi security services. Norden claims that the thousands of discs were discovered by the Russians at the war's end and passed to the Communist security services of the GDR (East Germany). To date not a single one of these discs has been found in the GDR's archives.

Norden's daughter Brigitta Hughes is unsurprised that her father's book is riddled with half-truths. In his lifetime she remembers her father as a man who without exception knew how to captivate every listener with his stories. Given that we have been unable to find so few truly reliable sources for Kitty Schmidt's life and salon, and that solid facts are so sparse, are we to simply assume that Norden's book was not seriously researched, and that his main assertions are more fiction than truth? Because almost none of his central claims can be proved, the probable verdict must be that Norden, lacking reliable data, and faced with the wall of silence put up by Kitty's family, because of what he himself called his 'chronic money troubles' gave his own fantasies free rein.

Peter Norden called his book a 'documentary novel'. However, despite his own claims of years of research, he unfortunately left no documentation behind. The book lacks any indication of the real identities of any of the witnesses that he spoke to in the course of his research, so we don't know who told him what. Evidence of his research seems to be forever lost. Peter Norden died on 19 April 1995, destitute and deeply in debt. At the end of his life he was living in a care home for artists on the Viktualienmarkt in Munich. Because of his debts, his heirs declined their heritage. We have no idea what became of any property or papers that he may have possessed.

In an attempt to correct the claims made by Peter Norden, Jochem Matei decided to commit his own memories to paper. With the working title 'Salon Kitty II – how it really was', he wrote:

> To set down things correctly . . . my mother received Herr Norden in 1970 and tried to put right such untruths as the claim that my grandmother was born in Wedding and trained as a hairdresser. She said that her mother Kätchen 'Kitty' Schmidt had been born in Hamburg's Grossen Allee and was a salesman's daughter and not a hairdresser. Apart from that, Herr Norden had invented stuff about the listening devices in order to sell his book . . . It is true that my grandmother, Frau Kitty Schmidt, ran a well-known salon, which I'm very proud about. She had a good name among people throughout the whole world. Even though she ran a delicate business, which today is still delicate. Everyone I have spoken to will attest to that.

In a video interview with his friend Manuel Stahl in 1995, Jochem read from the first pages of his projected book; it was never published, however, and the manuscript, if it existed, has disappeared.

The Italian film director Tinto Brass, who had made a name for himself in the late 1960s and early 1970s for his experimental, avant-garde movies, hired Peter Norden to work on a film script about the salon. The resulting movie, *Salon Kitty*, an Italian, German and French co-production, was based on parts of the book, although it strayed for long stretches into an unbridled voyeuristic and perverse fantasy.

At its premiere in Munich in March 1976, the media was presented with this description of the film's content:

Germany: 1940. In the Reich capital Berlin the latest victories in the war are celebrated. Paris is in German hands! While people in public passionately discuss the special reports from the Western Front, in the circles around SS-leader Heydrich a piquant plan is put into effect that is immediately declared a state secret. It involves, according to the task given to Untergruppenführer Wallenberg, creating an eavesdropping centre for foreign diplomats and the Reich's leaders. And it's there, where every man can honestly let their inhibitions fall and give their real opinions openly: in the bed of a beautiful woman, especially in a brothel's bed.

The film screenplay tells a now familiar tale: 'Untergruppenführer Wallenberg' – a transparent alias for Walter Schellenberg – an ambitious secret service chief, sees a chance to advance his career by converting a high-class bordello into a listening centre. He chooses the high-bourgeois establishment at Giesebrechtstrasse 11 that is known to its high-class patrons as 'Salon Kitty' to realise his plan. Kitty herself is forced to agree to the scheme. A conventional brothel is thus transformed into a criminal bordello with the SS having their fingers deeply in the pie. A den of luxury is created and equipped with 120 microphone bugs. The intimate conversations of the 'guests' are now overheard underground through earphones and recorded on discs. Obviously, Kitty's own working girls must be exchanged for spies. A special squad of girls from the BDM (Bund Deutscher

Left: Weimar Berlin was alive with fun, partying and culture. At this popular club, Resi, patrons could call different tables to chat and flirt – a light bulb on the table indicating their 'availability' – and the pneumatic tubes, pictured here, could be used to send gifts between tables.

Below: Kitty Schmidt, here wrapped in furs, pictured some time between the wars.

Above: The liberal attitudes of the Weimar Republic allowed a more broad-minded attitude towards sexuality and sex work. Here, sex workers are pictured on Berlin's Friedrichstrasse in 1930. It would not be long before this was criminalised.

Above: While trouble was beginning to brew at home, Kitty (left) and Kathleen Schmidt took a holiday on Sylt island in the early 1930s.

Right: At around the time Kitty and Kathleen were enjoying themselves, as in the image above, Nazi power was increasing and it would not be long until their absolute rule would dominate Germany. Here Hitler and Himmler are at the 1938 Nuremberg rally, after total Nazi control had been established.

The stark contrast between these two images provides a very poignant visual representation of Nazi control and the erasure of the liberalism of Weimar Germany. Club Eldorado (above), Motzstrasse 15, Berlin, was an iconic Weimar venue. This gay cabaret bar was closed and taken over by the Nazis in 1933 and made an HQ of the SA Brownshirts (below). Ironically, SA leader Ernst Röhm had been a regular patron there until it's closure.

Once the Nazis had full control, the direct effects of their power began to be felt. Intimidation and imprisonment became a regular occurrence, as seen by the raids carried out by Criminal Police and Gestapo officers, control of print media (above) and the establishment of prison camps like Ravensbrück the women's concentration camp north of Berlin (below).

© Bettmann / Contributor / Getty images

© ullstein bild Dtl. / Contributor / Getty images

Kitty Schmidt in a Greta Garbo-style hat, *c.* 1920s.

Right: Giesebrechtstrasse 11 after the war; the upper floors were damaged by Allied bombing. Following this, Kitty moved her business to the ground floor.

Below: A bomb-damaged Giesebrechtstrasse 11. In this image the sign reading 'Pension Schmidt' can clearly be seen.

Above: This house of horrors on Prinz Albrecht Strasse was home to the SS and Gestapo HQ, and was where Kitty Schmidt was held and brutalised.

Below: Heinrich Himmler followed by Reinhard Heydrich in full dress SS uniforms.

Top left: Heydrich, 'the man with the iron heart', at the height of his power.

Top right: Walter Schellenberg on trial after the war. Schellenberg oversaw the transformation of Salon Kitty from brothel to spy listening post.

Below right: Propaganda Minister Josef Goebbels with his lover, Czech film star Lída Baarová, at the premiere of Leni Riefenstahl's film *Olympia*, held on Hitler's birthday, 20 April 1938.

Mädchen) the female equivalent of the Hitler Youth, is recruited and trained for this task.

One of the 'lust spies' is rebellious: Margarete, raised in her parents' bourgeois house and filled with Nazi ideals, has a secret love of her own which Wallenberg at first knows nothing about. Margaret is in love with a Luftwaffe officer, who confides to her in bed that he is planning acts of anti-Nazi sabotage. Although Margarete does not betray him, he is nevertheless arrested and executed. How? Margarete realises that every whisper in the brothel reaches Wallenberg's ears. She vows vengeance.

Kitty also rebels against her role as merely a glamorous neutral onlooker. She offers Margarete the opportunity to overhear and record Wallenberg in his own decadently furnished apartment by staging a seduction scene in which she turns the tables on him by breaking down his reserve and teasing his secrets out of him. He blurts out his own intimate deadly knowledge of the intrigues within the SS's leadership clique, and thus signs his own death warrant. Margarete releases her recording and Wallenberg is shot. Salon Kitty falls victim to Allied bombs in 1943 and thus ends the first eavesdropping scandal carried out by a government.

The Austrian actor Helmut Berger – best known for his part in the similar Nazi sexploitation movie *The Damned* directed by Luchino Visconti – played the lead role as Wallenberg in the film, while the Swedish sex symbol Ingrid Thulin – renowned for her roles in Ingmar Bergman's films such as *Wild Strawberries* – co-starred as the brothel's madam, Kitty. While the film did well in cinemas, and still makes money in digital form on home entertainment platforms, the critical world was not as merciful as the public. Film critics branded the combination of Nazism and porn as 'Nazisploitation'. Brass's movie is still today regarded as a classic of this sub-genre. Newspapers throughout Europe condemned the tasteless blending of National Socialism with pornographic eroticism, and deplored the fact that actors of the quality of Berger and Thulin had trashed their reputations by participating in it.

Before the film's release in 1975, the 69-year-old Kathleen Matei tried to take legal steps to stop it – just as she had with Peter Norden's book. Once again she used the services of the lawyer Dietrich Scheid, who stated: 'Frau Matei fears that the good name of her mother will be smeared by this film. She must know that Kitty Schmidt in her time was valued as a discreet, polite and civilised woman.' Discreet, polite and civilised is hardly the character portrayed by Ingrid Thulin in the movie. Rather her character is impulsive, loud and theatrical – a 'movie star' diva given to outbreaks of rage. Upon the declaration of war on 1 September 1939 and Hitler's conquest of Poland, she gathers her guests and girls to pop the Champagne corks, drink and dance on tables, yell 'Heil Hitler!' and sing 'Deutschland, Deutschland, über alles' with gusto.

Nonetheless, the character Kitty lets it be known that all this exaggerated jubilation and cheer is a mere masquerade, and that she herself is no Nazi. In a later scene when she is accused by one of her prostitutes working as an SS agent of not being a good National Socialist and having no ideals, she answers in a manner brooking no misunderstanding: 'First and foremost, before any ideals, I am a madam . . . money, that is the only thing that you should think about.' She answers her accuser with some amusement: 'Naturally [money], darling . . . that is all that a good professional should be thinking of. That is what gives you freedom.'

In the course of the film we soon realise that Kitty is a very strong woman who is always there for her girls whenever they have a problem. She is a kind of mother figure, feisty, cunning and courageous. She is not scared of standing up to Hitler's henchmen and is finally triumphant. Kitty wants to keep her house 'clean'. Therefore, knowing that the SS officer Wallenberg is misusing her employees as spies in his schemes of betrayal and murder, she conspires with Margarete – played by the Anglo–Italian actress Teresa Ann Savoy – and the bravest of her courtesans, to bring Wallenberg down using his own weapons.

The 'Kitty' character portrayed in Tinto Brass's movie bears little resemblance to the real historical Kitty Schmidt. The figure portrayed in black stockings and suspenders, with lascivious gestures, erotic dances and songs, is – even allowing for artistic licence – a travesty of the truth of what our research has revealed. In some respects, however, Ingrid Thulin's character is modelled on the real Kitty – her hairstyle, her age, her clothes and elegance. The way that Kitty sought with her family to survive the turmoils of war is also accurately portrayed. The presentation of Kitty Schmidt's driving ambition to create a first-class 'salon' in which both her guests and her employees could feel comfortable also seems to us to reflect the reality. In the film's final scene Kitty and Margarete toast with Champagne Wallenberg's death and their victory over their SS tormentors just as the British bombs fall on the salon.

The film's direction and screenplay contain a high degree of fantasy, even if the décor and details accurately represent the zeitgeist in which the movie is set. The film shows the SS forcing Kitty to relocate her salon to a villa in Berlin's leafy and prosperous western suburb of Grunewald despite her vehement protests. (It should be noted that the lakeside villa in which Heydrich convened and chaired the notorious Wannsee conference in January 1942, which set the scene for the Holocaust, is also located in Grünewald, where both Heydrich and his 'frenemy' Admiral Canaris had their neighbouring homes.)

The movie depicts the salon as having the size and atmosphere of a *Cabaret*-style club in which a sizeable choir finds a place. It shows the celebration of Roman Empire orgies in which naked guests, along with prostitutes, shamelessly cavort, mingling with elegantly clad ladies and gentlemen in suits or uniforms. The love grottos and bathrooms could easily pass for those found in a luxury five-star hotel. Even the splendidly appointed eavesdropping centre in the cellar resembles a broadcasting studio, complete with sophisticated recording equipment and blinking red lights. Such kit could barely fit into the cramped original underground cellar at Giesebrechtstrasse 11.

More realistic is the film's depiction of the salon's guests and customers. From the outset, Tinto Brass ruled out portraying well-known historical figures in his film. Nevertheless, the whole panorama of contemporary German high society makes an appearance: industrial magnates and bankers; army generals and officers on home leave from the front, clad in brown and black uniforms with swastika armbands; diplomats from friendly countries and newspaper correspondents.

And what of the ladies of pleasure moonlighting as secret agents? They stand at the centre of Brass's direction. These courtesans, who in the movie come from respectable households, are 'good' Germans, and above all have the correct National Socialist beliefs. 'Attitudes above all' is the SS demand during the recruiting of their prospective Mata Haris. Much less is portrayed of the reality of the prostitution practised in *Salon Kitty*, thus leaving plenty of room for speculation and interpretation.

Tinto Brass's cinematic spectacle offers strongly dramatic glimpses into the possible mindsets of these ladies. On the one hand Brass shows their hopes and dreams; on the other he also portrays their fears and deep despair. Naturally these tensions demand our full attention as we wait to find out how the drama is to be played out, and how the agents and other prostitutes will survive the extreme levels of stress and danger they are enduring by fulfilling the tasks set by their NS masters. A sex game played by one of the girls with a powerful man ends fatally. Another pleads with one of the regular clients to take her with him to America before, in despair, she takes her life. A third young woman becomes pregnant but hides her condition because she wants to keep her baby rather than be compelled to have an abortion. Teresa Ann Savoy's character delights in her role as the film's chief protagonist and heroine, falls in love with one of her clients and shoots another out of rage.

Such extreme emotions, so many wild adventures and dramatic scenes never took place in the real Salon Kitty. And yet it would be good to know more of the actual human tragedies that unfolded behind the scenes of the fabled Nazi espionage bordello. To discover more of the pains and tears that lay behind the laughter and the make-up of the servants of love who worked there. That must remain an area for fantasy and fiction. Incomplete and flawed though it is, Tinto Brass's *Salon Kitty* provides an interim first report.

The next screen visit to Salon Kitty was made by the internationally renowned German film director Rosa von Praunheim in his documentary film *Meine Oma hatte einen Nazipuff* (*My Granny had a Nazi Brothel*), first shown on German television on 4 November 1993. This film was the first to publicly interview at length Jochem Matei about his grandmother Kitty Schmidt, his mother Kathleen Matei and his own memories and experiences of the establishment after the war. Von Praunheim also uncovered and interviewed several witnesses whose recollections we have already quoted, including Hans-Oskar Schäfer, the establishment's 'house doctor' since 1943, who testified to Kitty Schmidt's friendly attitude towards the Jews; the next-door neighbours Magda and Hans Frintrop, who lived in Giesebrechtstrasse 10 from 1942; and the singer Evelyn Künneke who Kitty Schmidt unsuccessfully attempted to recruit to work in her brothel.

Rosa von Praunheim also interviewed Peter Norden regarding the research for his book. He critically questioned Norden about his claims, particularly comparing them with Jochem Matei's recollections. In interviewing Norden, von Praunheim also focused on the wax recording discs allegedly used in the cellars of Salon Kitty, asking why none of the discs had ever been discovered. Norden speculated that they had either been destroyed in the war or removed to Russia. Von Praunheim interviewed Reinhard Exner, an expert from Berlin's Radio Museum, where an example of such a disc was preserved. Exner pointed out that by the time of the Second World War the wax discs were already obsolete, and had been replaced by magnetic tapes, developed in 1935 and by 1938/9 already in use by German radio.

All told, Rosa von Praunheim's documentary film made a worthwhile contribution to the real history of Salon Kitty. He was the first to attempt to disentangle true facts from myths and rumours. He also visited the scene of the 'action' in Giesebrechtstrasse 11 with his cameras, shooting footage of the original furnishings of the brothel, complete with erotic pictures which Jochem Matei said came from the time of the original Salon Kitty. Von Praunheim also presented for the first time a wealth of photos from the private albums of the Schmidt-Matei family. Although the film was shown primarily from Jochem Matei's viewpoint, and can therefore be justifiably accused of being a one-sided and very subjective portrait, it should also be remembered that Matei was by then the most important living witness to the time and events that he described.

Around ten years after von Praunheim's documentary appeared, in 2004 another Berlin filmmaker, Claus Räfle, returned to the legendary high-society brothel and its denizens. Räfle interviewed many of the same witnesses as von Praunheim for his film *Salon Kitty*, including Jochem Matei and his wife Irena, the actor Ernst Stankovski, and the one-time neighbour Magda Frintrop. But he offered a less subjective and more fact-based portrait of the subject than his predecessor. Räfle traced the style of Kitty Schmidt's high-class and exclusive brothel to the example set by the 'Everleigh Sisters' – Ada and Minna Everleigh, who set up and ran a similar establishment called the Everleigh Club in Chicago between 1900 and 1911. The club, described as 'the most elegant, expensive and best-run brothel in the western USA', was a successful and highly profitable enterprise which made the sisters millionaires in a short space of time.

In contrast to the open – albeit exclusive – whorehouse operated by the Everleighs, in running her salon, Kitty Schmidt had to disguise the operation as an 'artists' pension'. In doing so, it helped that her daughter Kathleen was a budding dancer and showgirl who moved in Bohemian circles. That Kitty openly offered love for sale in her 'Pension Schmidt' was remembered in Räfle's film by her former neighbour Magda Frintrop in almost nostalgic and idyllic terms. She spoke of the album with pictures of Kitty's girls and the Champagne that generously accompanied it. Frau Frintrop also testified that, like Evelyn Künneke, as a twenty-year-old trainee actress she too had turned down an offer from Kitty to work in the salon. At the time of her interview the 85-year-old Frintrop still lived in a neighbouring house.

The research of the historian and archivist Joachim Kundler, who worked on the film, bore further witness to Kitty Schmidt's discretion. His searches in official archives revealed that not once during the Third Reich was Salon Kitty listed among the forty or so brothels in Berlin that were officially tolerated by the Nazis. Another participant in the programme, Werner Raykowski, a former employee of the Foreign Office, confirmed that the salon was well known to the authorities, and alleged that it had been established 'with the financial support of the Propaganda Ministry'. A third expert who took part, the publicist and author Lutz Hachmeister, spoke of SD chief Reinhard Heydrich's admiration for British spy novels, and said that the British Secret Service was the main model for the SD. Hachmeister added that he could well see how the idea for setting up a luxury spy brothel sprang from Heydrich's fertile imagination.

One controversial eyewitness and former resident at Giesebrech-tstrasse 11 interviewed for the film was the veteran Dutch-born actor and singer Johannes Heesters, then aged over 100. The star, born in 1903, made his successful stage and screen career in Germany from the 1920s. Much admired for his acting style by Hitler, whom he met several times, Heesters was on Goebbels' list of officially approved artists, and continued his spectacularly stellar career under the Third Reich. He visited Dachau concentration camp, where he is said to have performed before the SS guards.

In the interview Heesters told the 'amusing' tale of how, after he was bombed out of his Berlin home during the war and was in search of a new billet, friends as a 'joke' brought him to Salon Kitty. Heesters decided to make his new home at the salon and remained there for the rest of the war. He told the interviewer that the real goings-on there were so widely well known that taxi drivers always laughed knowingly when he asked them to drive him 'home' and gave Giesebrechtstrasse 11 as his address. He added that among the customers at the brothel he recognised Italy's Foreign Minister Count Ciano, who made several visits. Johannes Heesters died as recently as 2011, still performing at the age of 108.

An anonymous Berlin witness interviewed for Räfle's film had been employed at the salon as a working girl after the war. Though wreathed in shadows for the film to disguise her identity, and in her eighties, the woman evidently maintained the elegant style that she had learned from Kitty in her youth, wearing a long red dress and with fashionable make-up and hairstyle. She recalled the expensive cocktail dresses that Kitty insisted on her girls wearing, as she believed that appearance was all important. Though the salon's time as a spy brothel predated her employment there, she said that some of her older colleagues told her that they had doubled as Nazi spies and courtesans.

During the making of his film, Räfle visited the cellar at

Giesebrechtstrasse 11 in the company of the caretaker at the time, Eberhard Rick, who recalled that his stepfather, who had done the same job during the war, spoke of the cables and cans that had been found there and removed during renovations carried out in the 1960s.

A further eyewitness found by Räfle was the neighbourhood apothecary in Giesebrechtstrasse, Jürgen Meyer-Wilmes, who spoke of Kitty's Jewish neighbours and confirmed the story that Count Luckner, the 'Sea Devil', had rescued the Jewish woman Rosalie Janson by giving her the identity of a German victim of Allied bombing, Frieda Schaefer, who had then been sheltered by Kitty Schmidt under the Nazis' noses as a kitchen worker in the salon. Räfle even found Count Luckner's personal diary for July 1939, which listed Kitty's name, telephone number (321032) and address in his handwriting.

The actor Ernst Stankovski spoke in the film about life at Giesebrechtstrasse 11 after the war when he had stayed at the pension, when it was still operating as a 'harmless' brothel business run by Kathleen Matei after her mother's death. Räfle also touched on the subject of the mysterious wax discs said to have been used by the SD. Christian Booss, a Federal Government spokesman who had investigated the East German secret service archives following German reunification, confirmed that no wax discs with recordings from Salon Kitty had ever been found. Claus Räfle's conclusion: 'What remains is a heap of wild speculations over secret services, politics, seduction, and a woman who really only wanted nothing more than to run a superior brothel business in a side street off the Kurfürstendamm.'

Even today, the spell that the legend of Salon Kitty continues to exert over the imaginations of many people shows no signs of disappearing. The high-class brothel and its secrets have frequently been an attractive stage on which both filmmakers and novelists have projected their fantasies and their fictitious stories.

In Peter Berling's novel *The Chauffeur*, for instance, the character 'Kitty', influenced by her proletarian background, has a left-wing attitude. In Berling's version of the story, following the failure of her flight to Amsterdam, Kitty lands in a concentration camp where she is persuaded to co-operate with Heydrich and Schellenberg's plans to erect an eavesdropping centre in the cellar at Giesebrechtstrasse 11 that was once used to store potatoes. Bering portrays the cellar with recording devices each linked to rooms in the brothel with the code names 'Hawaii', 'Madagascar', 'Shanghai' and 'Honolulu'.

Harald Gilbers' novel *Germania* – the name that Hitler and Albert Speer intended to give Berlin if their grandiose plans to transform the city on a giant scale had ever been realised – is set in 1944. A police commissar, Richard Oppenheimer, with a hidden Jewish heritage, is on the trail of a serial sex killer and is led to Salon Kitty, where one of the victims, Edith Zöllner, had once worked as a prostitute under the name Friedericke. Gilbers imagines a party held at the spacious salon on the day that Hitler took power in which both Jews and members of the SA took part. Gilbers shows his Kitty character's feelings of friendship towards the Jews after she discovers Oppenheimer's Jewish heritage and presses a banknote into his hand with the words: 'The times must be very difficult for you.'

The murder victim in Bela Bolton's detective story *Codeword Rothenburg*, set in Berlin in early 1941, had also worked in the 'Pension Schmidt' as a prostitute. The brothel does not feature in official police files because it is listed as a 'state secret' by the Abwehr foreign intelligence service. Kitty Schmidt is described by the book's central character, police commissar Axel Daut, as presiding over an 'elegant establishment'. He describes her appearance and expensive clothing as giving the impression of a 'Grande Dame'.

The Croatian author Daša Drndić uses information culled from Peter Norden's book and Walter Schellenberg's memoirs in her Holocaust novel *Sonnenschein* (*Sunlight*). In the novel, a Jewish mother searching for her son who had been kidnapped by the Nazis comes to Salon Kitty. Another novel featuring the brothel – although disguised under the name 'German Harem' – is Thor Kunkel's *Endstufe*, which features rumours that the Nazis made pornographic films there.

The bestselling debut novel *HHhH*, by the French author Laurent Binet, which won the prestigious 2010 Prix Goncourt, tells the story of, the assassination of Reinhard Heydrich in Prague. It also features Salon Kitty, portraying Heydrich's conversion of the establishment to an espionage post. Binet characterises Kitty Schmidt as 'a brothel madam from Vienna . . . educated, competent and fully committed to her job.'

Binet's book was filmed in 2018 under the title *The Man With the Iron Heart* – the description Hitler is said to have bestowed on Heydrich. The film features a scene set in Salon Kitty – though the brothel is not named. A high-ranking Wehrmacht general is portrayed in the salon along with naked or lightly clad attractive young women. When one of them, dressed only in stockings and a silk kimono, takes him to a private room, she stands in front of a Venetian mirror and puts her finger to her lips, thus letting him know who is behind the two-way mirror. It is none other than Reinhard Heydrich, who is noting everything he hears in a black notebook. Beside him is a cameraman preparing to film the couple making love.

Later the general is shown in conversation with Heydrich. The SS-Gruppenführer demands the general's co-operation, which he decisively rejects. Heydrich then plays his trump card, telling him, 'You do your job, General, and I do mine, and mine – among other things – includes surveillance. Yes, I observe, I notice things and I inform. I can inform the Führer's Chancellery of your taste for young whores.' Heydrich then shows his victim his notes listing the names and ages of the prostitutes that the general has seen in the Berlin brothel, together with the dates of his visits.

Heydrich adds: 'You are a high-ranking officer of the German

Wehrmacht, screwing impure women and bringing disgrace upon your family. No court martial would have any tolerance of that.' Having heard this, the general speedily decides to give Heydrich all the information he wants about the regime's enemies within the Wehrmacht.

Salon Kitty not only features in film dramas, but also, for example, in the BBC comedy series *Private Schulz* in the early 1980s. The fascination for Salon Kitty clearly continues.

CONCLUSION

– Researches and results

The former 'Salon Kitty' brothel near Berlin's famed Kurfürstendamm boulevard is still known today because of the sometimes garbled and contradictory stories that during the Second World War the Nazi Party's security organs converted the establishment into an espionage post for their own nefarious purposes. We have spent many years in several European countries from Sweden and England to Slovenia and Italy, as well as the USA, and above all in Berlin, researching how credible the rumours and myths that have gathered around Kitty Schmidt and her salon really are.

Our mission was to ferret out provable facts in order to answer the core question: was 'Salon Kitty' under the Third Reich more than a high-class bordello for the use of the rich and powerful in Berlin? In particular we set out to answer these specific questions: was it true that during the war spies worked as prostitutes employed by the Reich Security Main Office (RSHA) or other Nazi espionage organisations to extract information relating to the war from their clients? Were there any valid clues remaining that listening bugs were fitted connecting the brothel's third-storey love rooms with the cellar, where an elaborate installation was set up to record the conversations? Finally, what was the real role played by the notorious madam of the house, Kitty Schmidt, and what do we really know about her?

Before putting the pieces of the puzzle together that we have assembled from official documents, and from literature, films, documentaries and photographs, as well as from personal interviews and memoirs, we have to identify the socio-political sphere and ideological space in which this Nazi espionage project played out, and how plausible their espionage efforts were.

Such a strategically planned enterprise, as coldly conceived as a chess move, to winkle out information relevant to the war in a 'sinful temple of fleshly lust' was in flat contradiction of the officially propagated Nazi crackdown on sexual immorality. Probably the plan was conceived by Hitler's security and intelligence services with the idea that 'the enemy' would not imagine such a brilliant scheme, and that, besotted with lust, they would fall straight into the trap. After Hitler's seizure of power, sexual relationships and who could be intimate with who were strongly regulated. The liberal position towards free and commercial love that had characterised the Weimar Republic in the 1920s was demonised by the Führer as 'Bolshevik contamination of our sexual morality'. Nazi ideology officially permitted only one form of sexual relationship: within a marriage in a community for the purpose of 'presenting the *Volk* with healthy children and to bring those children up as upstanding German women and men'. Though not strictly legislated for, this was understood on all sides.

In stark contrast to this doctrine, as we have shown in previous chapters, the Führer and some of his closest cronies and hangmen did not adhere so strictly to their definition of sexual morals. Piquant details have come down to us regarding the amorous debauches of members of Hitler's intimate circle — for example, SS-Reichsführer Heinrich Himmler's illegitimate children with his secretary; Propaganda Minister Josef Goebbels countless affairs with film actresses that won him the nickname the 'Bock of Babelsberg'; Reich Labour Minister Robert Ley's uninhibited affair with an underage girl'; or War Minister Werner von Blomberg's wedding – sealed by the presence of Hitler and Goebbels – with a young woman who had previously worked as a naked model and prostitute.

A prominent practitioner of this double and triple morality was the head of the RSHA, none other than Reinhard Heydrich. His subordinate and Chief of the SD's Foreign Department, Walter Schellenberg, writes in his memoirs of the frequent nights on the town and excessive escapades enjoyed by his boss. Heydrich's unquenchable desire for sex was, among other factors, the trigger for setting up his own Nazi brothel in order to trap foreign diplomats and his own party comrades into betraying indiscreet secrets.

While the Nazi bigwigs partied behind the scenes, the restrictions governing the everyday existence of the people they ruled over were ever more strictly applied and executed. Under a basic law to fight crime decreed in December 1937, people – primarily women – who frequently changed sexual partners and who had already been branded for their immoral lifestyles could be classified as 'asocials' and risked being sent to concentration camps under that category. Already in 1934, 20,000 women were officially registered as prostitutes or constantly changing partners. Paradoxically, such women detained in camps were exploited by the Nazis and compelled or pressurised into working as prostitutes in the camp brothels. The asocial category, making up some 110,000, were the largest group of non-Jewish Germans to be imprisoned in the camps between 1937 and 1943. Most females were detained in Ravensbrück near Berlin from where many of them were taken to other camps or Wehrmacht brothels as sex workers.

In May 1941, a year before his assassination, Heydrich closed one of the last loopholes in the law, when he ordered the closure of those brothels in the Reich that had not already been shut down. The fact that Kitty Schmidt's establishment in the Giesebrechtstrasse was not officially registered and continued to operate strongly suggests that probably even before the outbreak of war in 1939 it enjoyed a degree of official recognition and protection as a 'state matter'.

We can also be fairly certain that some sort of espionage operation did indeed take place in Salon Kitty, whether it was initiated by the Gestapo or the SD, and whether the idea originated with Criminal Police Chief Arthur Nebe, Walter Schellenberg or – as most sources suggest – Reinhard Heydrich. The question that remains open is to what extent Kitty Schmidt and her ladies can be defined as spies. Most probably, in the terminology of the RSHA, the courtesans who worked at Salon Kitty were not professional 'agents' but were classified as *V-Leute* – or *Vertrauens-Leute* – trusted informants. In practice this would have meant that they were interviewed and tested to ensure their loyalty to the Nazi regime, and regularly submitted reports about their contacts with clients. They therefore formed part of that vast social group in a totalitarian society who observed and informed on their contacts and neighbours – a powerful weapon in the hands of the Gestapo and SD.

It is more difficult with the scant and contradictory available evidence to decide on the exact role of Kitty Schmidt herself. Did she, either voluntarily or even with enthusiasm, as some reports indicate, support the secret espionage activities that went on in her brothel? If so, she too was doubtless a leading 'V-Frau' for her SS employers. Or was she, as Peter Norden avers, and other sources allege, pressurised or forced to co-operate in turning over her establishment to the dirty purposes of the RSHA and other intelligence agencies of the Reich?

If the latter, then she performed a role familiar in espionage – of a classic agent operating under the orders of her spymasters, paid for her services but also mistrusted and constantly under the watchful eyes of her employers, and permanently under threat of draconian punishment. If she was indeed paid for her 'services', then that probably took the form of privileges rather than hard cash – above all that she was permitted to continue running her salon as a commercial enterprise. And that she continued to obtain plentiful supplies of luxuries like Champagne, truffles and caviar in the middle of the war.

Whether the women at Salon Kitty were 'V-Leute' or paid agents, was the information gleaned by the SD obtained from them by verbal or written reports or by sophisticated listening devices as detailed by Peter Norden in his 'documentary novel'? To what extent were such devices real or the products of Norden's fantasies and fertile imagination? Where did he obtain his information and who told him the details of the women in the 'love rooms' and the activities of the SD officials in their cellar listening post? These questions have long preoccupied us, and Norden's claims can neither be completely verified or entirely disproved. Norden himself made no secret of the fact that his story mixed truth and fiction. Many of the technical details he repeated in his contribution to Rosa von Praunheim's 1993 documentary film were made a good twenty years after the publication of his book. He claimed that he himself had spent twenty years researching his book. If so, that means that in the late 1940s or early 1950s he found witnesses who knew of the technicalities in the Giesebrechtstrasse and were willing to divulge them.

There is a considerable body of evidence from survivors of the Nazi era – as well as from our own inspection of Giesebrechtstrasse 11 – that the Nazis employed listening bugs. For example, Eugen Dollmann, chief interpreter between the Axis powers, reported in his memoirs that Reinhard Heydrich told him as early as April 1938 that he was contemplating setting up a brothel to spy on the Reich's enemies, and that he intended to install listening devices to enable him to do so. The SD agent Alfred Naujocks, tasked by Heydrich with installing the listening equipment, confirmed after the war that he had done so. Naujocks added that he had, whether accidentally or deliberately, left the listening bugs on during one of his chief's visits to one of the love rooms – the same charge that Heydrich had levelled against Schellenberg. This caused a furious Heydrich to send him to the Russian front as a punishment.

Walter Schellenberg describes in his memoirs how he had been in overall charge of the operation to convert Kitty's Salon into a listening post, complete with the installation of double walls and state-of-the-art listening bugs capable of picking up every word spoken in the love rooms, that were run by professional technicians of the security services. Heinrich Himmler's personal masseur, Felix Kersten, wrote in his memoirs that the Reichsführer had boasted of being able to listen to 'the intimate conversations of powerful gentlemen' recorded on such devices.

Kitty Schmidt herself, in an interview with the prominent journalist Klaus Harpprecht conducted shortly before her death in 1954, spoke about the microphones that had been hidden in her salon and the listening devices in the cellar which the young ladies who worked for her knew all about. An anonymous former sex worker, interviewed for Claus Räfle's documentary film in 2004, who had been at the salon later in the war after the listening action had ended, also spoke about the hidden microphones, which she said had been a common subject of gossip among her co-workers. An article published in 1959 in the German news magazine *Stern* informed its readers that Heydrich had had around forty-eight microphones installed at Giesebrechtstrasse 11, with their cables hidden under carpets. He had also placed hidden cameras in almost all the love rooms. Although no traces of such devices remained during our visit to the property in 2016, we were informed by the janitor, Eberhard Rick, that during renovation work carried out in the 1970s 'remarkably long cables' had indeed been discovered that could have connected the house's third storey with the cellar, along with 'strange sockets' with an unknown function.

All this strongly suggests that there is a high probability that the Nazis did indeed install listening devices at Salon Kitty during the war in some form or other, although we do not know whether these used the fabled wax discs. Nor do we know exactly when or why the listening operation was wound up. Possibly the action was ended by Ernst Kaltenbrunner, who succeeded Heydrich as chief of the RSHA after Heydrich's death in June 1942, and who 'quite by accident' was a neighbour of Salon Kitty, living at Giesebrechtstrasse 12. In any event, the point of no return for the espionage operation at the salon came no later than 1943 when the house was hit by an Allied air raid, and the third and fourth storeys suffered massive damage.

Mystery also surrounds the ownership of Giesebrechtstrasse 11 and the financing of the eavesdropping project. Although Kitty Schmidt's grandson Jochem Matei believed that his grandmother was the owner of the property and that he had been cheated out of his rightful inheritance, others think that she only rented the premises. During the time that the Nazis were using the salon for their own purposes it is likely that some kind of 'special relationship' existed between Kitty and the authorities. We believe that an agreement was probably reached between Heydrich, Schellenberg and Foreign Minister Joachim von Ribbentrop that Joseph Goebbels' Propaganda Ministry would finance the operation – bearing in mind that both Ribbentrop and Goebbels were probably among the salon's clients. Heydrich and others certainly claimed that Goebbels' Ministry bore the costs.

Whether or not this supposition is correct, it is clear that Kitty Schmidt ran a lucrative business there, considering that she occupied 500 square metres on the third storey, along with the entrance hall and two apartments on the first storey where she lived along with her sister Elsa, her daughter Kathleen, and her infant grandson Jochem. The sole official document that we found on the subject during all the years of our research was a plan of the 'Pension Zammit' on the ground floor of the property, where 'Salon Kitty' was relocated after the upper floors of the building were wrecked by the Allied air raid. On the plan, drawn up in April 1954, two months after Kitty's death, the property company Hackenberger & Loll are listed as the owners. It seems likely, therefore, that even if Kitty was the original owner, at some point during her declining years, she sold the property and became a tenant.

Turning once again to Kitty Schmidt herself, from the outset of our research, we tried to discover as much as possible about her life, and especially her role as a brothel madam and the exact nature of her 'co-operation' with the Nazis. With the help of official documents recording changes of address and so on, and above all with the recollections of her grandson in interviews and on various documentary films, and the memories of other witnesses, we have established a broad biographical outline of her life and personality.

Especially valuable to us were the recollections of Karin Zickerick, the only living eyewitness who still remembered Kitty. Karin spent much of her childhood visiting Giesebrechtstrasse 11 and gave us her impressions in several long interviews. Our research took us to Slovenia and the relatives of Jochem Matei's wife Irena, where we found an unexpected trove of family documents, including some 500 photos, a postcard written in Kitty's hand, and a video film of her daughter Kathleen's funeral. These led us in turn to Jochem Matei's best friend, Manuel Stahl, and other videos in private hands.

The established facts are that Kitty Zammit-Schmidt was born in Hamburg on 25 June 1882 as one of eight children. Two of her siblings died in childhood, and her father died in 1908 when, as a 26-year-old, she had already emigrated to Britain. Her marriage there to a Spaniard named Zammit only lasted a few years before her husband committed suicide, leaving her with a young daughter Kathleen. Her sister Elsa persuaded Kitty to return to Germany late in 1918 as the First World War ended. She lived at first with thirteen-year-old Kathleen at Berliner Strasse 10 in the capital's Wilmersdorf district. By the 1930s she had opened her first 'salon' at Budapester Strasse 27, where she was officially registered as living between 1933 and 1938, describing herself as an 'artist'. Kitty enjoyed life to the full in the 'Golden 1920s' of the Weimar Republic, with its open eroticism and club nightlife. She became a well-known, fashionably dressed personality about town and made many friends among Berlin's Bohemian and artistic circles.

Kitty Schmidt opened her second salon at Kurfürstendamm 63 before finally locating to nearby Giesebrechtstrasse 11 – the site of the legendary Salon Kitty. Kitty was evidently greatly loved by the women who worked for her. Despite her keen business brain, she acted in a motherly role towards them. She placed great stress on them having a smart and elegant appearance like herself. Kitty's neighbours uniformly described her as friendly, sociable and always ready to help. As a child Karin Zickerick knew her as 'Auntie Käthe' and enjoyed spending much time with her. Jochem Matei recalled his grandmother's contradictory character combining generosity with financial thriftiness. A graphological analysis of her handwritten postcard from the family archive confirmed this, finding her to be optimistic, temperamental, intelligent and self-confident. All these positive characteristics would come in useful in her dealings with the Nazi power brokers who probably were among her clientele before the outbreak of war in 1939.

All witnesses to have spoken out on the subject attest that Kitty Schmidt never expressed support for Nazi racial ideology and had several Jewish friends. Before 1941 five Jews lived in apartments at Giesebrechtstrasse 11 who were all deported to their deaths during the Holocaust. There are several reports that Kitty helped Jews escape to safety from Nazi persecution, and even hid one on her premises during the war under a false identity working as a kitchen helper.

Much of Kitty's life after the Second World War ended still lies in the shadows. Her salon, rebranded as a pension guest house, was a shadow of its former self, and though the brothel business continued on a much smaller scale, Kitty herself in her last decade retreated into the bosom of her family. She became seriously ill in November 1953 and died on 23 February 1954 in Giesebrechtstrasse 11 aged seventy-one.

Kitty's funeral was held four days later attended by her family and hundreds of other mourners. She was laid to rest in the nearby Waldfriedhof cemetery in Heerstrasse. After the death of her mother, Kathleen Matei took over the business under the name 'Pension Florian' and ran it as a guesthouse for artists and actors in tandem with the much reduced brothel. After Kathleen's own demise, Kitty's grandson Jochem Matei tried to run the pension as a home for foreign asylum seekers, but lacking his grandmother's and mother's business acumen, and facing opposition from his neighbours, the project rapidly declined and Jochem himself lapsed into alcoholism.

The new and mostly previously unpublished material that we have uncovered filled some of the gaps in Kitty Schmidt's biography and clarified many of the rumours, myths and legends surrounding Salon Kitty. The answers to some questions, however, remain unclear. Above all it is still uncertain whether 'Madam Kitty' was a 'trusted informant' or a willingly co-operative agent of the Nazis. Or was she compelled to play that role? To put it another way, was she a Hitler sympathiser or was she finally a victim of Nazi ideology and their machinations? Alfred Naujocks is the only witness to have once stated that long before the establishment of the Nazis' spying operation in Giesebrechtstrasse, Kitty Schmidt worked as an agent for the security services in Poland and the Balkans. In the course of our research we have found no evidence to suggest that there is any truth to this story.

Peter Norden's book is the sole source of the story that when Kitty attempted to flee to the Netherlands in June 1939, she was detained by Nazi agents who threatened to send her to a concentration camp unless she co-operated with their plans. We do know that during the 1930s Kitty Schmidt visited England more than once, but we cannot either confirm or rule out Norden's claim that she was caught attempting to go there permanently, and that her escape attempt was used to compel her to agree to the conversion of her brothel into an espionage centre.

Despite the fact that we have spent years researching the subject, we still find it difficult to reach a certain verdict on Kitty Schmidt's exact role during the war years. We cannot simply damn this woman as an ideologically convinced National Socialist or even as an opportunistic assistant of their schemes. Still less, can we whitewash or even glorify her as a sort of hidden 'heroine of the passive resistance'. Kitty Schmidt's historic role from today's perspective is difficult to define and presents more questions than answers.

What is certain is that this single mother, beginning with no financial resources, was at the epicentre in Berlin of the most turbulent and brutal years of the twentieth century. For her willing call girls she was – at least according to their later statements – a well-meaning 'brothel mother' with her heart in the right place. But we can – and probably must – pose questions about her personal motivations and morality. For example, should we see her as an amoral matchmaker, an exploiter of young and naïve girls who didn't hesitate to bring her own artistically inclined daughter into her business? Was she really a fashionable and elegant society lady, a cultivated mistress of her business, or an unscrupulous slave driver, heavily made up and with expensive tastes? A clever and resourceful businesswoman with prematurely modern management skills in a male-dominated world? Or was she simply a cold, calculating and greedy war profiteer, benefitting from masculine sabre-rattling and animalistic drives? Did she belong to the elite of perfect spies who leave no trace behind them, or was she only a treacherous informer and a willing and trusted servant of the SS, prepared to do anything in the name of the party and the state?

How can we place this 'Aryan' woman of whom eyewitnesses have only nice words to say, who literally no one spoke of badly? Many, indeed, declared that she was no Nazi, and went out of her way to be friendly to the Jews. Yet they are speaking of the same woman who entertained the worst war criminals in world history and the organisers of the Holocaust, who drank Champagne with them and provided the services of her loyal and well-paid young ladies for them to use and exploit. Was Kitty Schmidt an amazingly strong or a contemptibly weak person? Maid or minion, victim or criminal?

We cannot answer such questions with any certainty. Without a doubt Kitty Schmidt's life leaves many puzzles behind. What we have learned from surviving sources and everything that has been written and spoken about her, we have related in this book. We have considered the various views, opinions and angles on whether Kitty Schmidt can be described as an opportunist, profiteer, collaborator or victim of National Socialism. The most historically accurate and fairest answer that we can give from our present state of knowledge is that she was probably a bit of all these things: a very capable, careful and intelligent survival artist in times of extreme chaos and violence. Her tragedy, if it can be so described, is that her whole life of more than seventy-one years – and probably for all eternity – is reduced to the short time in the early war years revolving around her much mythologised and still mysterious role when 'Salon Kitty' played a very successful, if unofficial, part at the very heart of Hitler's criminal state. As a German Aryan courtesan and madam, it is her morally dubious reputation, being as she was in prominent association with the Nazis' times and crimes, that will be carried through history.

AFTERWORD

'Is this still a brothel?'

Although today there is no memorial plaque on Giesebrechtstrasse 11 in memory of 'Salon Kitty' or its onetime resident Kitty Schmidt, many Berlin tourist guides still include a stop at the former brothel on their itineraries. They all know that scary or mysterious stories of what went on there are still attractive to tourists, making history come alive. But it is not only at the site itself where such stories are told. A brief foray through Berlin's tourist literature yields similar results. For example, Andrea Steingart's book *Schauplätze Berliner Geschichte* includes an entry, among such places as Hitler's former Führerbunker, or Goebbels' former residence, listing the address Giesebrechtstrasse 11 as the 'former Salon Kitty' together with the appropriate bus and U-Bahn stops. On the initiative of the historian Florian Schimikowski, the German Espionage Museum in Berlin is planning to give Salon Kitty a permanent exhibition space in the near future.

Today, the upper floors of Giesebrechtstrasse 11 are divided into private apartments and the offices of lawyers, a tax advisor, an insurance company, an educational institute for psychodrama, a PR agency and a dance studio. Ironically, given its history, there is also a firm selling tape recorders and other office equipment. On the ground floor a shop currently sells exclusive designer lighting and luxury furniture. The old doors, part of the walls, the lift, as well as the internal stairs dating from the war years are still extant, though renovated to give a modern appearance. The space that once housed 'Salon Kitty' on the third storey has been adapted to accommodate two large apartments. A further space behind these two flats that was destroyed in the 1943 air raid has never been rebuilt.

A married couple, Norbert and Rita Christian, have occupied one of the flats since 1972. Ever since the publication of Peter Norden's book the pair have had to deal with a constant stream of uninvited rubbernecking visitors curious to know the truth behind the myths and legends. The question they almost always ask is: 'Is this still a brothel?'

Norbert Christian told us in an interview in 2016:

I can absolutely well imagine that it was possible that an eavesdropping action was mounted here to obtain information impossible to obtain in other ways. You know how people in the throes of passion give lots away. Perhaps someone or other spoke out of turn in such situations – that is certainly easy to imagine. If someone said something indiscreet about Adolf Hitler, then perhaps a couple of days later they'd be called in by the Gestapo . . . The listening devices were certainly hidden, but the people going in and out were not invisible. I think that Frau Schmidt must have known about it, or at least suspected it.

Rita and Norbert Christian still remember their former neighbour, Kathleen Matei. They say she never spoke about her mother, was very taciturn and kept herself to herself.

A visitor to Berlin today who stands on the famous Kurfürstendamm by the street sign 'Giesebrechtstrasse' and looks along the few steps to where No. 11 stands, can still easily visualise the discretion and elegance of the buildings along this short and unspectacular side street. If such a visitor lets their thoughts run free, it is still possible to imagine today the chauffeur-driven cars or taxis carrying Nazi bigwigs, industrialists and foreign diplomats drawing up to drop off their passengers and later stopping by to collect them.

Inside the house itself, the creaking stairs, the old, cramped lift and the old iron door knockers could, if they could speak, tell dozens, if not hundreds, of sad and strange stories of what once played out here. In the apartments on the third floor the large living rooms and the smaller side rooms also have their tales to tell. In the courtyard the steps leading down to the cellar once saw the Nazi listening technicians go up and down, unseen and undisturbed, to install their equipment. Inside the cellars, converted again during the war into air raid shelters, the visitor does not need much fantasy to conjure up the scene where the SS eavesdropping specialists once sat, and where the old gas pipes were adapted to contain cables. Still visible is the walled-up tunnel leading to the residence next door of the RSHA chief Ernst Kaltenbrunner. The topmost storey of the old house, hit and destroyed by British bombers in 1943, was never restored. This still open wound serves as a memorial to a truly terrible war.

ACKNOWLEDGEMENTS

A big 'thank you' must go in the first instance to Miri Peraic who welcomed us in Slovenia and shared a collection of more than 500 family photos and documents, including a handwritten postcard of Kitty Schmidt. We are grateful to Yassien Shaker for allowing us unrestricted access to video material inherited from his late father Manuel Stahl, enabling us to obtain a very personal insight into the childhood of Jochem Matei as well as his mother and grandmother.

Karin Zickerick, the last living witness to have known Kitty Schmidt personally, helped us with her memories to gain a better picture of Kitty, the madam of her high-society bordello, and her daughter Kathleen. We are grateful too, to Inger Anne-Marie Öster, Kitty's great niece and sole surviving descendant, for allowing us to examine and reproduce pages and photos from her family album.

Eberhard Rick, the House Manager of Giesebrechtstrasse 11, gave us a guided tour of the property and its cellars. We are indebted also to Rita and Norbert Christian for their hospitality in their apartment on the third floor of the former 'Salon Kitty', and for sharing their memories.

We gratefully acknowledge the assistance and historical insights of the Berlin historian and archivist Joachim Kundler. We are also grateful to Helmut Krauss, custodian of the Waldfriedhof cemetery, for taking the time to show us the last resting place of Kitty Schmidt, and of Kathleen and Jochem Matei.

For his many rich descriptions and exceedingly vivid memories of Kitty's Salon and Kathleen Matei after the Second World War we would like to thank the actor Berno von Cramm. Felicitas Schirow was also admirably honest and forthcoming in her conversation with us regarding her work as a former prostitute with Kathleen Matei. We are very grateful to Brigitta Hughes, daughter of Peter Norden, and to his ex-wife for interviews giving us valuable insights into the writer's life. We would like to thank the film director Alexander Tuschinski, who in the course of our research facilitated a contact with Tinto Brass, director of the 1970s film *Salon Kitty*.

For a graphological analysis of the only extant document in Kitty Schmidt's handwriting we are grateful to Wolfgang Caspart. We are also indebted to Count Felix von Luckner researcher Jürgen Stumpfhaus for offering us his insights into the 'Sea Devil's' biography.

We would also like to express our thanks to Christina Kunkel, from the Institute for Contemporary History in Munich, and to Ulrich Räcker-Wellnitz, former director of the City Archive in Wilhelmshaven, for their help in our research.

For their unstinting assistance, we are also extremely grateful to the filmmakers Rosa von Praunheim and Claus Räfle who, with their documentary films *Meine Oma hat einen Nazipuff* and *Salon Kitty*, contributed significantly to uncovering the history of the brothel before we began our research.

No small part was played in the completion of the book by Brigitte Mayr, for whose work we can never thank her enough. The same goes for the publishers of the original German edition, Berlin Story Verlag, especially our editor Wieland Giebel. We are also indebted to cameraman Christoph Ainedter and the photographer Birgit Probst for taking pictures in Berlin on our behalf. We have also drawn on the knowledge of Berlin of our personal friend Roger Rotzinger, who often chauffeured us across the city, along with his friend Mario Hahne of the Cumulus Kniepe who introduced us to Felicitas Schirow. We would also like to acknowledge the contribution of film producer Mark Boot whose idea to make a new film of the Salon Kitty story set us off on the trail of this adventure. Nadin Hadi from our office in London greatly assisted our research in Great Britain. Our final thanks must go to our nearest and dearest at home: Maleerat, Bernd and Sofia, who gave us the strength and time to see this book through to completion.

URS BRUNNER, JULIA SCHRAMMEL

For the expanded English edition of this book Nigel Jones would like to thank Professor Robert Gerwarth, most recent biographer of Reinhard Heydrich for his advice. Nigel also wishes to acknowledge the work of Himmler's biographer Peter Padfield, and that of Richard Bassett and Michael Müller, biographers of Admiral Wilhelm Canaris, along with Sarah Helm's study of Ravensbrück concentration camp and Catrine Clay's history of the Lebensborn project. He also owes a debt to Daniel Siemens and Giles MacDonogh for their studies of the Nazi 'martyr' Horst Wessel.

NIGEL JONES

CHRONOLOGY

25 June 1882: Birth of Kätchen 'Kitty' Emma Sophie Schmidt in Hamburg.

20 April 1889: Birth of Adolf Hitler in Braunau-on-the-Inn, Austria.

Circa 1900: Kitty Schmidt travels as a piano teacher and governess to Great Britain and meets a Spanish diplomat named Zammit who becomes the love of her life.

15 October 1906: Birth of Kitty Schmidt's daughter Kathleen in Cardiff, Wales.

Circa 1906–1917: Kitty marries the Spanish Consul Zammit who later takes his life with a pistol (date and year unknown).

1918: First World War ends. Kitty returns to Germany and resides in Berlin with her daughter.

1919: Kitty rents out rooms in Berlin. She lives with her thirteen-year-old daughter Kathleen at Berliner Strasse 10 in the Wilmersdorf quarter where she remains registered until 1932.

Circa 1922: In the city where approximately 120,00 prostitutes ply their trade, Kitty Schmidt opens her first 'salon' at Budapester Strasse 27.

8–9 November 1923: Failure of Hitler's 'Beer Hall Putsch' in

Munich.

1925–6: Hitler's manifesto/autobiography *Mein Kampf* is published in two volumes.

24 October 1929: Wall Street Crash in New York. Beginning of the worldwide Great Depression.

July 1932: Reinhard Heydrich is leader of the SS Security Service, the SD.

30 January 1933: As leader of the strongest party in the Reichstag, Nazi 'Führer' Adolf Hitler is appointed Chancellor. The Nazis begin to impose their grip on Germany with the opening of the first concentration camps where their political opponents, and later Jews, Roma-Sinti, homosexuals and other 'asocials' are imprisoned.

Summer 1933: Prostitution declared responsible for the spread of sexually transmitted diseases. Many privately owned brothels closed as a result.

1934: Officially only around twenty brothels remain open in Berlin. 'Night of the Long Knives' purge leads to demonisation of homosexuals. Hitler merges posts of Chancellor and President as 'Führer' after death of President Hindenburg.

1935: Kitty Schmidt opens her second Salon at Kurfürstendamm 63. 'Nuremberg Laws' forbid sexual relations or marriages between Jews and 'Aryan' Germans.

1936: According to Peter Norden, Kitty Schmidt begins to smuggle illegal currency to London. Hitler reoccupies the Rhineland. Germany gives military support to General Franco in the Spanish Civil War. Heydrich assumes command of Security Police (Sipo), Gestapo and Kriminalpolizei (Kripo).

Early 1938: Blomberg–Fritsch crisis. Göring, Himmler and Heydrich conspire to discredit top army generals with sexual scandals. Hitler assumes personal command of the Wehrmacht after Blomberg and von Fritsch quit.

12 March 1938: The 'Anschluss' – Hitler annexes Austria.

September 1938: Czechoslovak crisis: Hitler's threats against Czechoslovakia lead to the Munich Agreement in which Britain and France agree to Czechs ceding Sudetenland to Germany.

9–10th November 1938: Reichskristallnacht: nationwide pogrom against Jews – more than a thousand synagogues are torched, thousands of Jewish shops trashed, around a hundred Jews are murdered and many more are sent to Dachau concentration camp.

Early 1939: Kitty Schmidt opens her 'Pension Schmidt' at Giesebrechtstrasse 11 – the establishment later known as 'Salon Kitty'.

March 1938: Hitler occupies rump of Czechoslovakia.

April 1939: According to Peter Norden, Criminal Police Chief Arthur Nebe proposes to place agents in Salon Kitty to spy on clients. Kitty Schmidt politely but firmly rejects the proposal.

June 1939: According to Peter Norden, Nebe's proposal accelerates Kitty Schmidt's plan to flee to Britain and open her business there. She flees Berlin but is arrested near the Dutch border and is held and interrogated in a cell at the Gestapo HQ in Berlin's Prinz- Albrecht-Strasse. She is faced with a harsh choice: co-operate with the Nazis or go to a concentration camp.

1 September 1939: After a 'false flag' provocation organised by Heydrich, German forces invade Poland. Britain and France declare war on 3 September – beginning of the Second World War.

27 September 1939: Merger of the Security Police (Sipo) and the SS-Sicherheitsdienst (SD) in a new umbrella organisation, the Reich Security Main Office (RSHA) under Heydrich's command. According to Peter Norden this also marks the birth of the 'Reich Special Matter': Salon Kitty.

Late February 1940: According to Peter Norden Salon Kitty is refurbished within four weeks as a spy centre.

10 May 1940: Hitler's armies invade the Netherlands, Belgium,

Luxembourg and France, leading in June to the collapse and occupation of France and the retreat of British forces from Dunkirk.

22 June 1941: Hitler's armies invade the Soviet Union.

1 September 1941: All people of Jewish origin in the Reich are required to wear a yellow star.

7 December 1941: Japan attacks Pearl Harbor. Entry of the USA into the Second World War.

20 January 1942: The Wannsee Conference outside Berlin under Heydrich's chairmanship signals the 'Final Solution of the Jewish question' and opens the way for the Holocaust.

27 May 1942: Attack on Reinhard Heydrich in Prague by British-trained Czechoslovak partisans. He succumbs to his injuries on 4 June. SS-Reichsführer Himmler assumes command of the RSHA.

20 June 1942: Birth of Kathleen Schmidt's son Jochem Matei.

28 October 1942: Marriage of Kathleen Schmidt and Jean-Florian Matei at the Registry Office in Charlottenburg, Berlin.

Winter 1942–3: Battle of Stalingrad. The decisive turning point of the war shakes the belief of the German population in Hitler's victory.

30 January 1943: Ernst Kaltenbrunner is appointed chief of the RSHA in Berlin.

1943: Giesebrechtstrasse 11 is hit by a bomb in an Allied air raid. The third and fourth storeys of the building are burned out. Kitty Schmidt and her salon move to the ground floor.

1943: According to Felix, Count von Luckner, he finds the pass of a German woman killed in an air raid and gives the false identity to a Jewish woman fugitive. He arranges with Kitty Schmidt for her to be employed at Salon Kitty as a kitchen helper, thereby saving her life.

18 February 1943: Following the defeat at Stalingrad, Propaganda Minister Joseph Goebbels proclaims a policy of 'total war'. Restaurants, brothels and other places of pleasure are closed.

6 June 1944: British, American and Canadian forces invade

Normandy on D-Day, beginning the liberation of Western Europe.

20 July 1944: Colonel Count Claus von Stauffenberg places a bomb at Hitler's East Prussian HQ. The bomb explodes but Hitler survives. An anti-Nazi military putsch in Berlin, Paris and Prague collapses as news of Hitler's survival spreads. Stauffenberg and hundreds of his co-conspirators are executed.

16 April 1945: Russian forces encircle Berlin and the final battle for the capital begins.

30 April 1945: Hitler and his newlywed bride Eva Braun commit suicide in his Berlin bunker. Goebbels and his wife Magda follow them after murdering their own children.

7 May 1945: German forces unconditionally capitulate to the four Allied powers. End of the war in Europe. Berlin is divided by the Allies into Soviet, American, British and French occupation zones.

25 December 1945: Jean-Florian Matei dies in Wilhelmshaven of a lung infection.

23 February 1954: Kitty Schmidt dies aged seventy-one in her apartment at Giesebrechtstrasse 11.

27 February 1954: The funeral of Kitty Schmidt at the Waldfriedhof in Heerstrasse is attended by hundreds of mourners. Her daughter Kathleen Matei takes over the running of the pension and a reduced brothel business at Giesebrechtstrasse 11.

1956: First publication in English of Walter Schellenberg's posthumous memoirs mentions his alleged role in the setting up of Salon Kitty as a spy listening post.

1970: Publication of Peter Norden's 'documentary novel' *Salon Kitty* (*Madam Kitty* in its English edition). Kathleen Matei refuses all co-operation with Norden's work.

May 1975: Kathleen Matei's efforts to stop the release of Tinto Brass's film *Salon Kitty* by legal means fails.

March 1976: The movie *Salon Kitty* has its premiere in Italy.

4 February 1985: Jochem Matei meets his future wife, Irena.

December 1985: Jochem and Irena marry in a civil ceremony. They later have a church wedding on the first anniversary of their meeting.

March 1992: Property managers give Jochem Matei notice to quit Giesebrechtstrasse 11 after complaints about his efforts to turn it into a hostel for migrants.

23 August 1992: Kathleen Matei dies aged eighty-five. She is buried beside her mother on 10 September.

Late 1992: Jochem and Irena Matei leave Giesebrechtstrasse 11.

November 1993: Filmmaker Rosa von Praunheim presents his documentary film *Meine Oma hatte einen Nazipuff* ('My Granny had a Nazi Brothel') with contributions from Jochem Matei.

2004: Filmmaker Claus Räfle presents his documentary film *Salon Kitty*.

28 November 2009: Jochem Matei dies in Berlin aged sixty-seven. He is buried beside his mother and grandmother in the Waldfriedhof cemetery. His widow Irena returns to her native Slovenia to live with her sister Miri Peraic. She dies of cancer in September 2015.

BRIEF BIOGRAPHIES
– Prominent people in the Third Reich
linked with 'Salon Kitty'

BEST, WERNER (10.7.1903–23.6.1989)

A jurist and Nazi 'intellectual', SS-Obergruppenführer Best was Heydrich's deputy in the SD leadership and Governor in occupied Denmark. Earlier, Best had been an organiser and co-ordinator of the mass killings carried out by the Einsatzgruppen in Poland. From August 1940 to June 1942 Best was on the staff of the Military Administration authorities in France, responsible for initiating persecution of Jews. He led the drive for the 'Final Solution of the Jewish question' in Denmark, though many Danish Jews were smuggled to safety into neutral Sweden. After giving evidence for the defence in the post-war Nuremberg trials, Best was sentenced to death in Denmark but was reprieved. Released from jail in August 1951, Best was a main mover in the campaign for a general amnesty for Nazi criminals. He worked in German industry in later life.

CANARIS, WILHELM (1.1.1887–9.4.1945)

Admiral Canaris was head of the Abwehr military intelligence service and a 'frenemy' and rival to Heydrich. Moving into the intelligence world in the First World War, Canaris was active in right-wing conspiracy under the Weimar Republic, smuggling the killers of Communist leaders Karl Liebknecht and Rosa Luxemburg to safety. He became a mentor to Heydrich during the latter's service as a naval officer and the two men re-established contact when Canaris became Abwehr chief in 1935. Becoming disillusioned with the Nazi regime, Canaris pursued a policy of cautious opposition, filling the Abwehr ranks with anti-Nazis who plotted against the regime and sending envoys to warn foreign governments of Hitler's plans for war. This led to his dismissal and arrest after the failure of von Stauffenberg's attempt on Hitler's life. He was hanged at Flossenburg concentration camp during the last days of the war.

CIANO, GALEAZZO (18.3.1903–11.1.1944)

A professional diplomat, Count Ciano was appointed Italian Foreign Minister in 1936 by Benito Mussolini after his marriage to the Fascist dictator's eldest daughter Edda. During an earlier posting in China, he is reported to have had an affair with Wallis Simpson, later the wife of the Duke of Windsor, the former King Edward VIII. He was widely seen as the Duce's heir, but was an opponent of Italy's alliance with Germany and her declaration of war on Hitler's side. He was demoted to Envoy to the Vatican in 1943 after covertly working for a separate peace with the Allies. In July of that year, he voted for his father-in-law's effective removal from power at a meeting of the Fascist Grand Council. He unwisely fled to Germany with his family where he was arrested and returned to Fascist custody in Italy. Tried at Verona with other leading anti-Mussolini fascists, he was condemned to death and shot at Hitler's insistence. His diaries give an unrivalled portrait of Italy's part in the war. A frequent visitor to Berlin, he is believed to have been a client at Salon Kitty.

DIETRICH, JOSEPH ('Sepp') (28.5.1892–21.4.1966)

An early Nazi party member and Hitler crony, Dietrich was chief of Hitler's bodyguard and his chauffeur, and became an SS-Oberstgruppenführer and a general in the Waffen-SS. In 1934, during the Night of the Long Knives, Dietrich personally executed SA chief Ernst Röhm at Munich's Stadelhelm prison. During the Second World War he was a Panzer general in the Waffen-SS, having commanded Hitler's bodyguard which became the crack 1st SS Panzer Division Leibstandarte SS Adolf Hitler. Showing unsuspected military ability, he took part in most of the war's campaigns, serving on the Western and Eastern Fronts and in the Balkans. Indicted for his war crimes and sentenced to death in his absence in the Soviet Union, he was given a life sentence by a US military court in 1946. He was freed in 1955. Dietrich was reputed to be a frequent guest at Salon Kitty.

DOLLMAN, EUGEN (8.8.1900–17.5.1985)

An SS-Obersturmbannführer and diplomat, Dollman was appointed chief of the Nazi Party's press department in Italy in 1935. According to Dollman, Heydrich confided his plans to set up a brothel as a spy listening post to him during a visit to Naples in 1938. From 1939 he was the SS's special representative in Italy. He acted as interpreter at the meeting between Hitler and Mussolini on 20 July 1944, the day that Hitler had survived Count Stauffenberg's bomb. After the war, Dollman worked as a hotelier and translator in Munich.

FRICK, WILHELM (12.3.1877–16.10.1946)

As police chief in Munich in the early 1920s, Frick did his best to aid the Nazi Party's early rise and was tried with Hitler for high treason after the failure of the 1923 Beer Hall Putsch. Frick headed the Nazi Party faction in the Reichstag and was appointed Interior Minister in Hitler's first cabinet. In this post, which he held for ten years, Frick was responsible for the Nazi co-ordination of their criminal rule and for anti-Jewish legislation. He was the last Nazi governor of the occupied

Czech lands at the end of the war. Tried and condemned with other leading Nazis, he was hanged at Nuremberg in 1946.

FROMM, FRIEDRICH ('Fritz') (8.10.1888–12.3.1945)
A professional soldier, from 1933, Fromm was the chief of the Army Office in the OKW. In 1939 he became head of the Reserve Army in Berlin, responsible for implementing the 'Valkyrie' plan to crush any internal uprising. As such, he played a double game. Though aware that anti-Hitler conspirators were adapting Valkyrie for an anti-Nazi putsch following Hitler's assassination, he held himself aloof from the plot until he could see which side had won. After the failure of the bomb plot on 20 July 1944, he denounced the plotters and was briefly arrested by them. Freed by pro-Hitler officers, he sentenced Stauffenberg and his companions to death and had them immediately shot. Suspected by the Nazis of disloyalty, he was arrested and eventually executed early in 1945. He is thought to have been a client at Salon Kitty.

GOEBBELS, JOSEPH (20.10.1897–1.5.1945)
An intellectual and Doctor of Literature, Goebbels' club foot precluded his participation in the First World War. He became a bitter anti-Semite and a radical early Nazi Party member. Falling under Hitler's spell, he was appointed Gauleiter of Berlin in 1926, tasked with winning the left-wing capital for the party. His propagandist and public speaking skills helped him succeed, and he was appointed Propaganda Minister in Hitler's first Cabinet. A member of Hitler's inner circle, along with Göring and Himmler, he was among the foremost Nazi paladins. As Culture Tsar of the Reich, he was responsible for news, film, theatre and publishing, and used his position to conduct numerous affairs with actresses, despite his marriage to Magda Quandt, Hitler's favourite and unofficial 'First Lady' of the Reich. When the war turned against Germany, Goebbels proclaimed a fanatical policy of total war, and he remained loyal to Hitler to the last, following his

master in committing suicide in the bunker with Magda after killing their children. His Ministry may have financed Salon Kitty, and he was probably one of its clients.

GÖRING, HERMANN (12.1.1893–15.10.1946)
A flamboyant First World War air ace, Göring with his high-society background and contacts, was an important early recruit to the Nazi Party. Wounded in the 1923 Beer Hall Putsch, during his recovery he became a lifelong drug user. Returning from a lengthy exile, he became the Speaker of the Reichstag, facilitating Hitler's takeover. In April 1933 he was appointed Prime Minister of Prussia and became second only to Hitler in the party with the title Reichsmarschall. He became both Commander of the Luftwaffe and economics overlord, but made the mistake of handing control of the Gestapo to his rival Himmler. A leading player in the bloody Night of the Long Knives and the dismissal of Armed Forces Commander Werner von Blomberg (whom he vainly hoped to replace), Göring gave Heydrich the order in July 1941 to organise the so-called 'Final Solution of the Jewish question'. As the war turned against Germany, an increasingly indolent and obese Göring was blamed for the poor performance of the Luftwaffe, and steadily lost his former influence, immersing himself in drugs and plundering Europe for art works to add to his private collection. Dismissed from his party posts and arrested by the SS at the war's end for attempting to usurp Hitler's authority, he surrendered to the US Army in Bavaria. Weaned off drugs, he lost weight and regained much of his former intellectual ability to dominate the Nuremberg tribunal where he was the leading defendant. Condemned to death, he cheated the hangman on the eve of his execution by swallowing a phial of potassium cyanide in his cell.

HESS, RUDOLF (26.4.1894–17.8.1987)
Like Göring, a First World War flyer, Hess was a passionate early

follower of Hitler and served time with him in jail for his part in the 1923 Beer Hall Putsch. During their imprisonment Hess took down Hitler's dictation of *Mein Kampf.* Responsible for introducing Hitler to the concept of geopolitics, Hess was the Führer's secretary and official deputy after the Nazis took power. But, lacking a power base, he lost influence and in an apparent attempt to regain the Führer's favour, he flew to Scotland in May 1941 on a one-man mission to negotiate peace with Britain before the invasion of Russia. Arrested and interned on arrival, he was tried at Nuremberg and sentenced to life imprisonment. The last solitary prisoner in Berlin's Spandau jail, after several suicide bids, Hess finally succeeded in hanging himself in August 1987 after half a century behind bars.

HEYDRICH, REINHARD (7.3.1904–4.6.1942)

An opportunistic latecomer to Nazism, the youthful Heydrich joined the party in 1931 after being dishonourably discharged from the navy and was given the job of organising a security service, the SD, by SS-Reichsführer Himmler. His rise and his dedication to the pursuit of power was rapid and ruthless. He expanded his empire of terror from its Bavarian base to Berlin after the Nazis came to power and, with his boss Himmler, was the man most responsible for creating a totalitarian police state. In 1939 Heydrich united all the police, intelligence and security services of the Reich under his leadership in a new umbrella organisation, the Reich Security Main Office (RSHA). According to Peter Norden and others it was Heydrich who had the idea of converting Salon Kitty into a spy centre wired for sound and using his agents as prostitutes. A sexual philanderer, he also used the brothel for his own pleasure. A keen amateur aviator, Heydrich flew combat missions in the war until grounded by Hitler after being shot down behind Russian lines. Heydrich was personally responsible for many provocations and atrocities including the mass murder of Jews carried out by the Einsatzgruppen in Eastern Europe. In January 1942 he chaired the Wannsee Conference, which initiated the Holocaust. Made security boss of the occupied Czech lands, he was assassinated in Prague by British-trained Czechoslovak partisans.

HIMMLER, HEINRICH (7.10.1900–23.5.45)

The Reichsführer of the SS and Chief of the German Police was a devoted early follower of Hitler. The mild-mannered bespectacled son of a Bavarian courtier, Himmler carried a flag with Ernst Röhm in the Beer Hall Putsch. He found his life's work when he took over the SS – which had been formed as Hitler's bodyguard unit. Himmler steadily built the organisation into the Nazi Party's elite Praetorian Guard, and infused it with his own fanatical racial theories. In April 1933 he became Bavaria's Police Chief, and with Heydrich extended his control across the whole country. A main mover in the Night of the Long Knives, the SS displaced their SA rivals as the regime's spearhead and ideological core. Steadily building his own power base, Himmler succeeded Frick as Interior Minister in 1943. By then the SS were staffing the concentration camps and carrying out the Holocaust. Obsessed with preserving Germany's pure Aryan racial stock, Himmler was the initiator of the Lebensborn project and oversaw the mass extermination of European Jewry in the Holocaust. As the Reich crumbled, the SS became the last bastion of the regime, although Himmler proved totally incompetent as a military commander. When Hitler discovered that Himmler had put out peace feelers to the Allies in April 1945, he stripped him of all his offices, expelled him from the Nazi Party and ordered his arrest. Himmler attempted to join the Dönitz government but was rejected and went on the run in disguise. Apprehended by British soldiers, he was recognised and committed suicide with a cyanide phial concealed in his teeth.

HITLER, ADOLF (20.4.1889–30.4.1945)

The founder and Führer of Nazism, Hitler spent his early years in obscurity and poverty as a failed artist in Austria. A fanatical pan-German nationalist, he fled to Munich to escape the draft, but joined the German army on the outbreak of the First World War. He served throughout the conflict as a messenger on the Western Front, winning the Iron Cross, but never rising beyond the rank of corporal. He remained in the army after the war, witnessing the political chaos in Munich and being employed as an informer reporting on the city's political fringe and delivering lectures to his fellow soldiers. He joined the German Workers' Party in September 1919 and transformed it into the National Socialist German Workers' Party (NSDAP or Nazis) under his own autocratic leadership. After the bloody failure of the Beer Hall Putsch, he was imprisoned for a short spell during which he dictated his manifesto/ autobiography *Mein Kampf*. On his release he rebuilt the party and took part in elections. After the 1929 Wall Street Crash the Nazis became the largest party in the Reichstag and Hitler was appointed Chancellor on 30 January 1933. Within months, with the help of terror, violence and emergency decrees, the Nazis had become a one-party dictatorship owing total loyalty to Hitler as Führer. All other parties were banned, and political opponents were sent to the newly opened concentration camps to be tortured and murdered. Independent organisations were taken over. The SA was purged in 1934, and Hitler assumed personal command of the armed forces in 1938. His invasion of Poland in 1939 launched the Second World War, which ended with the defeat, division and occupation of Germany, millions dead and much of Europe in ruins.

KALTENBRUNNER, ERNST (4.10.1903–16.10.1946)

An Austrian, Kaltenbrunner was active in the illegal terrorist activities of the Nazis before the Anschluss, and became chief of the Austrian SS in 1936. After the Anschluss he became State Secretary for Security in Austria, rising to become an SS-Obergruppenführer and Police General. He succeeded Heydrich as Chief of the RSHA in January

1943 and was responsible for the investigations after the 1944 bomb attack on Hitler. Tried at Nuremberg with the other surviving Nazi leaders, he was sentenced to death and executed. Kaltenbrunner's Berlin house was next door to Salon Kitty.

LEY, ROBERT (15.2.1890–25.10.1945)

A head injury in the First World War left Ley with a severe stammer. In 1933, after the Nazis dissolved the trade unions, he became leader of the German Labour Front, (DAF), the largest Nazi organisation with 25 million members. The DAF organised the 'Strength Through Joy' holidays for German workers. A chronic alcoholic, and sexually incontinent, Ley retained his position thanks to his fanatical personal loyalty to Hitler. Ley escorted the Duke and Duchess of Windsor around factories and workplaces during their 1937 visit to the Reich. Arrested while hiding under a false name in Berchtesgaden after the war, he was due to be tried at Nuremberg with the other Nazi leaders but hanged himself in his cell.

LUCKNER, FELIX COUNT VON ('THE SEA DEVIL' – 9.6.1881–13.4.1966)

As commander of the armed sailing ship SMS *Seeteufel* ('Sea Devil') in the First World War, Luckner became a celebrated national hero for his exploits in destroying Allied merchant shipping. Captured and interned, Luckner boosted his reputation between the wars by writing books and lecturing about his adventures. A nationalist, he co-operated with the Nazi regime in cementing his status as a war hero and cultivated relationships with leading Nazis, including the Heydrich family. However, he never joined the Nazi Party and incurred their distrust as a keen Freemason. His motive in maintaining friendly relations with the regime were probably financial. A personal friend of Kitty Schmidt, and possibly a customer at her salon, he claimed after the war to have been instrumental in saving the life of a Jewish woman who worked in the salon's kitchen under a false identity provided by the count. After the war his public appearances in the USA made him a celebrity there.

MÜLLER, HEINRICH (28.4.1900–29.4.1945?)
A professional and non-political police chief in Bavaria before the Nazis took power, Müller co-operated with Himmler and Heydrich after the Nazi seizure of power, belatedly joining the party. He headed the Gestapo, acquiring the nickname 'Gestapo Müller' and was responsible for running the concentration camp system and for the persecution of Jews. He became an SS-Obergruppenführer in 1941 and took part in the Wannsee Conference in 1942. He disappeared from Hitler's bunker on 29 April 1945 and was probably killed attempting to flee from Berlin.

NAUJOCKS, ALFRED (20.9.1911–4.4.1966)
A thuggish Nazi tough before 1933, Naujocks joined the SD and became Heydrich's henchman in carrying out 'dirty jobs', including the 'false flag' seizure of the Gleiwitz radio station on the Polish border that precipitated the German invasion of Poland in September 1939 – earning Naujocks the sobriquet 'the man who started the Second World War'. Naujocks continued to organise similar 'greyzone' operations during the war, including financial fraud and the murder of Danish resistance fighters. He became an SS- Obersturmführer in 1943. Arrested by the Americans in 1945, he was jailed in Denmark as a war criminal but freed in 1950. He ended his career as a businessman in Hamburg. According to Peter Norden, Naujocks carried out the refurbishment of Salon Kitty as a spy centre.

NEBE, ARTHUR (13.11.1894–4.3.1945)
An official in Berlin's Criminal Police, Nebe joined the Gestapo and in 1941 took part in many atrocities in Eastern Europe – including

the mass murder of Jews and others with the use of explosives and experimental gassing. Playing a double game, Nebe was associated with the July plot on Hitler's life and went into hiding after its failure. Betrayed by a discarded mistress, he was arrested and executed. According to some accounts, Nebe was the first person to approach Kitty Schmidt in 1939 with the idea of using police agents as prostitutes in her salon.

OHLENDORF, OTTO (4.2.1904–8.6.1951)

A bureaucrat in the SD, after the invasion of Russia in June 1941, Ohlendorf led Group D of the Einsatzgruppen in Ukraine and the Caucasus – special police formations tasked with exterminating Jews, Roma and other 'enemies' of the Nazis in mass shootings. In November 1942 Ohlendorf returned to a post in the Economic Ministry. A leading witness at the Nuremberg trials after the war, Ohlendorf was condemned to death in 1948 at the 'Einsatzgruppen trial' and hanged at Landsberg in 1951.

PATZIG, CONRAD (24.5.1888–1.2.1975)

A naval officer, Patzig was Admiral Canaris's predecessor as chief of the Abwehr military intelligence service from 1932–5, warning his successor that he would be targeted by Heydrich. He returned to active service and was promoted to Admiral in 1937, retiring in 1943. A British prisoner of war for a year from 1945–6, Patzig became a senior adviser in the reconstruction of the German navy.

RIBBENTROP, JOACHIM VON (30.4.1893–16.10.1946)

A former Champagne salesman who married into a prominent German winemaking family, Ribbentrop joined the Nazi Party in 1932 and facilitated the meetings between Hitler and leading industrialists that helped him to power. A foreign policy adviser to Hitler with his own intelligence agency – the Dienstelle Ribbentrop, he was appointed Ambassador to Britain in 1936. Unpopular because of his arrogance and social gaffes, Ribbentrop became Foreign Minister in February 1938. He lost influence after the outbreak of war and went into hiding in Hamburg as Germany collapsed. Arrested in June 1945, Ribbentrop was tried at Nuremberg, condemned to death and executed. He is believed to have been a client at Salon Kitty.

SCHELLENBERG, WALTER (16.10.1910–31.03.1952)
Ambitious, intelligent and opportunistic, Schellenberg joined the Nazi Party and the SS after Hitler came to power in 1933. A protégé of Heydrich in the SD, Schellenberg rose rapidly, becoming chief of the Foreign Intelligence Department. He organised the abduction of two British secret service chiefs on the Dutch border in the so-called Venlo Incident in November 1939. He was responsible for the personal protection of leading Nazi functionaries. Arrested at the end of the war, he was a witness at the Nuremberg tribunal. He himself was later sentenced to six years' imprisonment for war crimes. Released on grounds of ill health, Schellenberg wrote his memoirs while dying of cancer in Turin. According to Peter Norden and other sources, Schellenberg was the main player in entrapping Kitty Schmidt and compelling her to convert her salon into a spy listening centre.

SIX, FRANZ (9.7.1906–9.7.1975)
Six joined the Nazi Party in 1930, and both the SS and SA in 1932. A media specialist and professor, Six combined an academic career responsible for the Nazi takeover of higher education with participation in the Einsatzgruppen massacres in Eastern Europe. Arrested and sentenced to twenty years imprisonment after the war, he was released early in 1952 and resumed a successful business and academic career unmolested.

TSCHAMMER und OSTEN, HANS VON (25.10.1887–25.3.1943)
Hans von Tschammer und Osten was an officer in the First World
War, joining the Nazi Party and the SA in 1929. He became a Nazi
Reichstag member in 1932. After the Nazis took power he became
their leading specialist in sports. From 1934 he was in charge of
ideological preparations for the 1936 Berlin Olympic Games. He
died in 1943 of a lung infection. Tschammer und Osten was a client
at Salon Kitty.

BIBLIOGRAPHY

Bassett, Richard, *Hitler's Spy Chief: The Wilhelm Canaris Mystery*, London, Weidenfeld & Nicolson, 2005

Cantrell, Arthur, *Flight of the Valkyrie 1939–43*, Bern, Scherz, 2013

Carre, Mathilde-Lily, *I Was 'The Cat'*, London, Souvenir Press, 1960

Ciano, Galeazzo (1947) *Ciano's Diary 1937–1943*, London, Heinemann, 1947

Clay Large, David, *Berlin: A Modern History*, London, Penguin, 2000

Cross, Robin and Miles, Rosalind, *Warrior Women*, New York, Metro Books, 2011

Dassanowsky, Robert von, 'The Third Reich as Bordello and Pigs Sty: Between Neodecadence and Sexploitation in Tinto Brass's *Salon Kitty*', in Magilow, Bridges and Vander (eds), *Nazisploitation! The Nazi Image in Low-Brow Cinema and Culture*, New York, Continuum, 2011

Doerris, Reinhard R., *Hitler's Last Chief of Foreign Intelligence*, London, Frank Cass, 2003

———, *Hitler's Intelligence Chief: Walter Schellenberg*, New York, Enigma, 2009

Friedrich, Otto, *Before the Deluge*, London, Michael Joseph, 1974

Gerwarth, Robert, *Hitler's Hangman: the Life of Heydrich*, New Haven and London, Yale UP, 2011

Isherwood, Christopher, *Christopher and His Kind*, London, Eyre Methuen, 1977

———, *The Berlin Novels*, London, Vintage Books, 1999

Gallo, Max, *The Night of Long Knives*, New York, Harper & Row, 1972

Grosz, George, *A Small Yes and A Big No*, London, Allison & Busby, 1982

Hanfstaengl, Ernst, *Hitler: The Missing Years*, London, Eyre & Spottiswoode, 1957

Hayman, Ronald, *Hitler and Geli*, London, Bloomsbury, 1997

Helm, Sarah, *Ravensbrück*, New York, Anchor Books, 2016

Johnson, Eric A., *Nazi Terror: The Gestapo, Jews and Ordinary Germans*, New York, Basic Books, 1999

Kater, Michael H., *Culture in Nazi Germany*, New York, Yale UP, 2019

Knightley, Philip, *The Second Oldest Profession: Spies and Spying in the Twentieth Century*, London, André Deutsch, 1986

Knopp, Guido, *The SS: A Warning from History*, Cheltenham, History Press, 2002

Lepage, Jean-Denis G. G., *An Illustrated Dictionary of the Third Reich*, Jefferson NC, McFarland & Co., 2013

Longerich, Peter, *Goebbels*, London, Bodley Head, 2015

———, *Hitler: A Life*, Oxford, OUP, 2019

MacDonogh, Giles, *Berlin*, London, Sinclair-Stevenson, 1997

McDonough, Frank, *Gestapo*, London, Coronet, 2015

Moorhouse, Roger, *Berlin at War*, London, Bodley Head, 2010

Mueller, Michael, *Canaris*, London, Chatham Publishing, 2007

Norden, Peter (trs. J. Maxwell Brownjohn), *Madam Kitty: A True Story*, London, Abelard-Schuman, 1973

Padfield, Peter, *Himmler*, New York, Henry Holt, 1990

Roland, Paul, *Nazi Women: The Attraction of Evil*, London, Arcturus Publishing, 2014

Rosenbaum, Ron, *Explaining Hitler*, New York, Random House, 1998

Stephenson, Jill, *Women in Nazi Germany*, London, Routledge, 2015

Ulrich, Barbara, *The Hot Girls of Weimar Berlin*, Los Angeles, Feral House, 2002

Wighton, Charles, *Heydrich: Hitler's Most Evil Henchman*, London, Odhams Press, 1962

INDEX